GONE TO AMERIKAY

VERTIGO

GONE TO

WRITTEN BY
DEREK McCULLOCH

ART BY
COLLEEN DORAN

COLORS BY
JOSÉ VILLARRUBIA

LETTERS BY
JARED K. FLETCHER

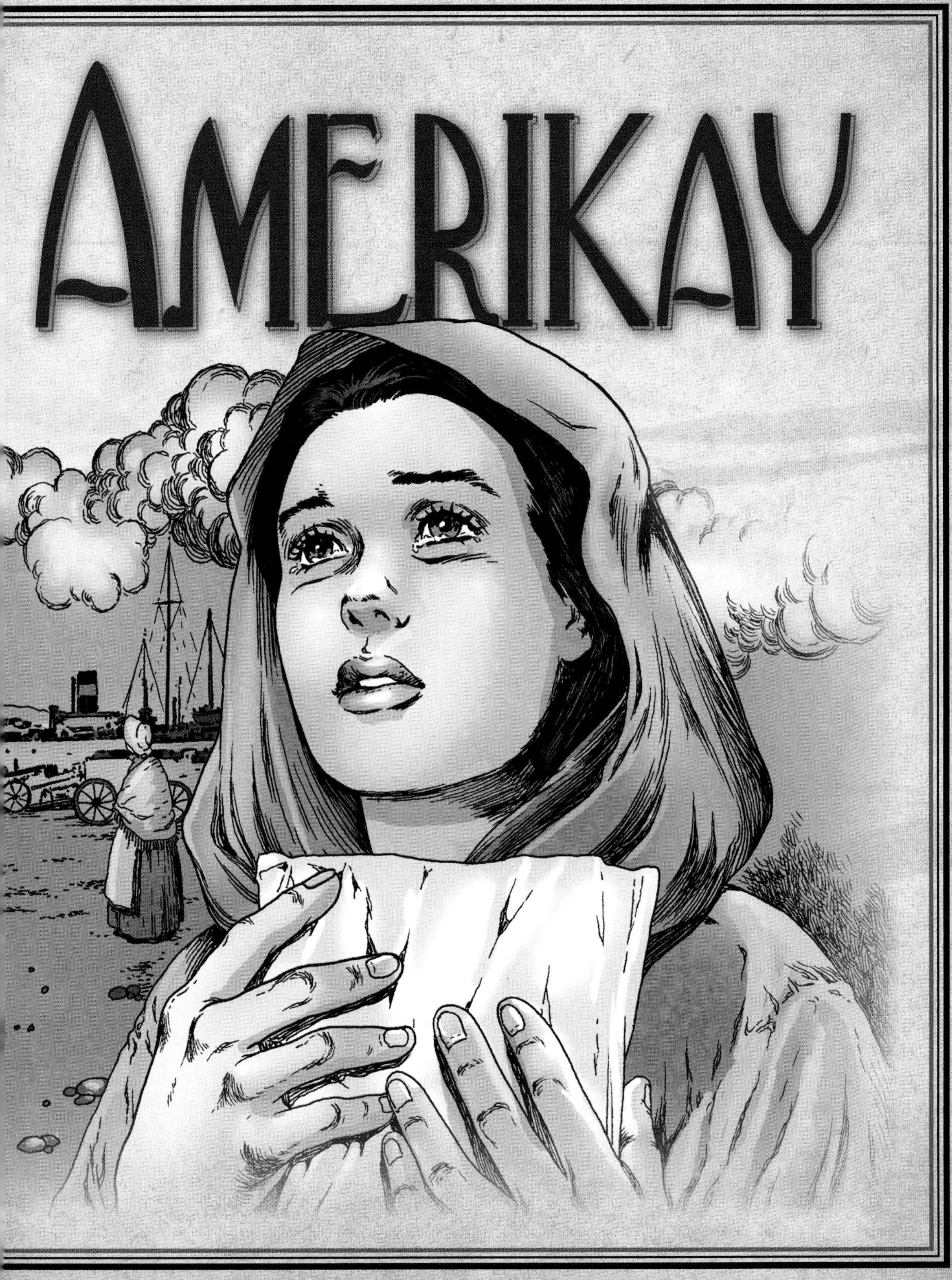
AMERIKAY

Dedications

This is dedicated, as always,
to Tara and Pearl—but also, with admiration
and gratitude to the great Irish gentleman
Philip Chevron—and with love to the
memory of Alice Sanderson (née Groark),
a tough Irish lady from Boston.

—Derek McCulloch

To Ronald and Anita Doran, my parents.
And their parents.

—Colleen Doran

Acknowledgment:
With special thanks to the US National Archives,
The American Irish Historical Society, and my models
Kacey Camp and Jed Brophy, he of the stratospheric
cheekbones. With gratitude to all my rural Appalachian
neighbors for their antique clothes and tools.
And great grandma's iron.

—Colleen Doran

Joan Hilty Editor **Joe Hughes** and **Sarah Litt** Assistant Editors **Robbin Brosterman** Design Director-Books **Curtis King Jr.** Publication Design

Karen Berger Senior VP – Executive Editor, Vertigo **Bob Harras** VP – Editor-in-Chief

Diane Nelson President **Dan DiDio** and **Jim Lee** Co-Publishers **Geoff Johns** Chief Creative Officer **John Rood** Executive VP – Sales, Marketing and Business Development
Amy Genkins Senior VP – Business and Legal Affairs **Nairi Gardiner** Senior VP – Finance **Jeff Boison** VP – Publishing Operations **Mark Chiarello** VP – Art Direction and Design
John Cunningham VP – Marketing **Terri Cunningham** VP – Talent Relations and Services **Alison Gill** Senior VP – Manufacturing and Operations **David Hyde** VP – Publicity
Hank Kanalz Senior VP – Digital **Jay Kogan** VP – Business and Legal Affairs, Publishing **Jack Mahan** VP – Business Affairs, Talent
Nick Napolitano VP – Manufacturing Administration **Sue Pohja** VP – Book Sales **Courtney Simmons** Senior VP – Publicity **Bob Wayne** Senior VP – Sales

GONE TO AMERIKAY
Published by DC Comics, 1700 Broadway, New York, NY 10019. Copyright © 2012 by Derek McCulloch and Colleen Doran.
All rights reserved. VERTIGO and all characters their distinctive likenesses and related elements are trademarks of DC Comics.
The stories, characters and incidents mentioned in this book are entirely fictional.
Printed in the USA. First Printing. DC Comics, a Warner Bros. Entertainment Company. ISBN: 978-1-4012-2351-9

SUSTAINABLE FORESTRY INITIATIVE

Certified Chain of Custody
At Least 25% Certified Forest Content
www.sfiprogram.org
SFI-01042
APPLIES TO TEXT STOCK ONLY

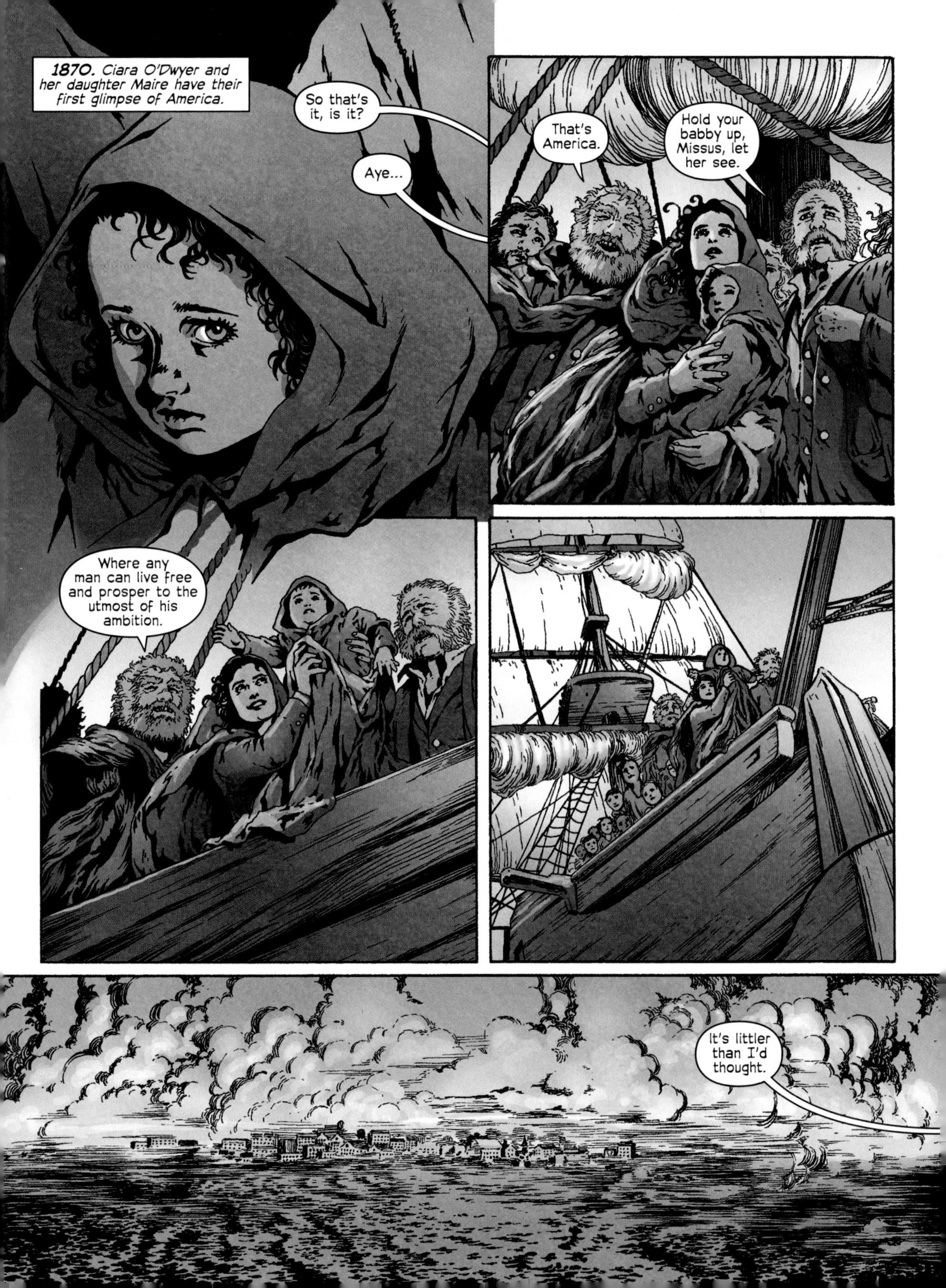
1870. Ciara O'Dwyer and her daughter Maire have their first glimpse of America.
So that's it, is it?
Aye...
That's America.
Hold your babby up, Missus, let her see.
Where any man can live free and prosper to the utmost of his ambition.
It's littler than I'd thought.

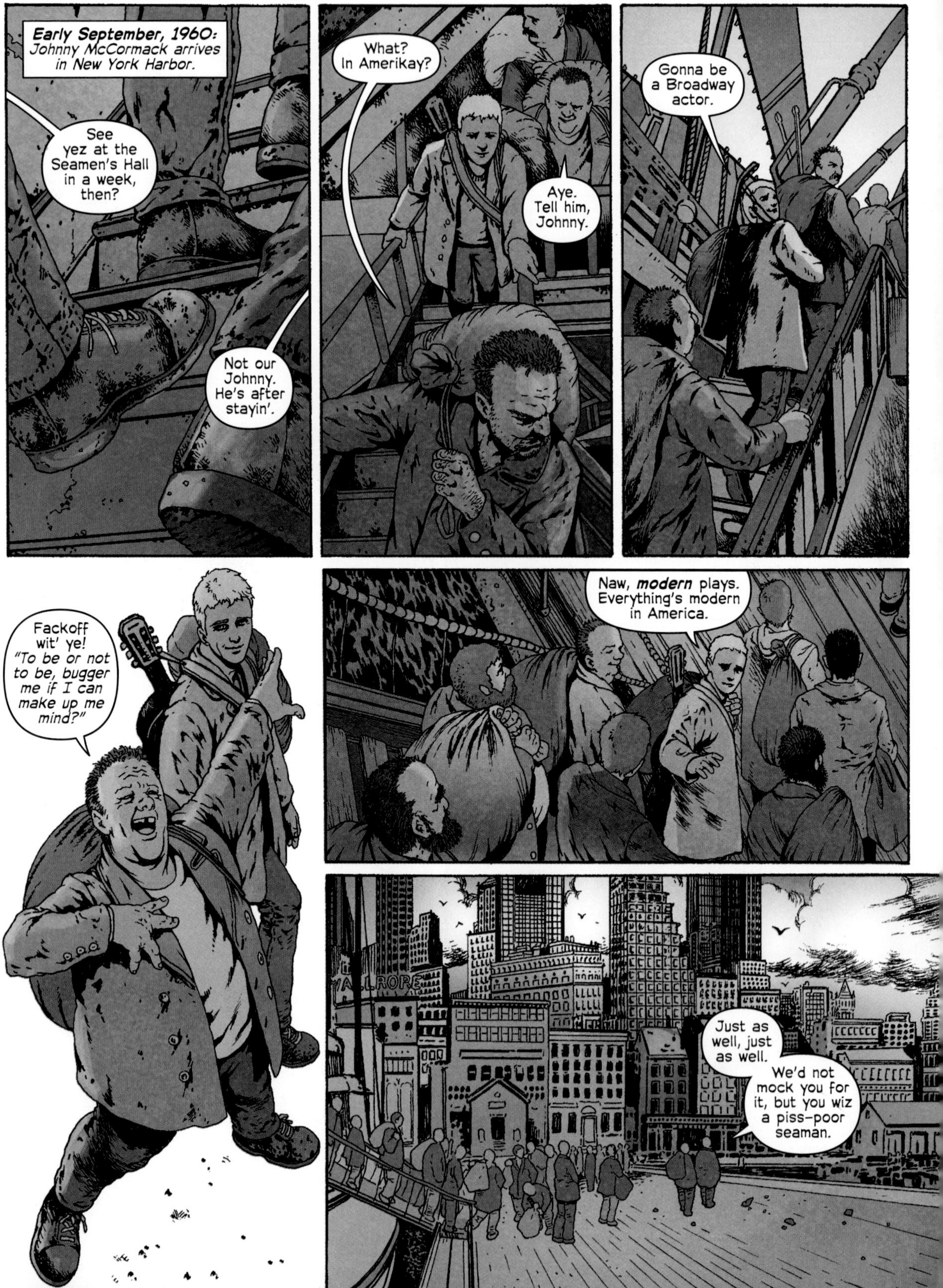
Early September, 1960: Johnny McCormack arrives in New York Harbor.
See yez at the Seamen's Hall in a week, then?
Not our Johnny. He's after stayin'.
What? In AmeriKay?
Aye. Tell him, Johnny.
Gonna be a Broadway actor.
Fackoff wit' ye! "To be or not to be, bugger me if I can make up me mind?"
Naw, modern plays. Everything's modern in America.
Just as well, just as well.
We'd not mock you for it, but you wiz a piss-poor seaman.

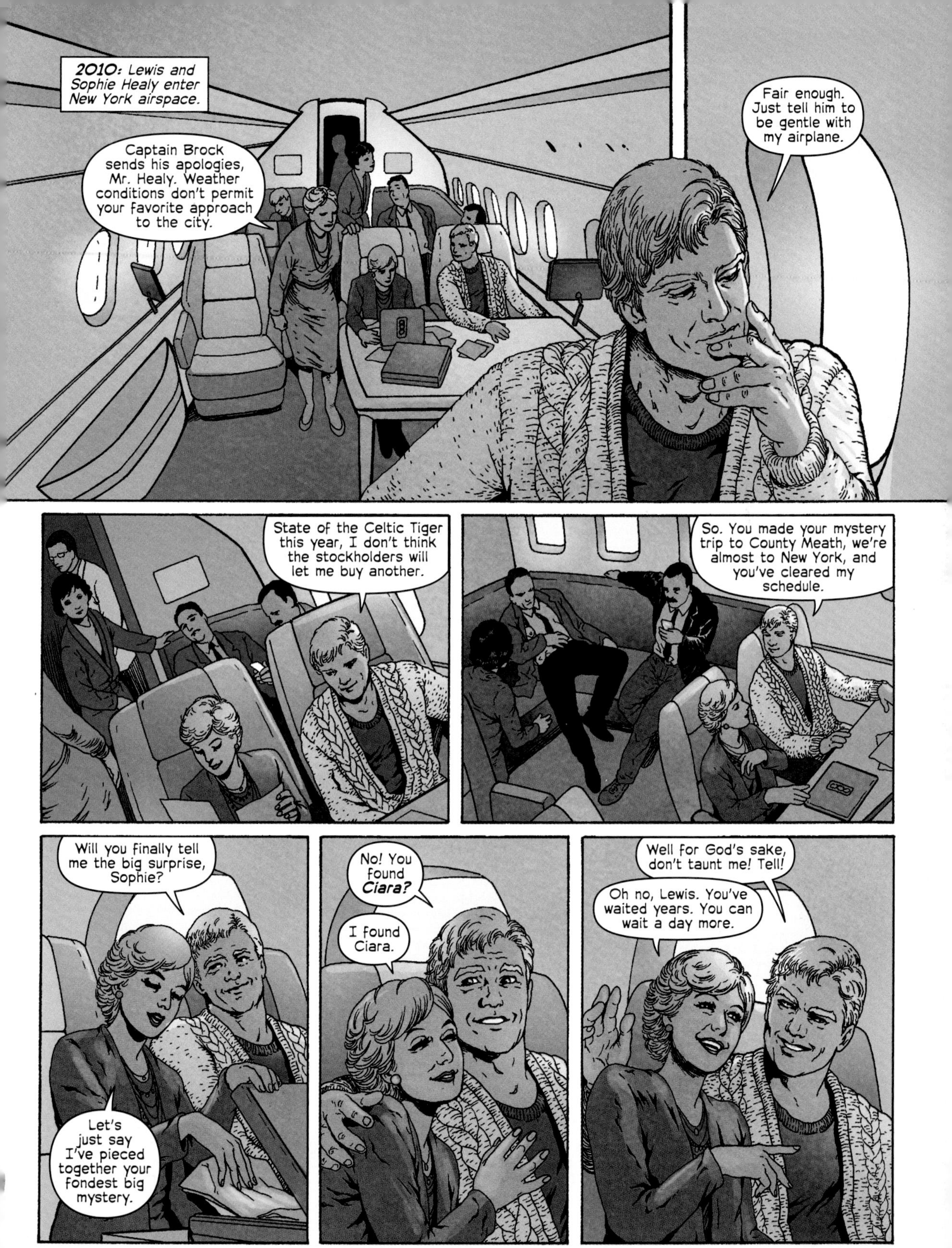
2010: Lewis and Sophie Healy enter New York airspace.
Captain Brock sends his apologies, Mr. Healy. Weather conditions don't permit your favorite approach to the city.
Fair enough. Just tell him to be gentle with my airplane.
State of the Celtic Tiger this year, I don't think the stockholders will let me buy another.
So. You made your mystery trip to County Meath, we're almost to New York, and you've cleared my schedule.
Will you finally tell me the big surprise, Sophie?
Let's just say I've pieced together your fondest big mystery.
No! You found Ciara?
I found Ciara.
Well for God's sake, don't taunt me! Tell!
Oh no, Lewis. You've waited years. You can wait a day more.

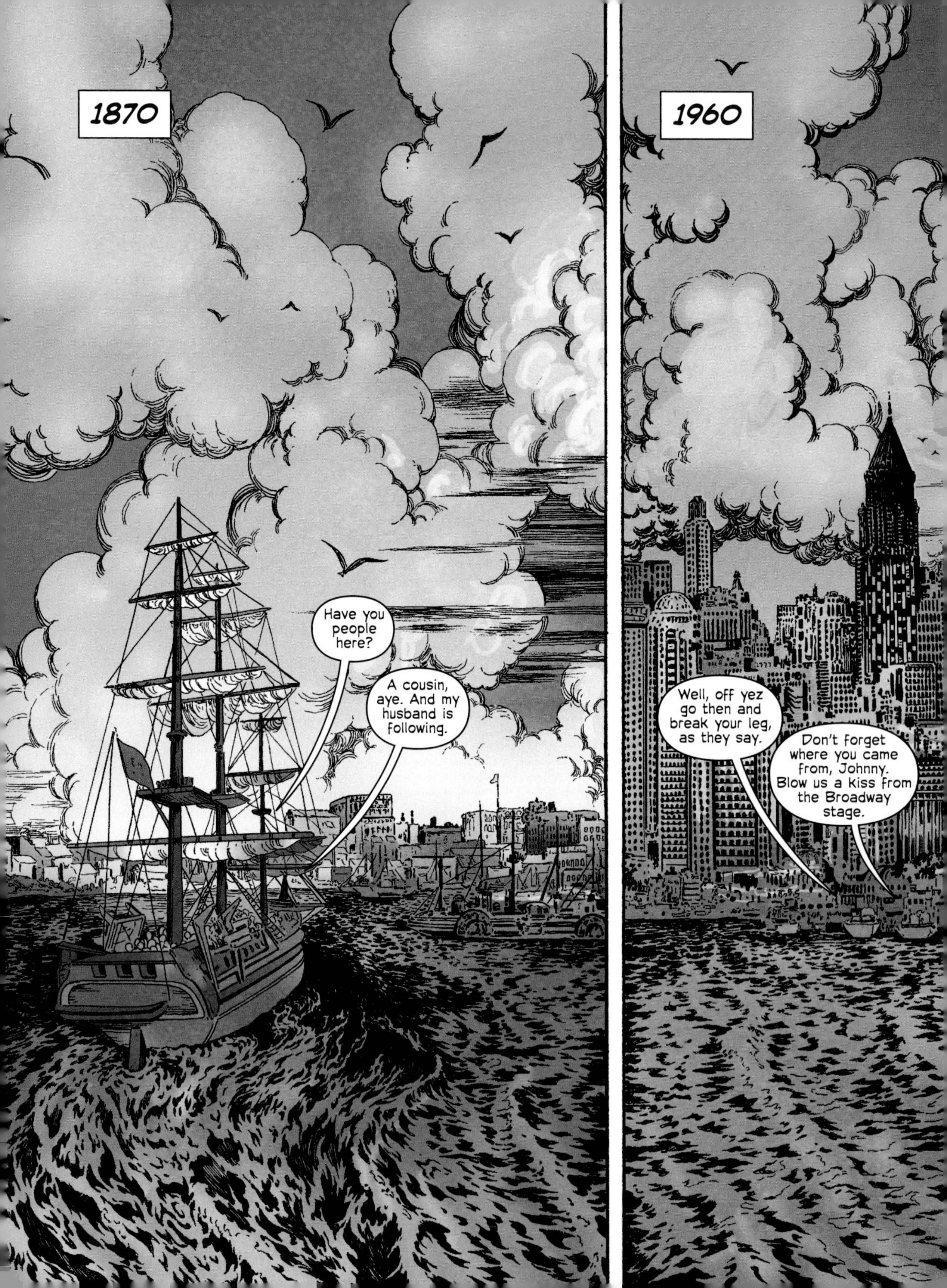
1870
Have you people here?
A cousin, aye. And my husband is following.
1960
Well, off yez go then and break your leg, as they say.
Don't forget where you came from, Johnny. Blow us a kiss from the Broadway stage.

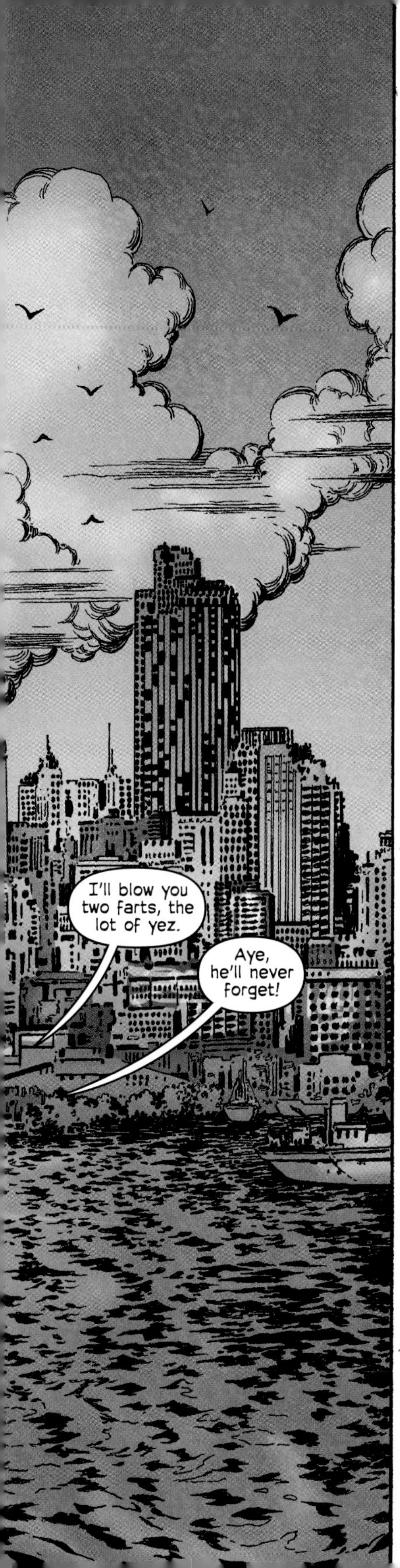
I'll blow you two farts, the lot of yez.
Aye, he'll never forget!
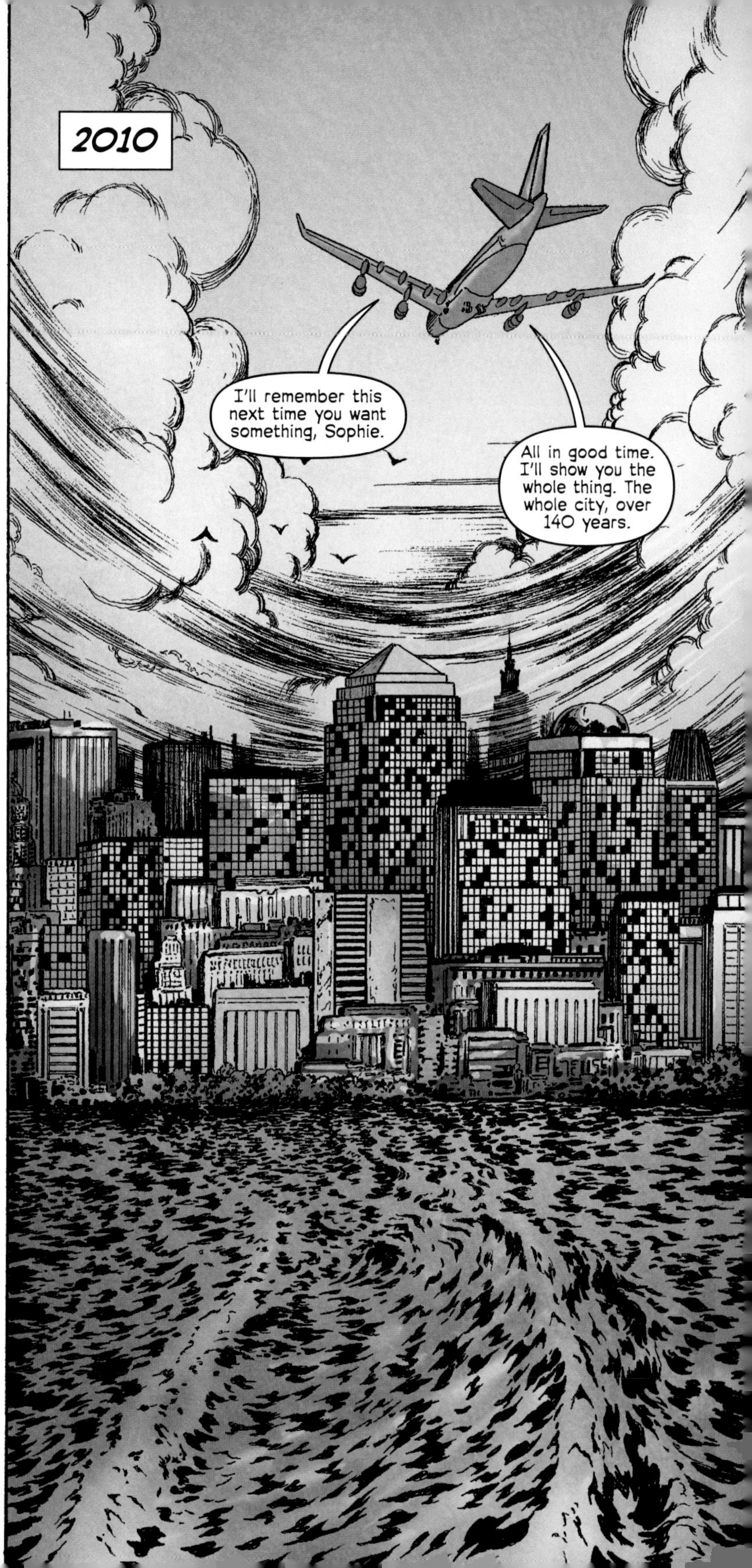
2010
I'll remember this next time you want something, Sophie.
All in good time. I'll show you the whole thing. The whole city, over 140 years.

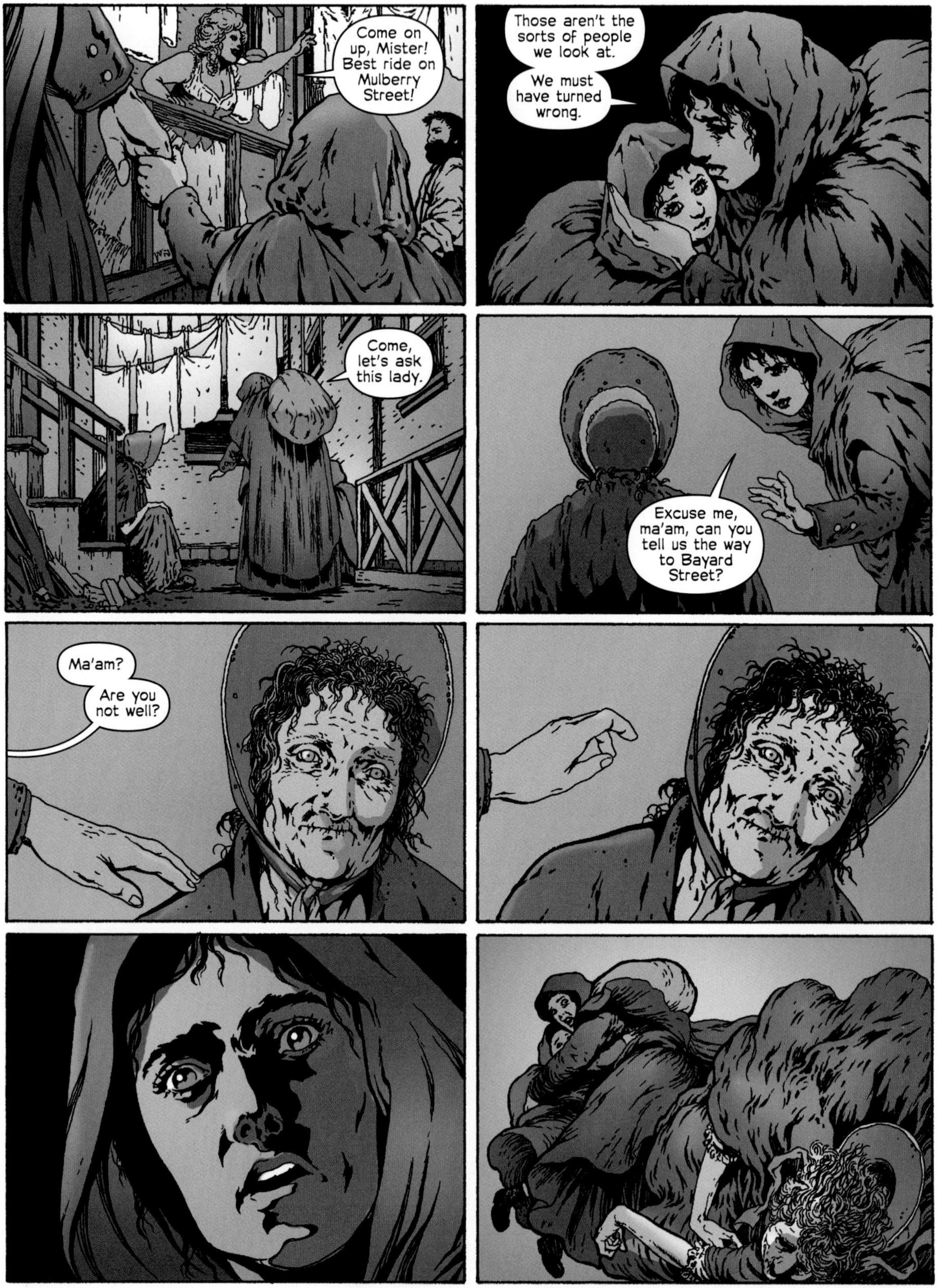
Come on up, Mister! Best ride on Mulberry Street!
Those aren't the sorts of people we look at.
We must have turned wrong.
Come, let's ask this lady.
Excuse me, ma'am, can you tell us the way to Bayard Street?
Ma'am?
Are you not well?

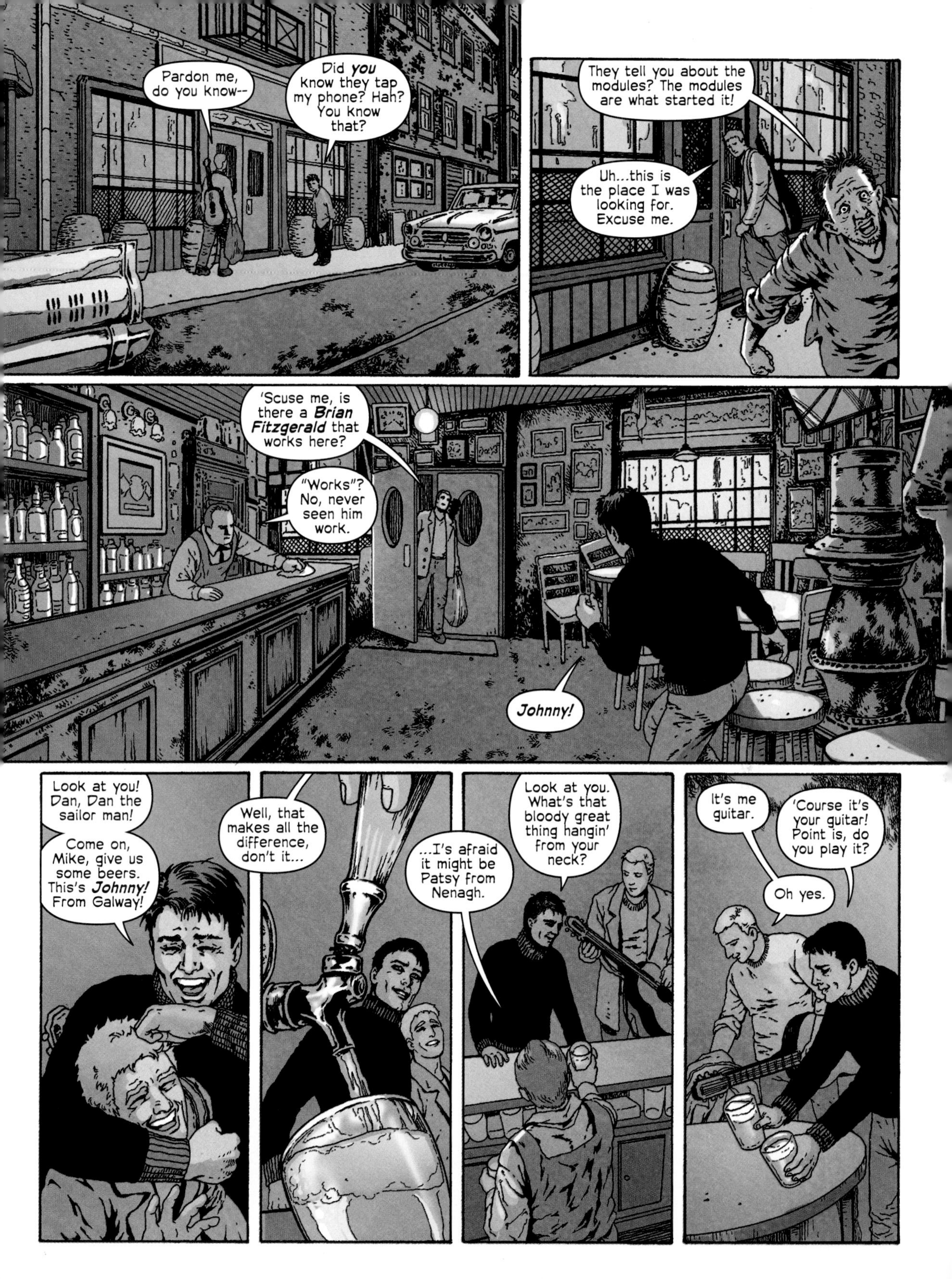
Pardon me, do you know--
Did *you* know they tap my phone? Hah? You know that?
They tell you about the modules? The modules are what started it!
Uh...this is the place I was looking for. Excuse me.
'Scuse me, is there a *Brian Fitzgerald* that works here?
"Works"? No, never seen him work.
Johnny!
Look at you! Dan, Dan the sailor man!
Come on, Mike, give us some beers. This's *Johnny!* From Galway!
Well, that makes all the difference, don't it...
...I's afraid it might be Patsy from Nenagh.
Look at you. What's that bloody great thing hangin' from your neck?
It's me guitar.
'Course it's your guitar! Point is, do you play it?
Oh yes.

Well, play us something then.

Um... heh...

♪ In nineteen hundred thirty, James McCready sailed away/From a weary Irish village forty miles from Galway Bay...

♪ He dreamed he'd find his fortune where the roads are made of gold/But the days were hard and he never knew that nights could be so cold...

♪ And back in dear old Ireland they're still asking to this day/Where's Jimmy gone? He's gone to Amerikay! ♪

Damn good. You can have that beer, Johnny From Galway.

That's your own song?

Er...yeah, made it up on the way over.

It's good, it's good. But you know, that ending, you need to really bang it out. You know, hammer it.

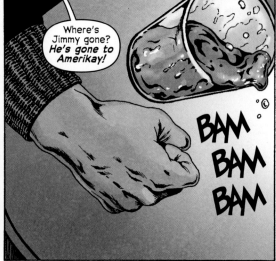

Where's Jimmy gone? He's gone to Amerikay!

BAM
BAM
BAM

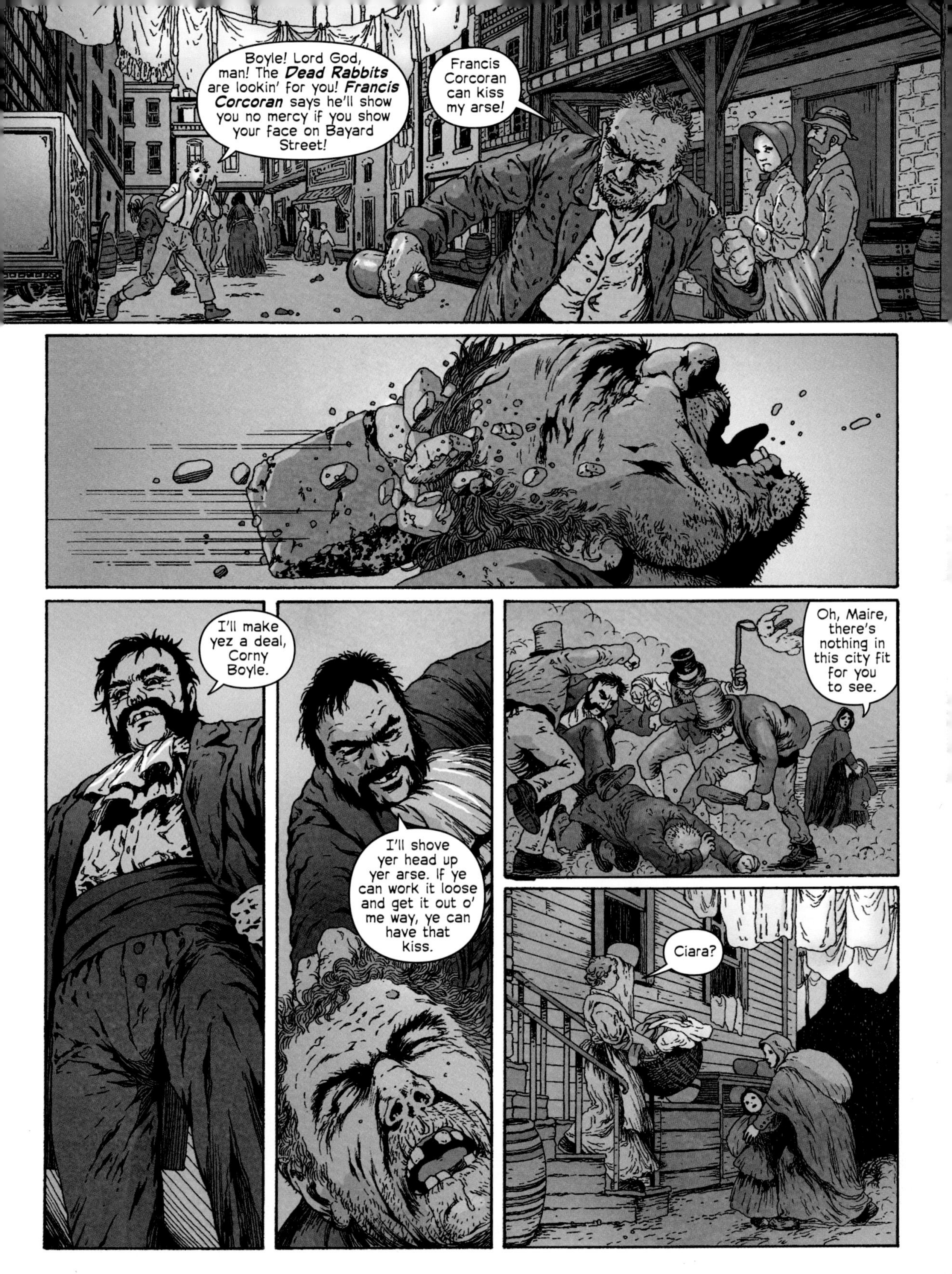
Boyle! Lord God, man! The Dead Rabbits are lookin' for you! Francis Corcoran says he'll show you no mercy if you show your face on Bayard Street!
Francis Corcoran can kiss my arse!
I'll make yez a deal, Corny Boyle.
I'll shove yer head up yer arse. If ye can work it loose and get it out o' me way, ye can have that kiss.
Oh, Maire, there's nothing in this city fit for you to see.
Ciara?

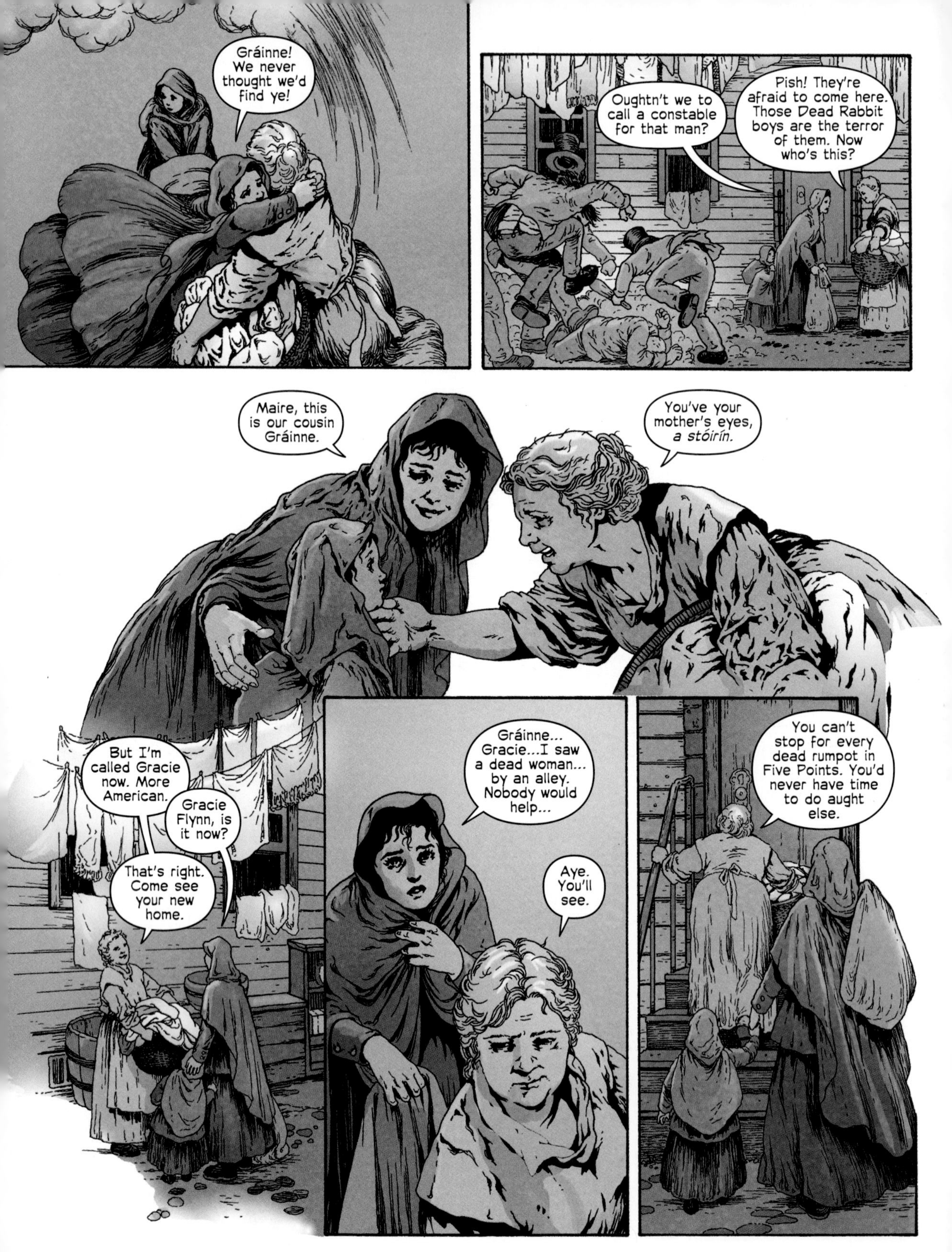
Gráinne! We never thought we'd find ye!
Oughtn't we to call a constable for that man?
Pish! They're afraid to come here. Those Dead Rabbit boys are the terror of them. Now who's this?
Maire, this is our cousin Gráinne.
You've your mother's eyes, *a stóirín.*
But I'm called Gracie now. More American.
Gracie Flynn, is it now?
That's right. Come see your new home.
Gráinne... Gracie...I saw a dead woman... by an alley. Nobody would help...
Aye. You'll see.
You can't stop for every dead rumpot in Five Points. You'd never have time to do aught else.

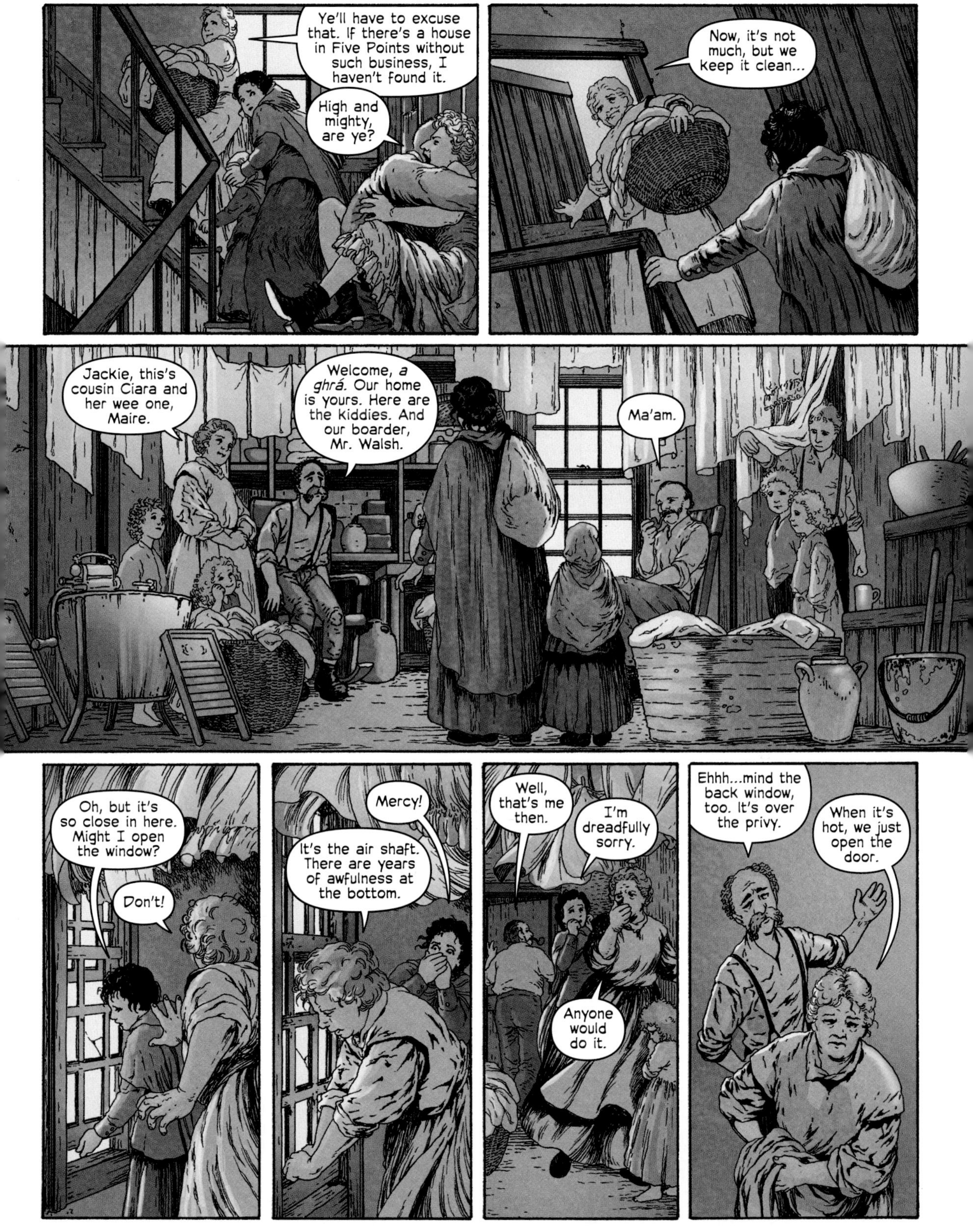
Ye'll have to excuse that. If there's a house in Five Points without such business, I haven't found it.
High and mighty, are ye?
Now, it's not much, but we keep it clean...
Jackie, this's cousin Ciara and her wee one, Maire.
Welcome, *a ghrá*. Our home is yours. Here are the kiddies. And our boarder, Mr. Walsh.
Ma'am.
Oh, but it's so close in here. Might I open the window?
Don't!
Mercy!
It's the air shaft. There are years of awfulness at the bottom.
Well, that's me then.
I'm dreadfully sorry.
Anyone would do it.
Ehhh...mind the back window, too. It's over the privy.
When it's hot, we just open the door.

Ucccchhh.

Heccchhh!
Huuuhhhh...

Ehhh.
Hair o'
the dog.

Sláinte.

Meet me at the
Cort at six. —Brian

APT FOR RENT
HARLEM - 2 bedroom Apt,
large ktchn. Call Ms. Jones,
KLondike 5-2196.

ROOM FOR RENT
CHINATOWN - Worth B
Centre and Bowery. Bo
good light. Call Mrs. I
KLondike 5-0

APT FOR
CHINATOWN -
no maint. Cal
KLondi

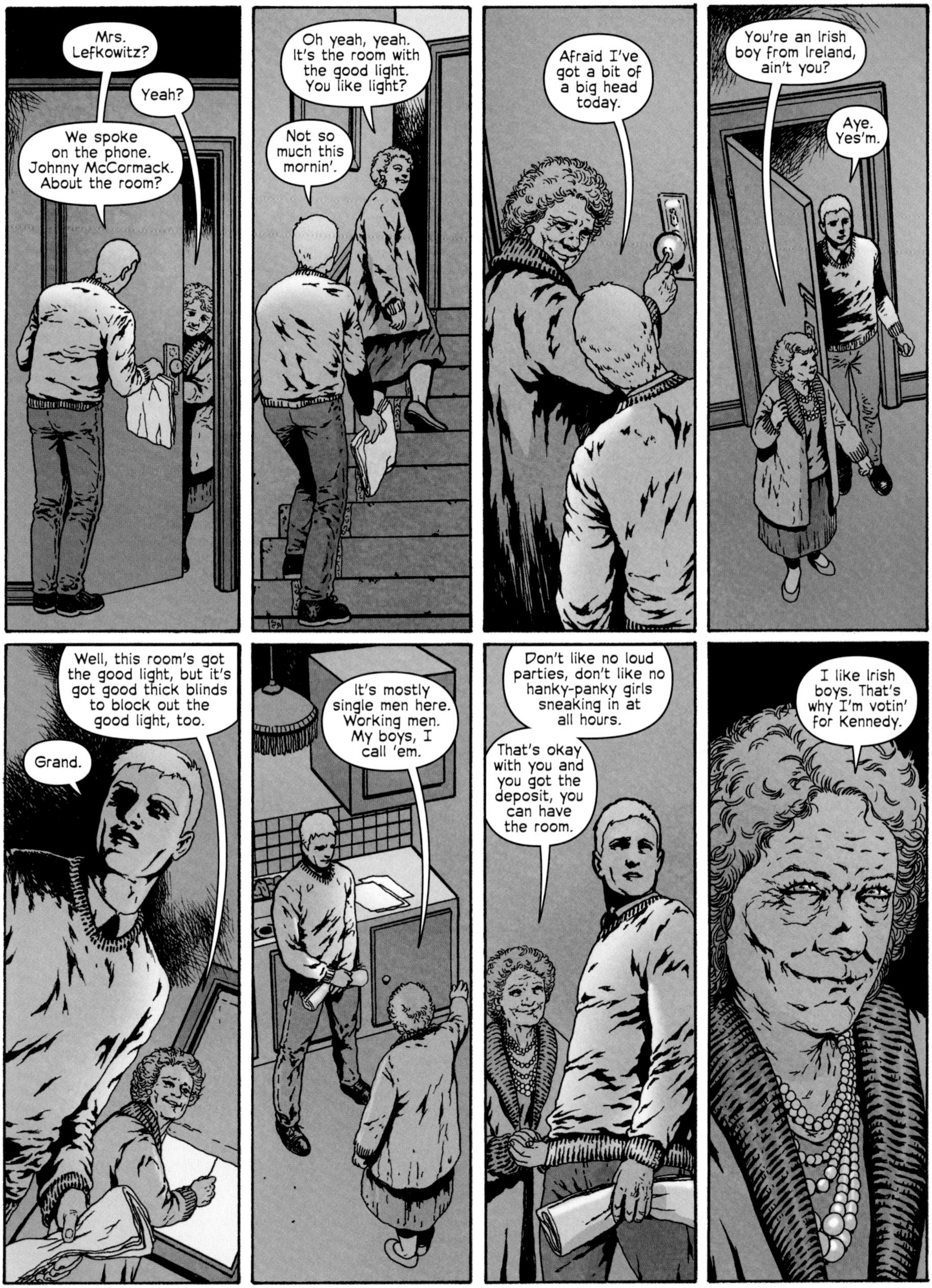

Mrs. Lefkowitz?
Yeah?
We spoke on the phone. Johnny McCormack. About the room?
Oh yeah, yeah. It's the room with the good light. You like light?
Not so much this mornin'.
Afraid I've got a bit of a big head today.
You're an Irish boy from Ireland, ain't you?
Aye. Yes'm.
Well, this room's got the good light, but it's got good thick blinds to block out the good light, too.
Grand.
It's mostly single men here. Working men. My boys, I call 'em.
Don't like no loud parties, don't like no hanky-panky girls sneaking in at all hours.
That's okay with you and you got the deposit, you can have the room.
I like Irish boys. That's why I'm votin' for Kennedy.

Come on! Stage door's through here.

So how'd you get this gig, then?

Friend of a friend's friend.

"Aren't we husband and wife?"

"I don't have to stay here!"

How's it work, then? Understudyin'?

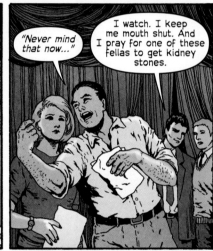

"Never mind that now..."

I watch. I keep me mouth shut. And I pray for one of these fellas to get kidney stones.

There's the great man.

Behan? Brendan Behan?

What the hell's that? What's going on?

Have you met him?

Sure. You want to?

"I've seen everything..."

We have some tea for you, Mr. Behan.

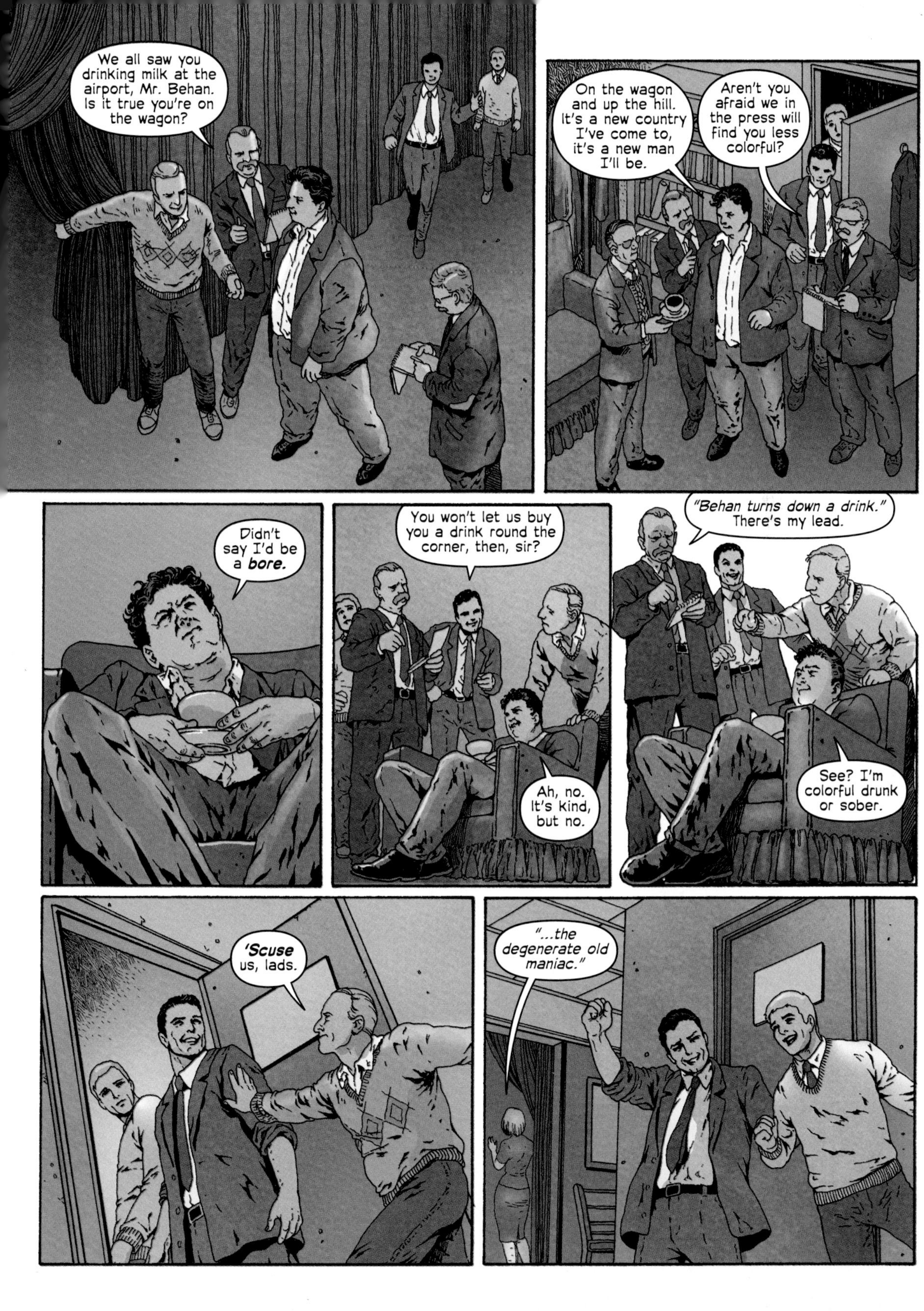
We all saw you drinking milk at the airport, Mr. Behan. Is it true you're on the wagon?
On the wagon and up the hill. It's a new country I've come to, it's a new man I'll be.
Aren't you afraid we in the press will find you less colorful?
Didn't say I'd be a ***bore.***
You won't let us buy you a drink round the corner, then, sir?
Ah, no. It's kind, but no.
"Behan turns down a drink." There's my lead.
See? I'm colorful drunk or sober.
'Scuse us, lads.
"...the degenerate old maniac."

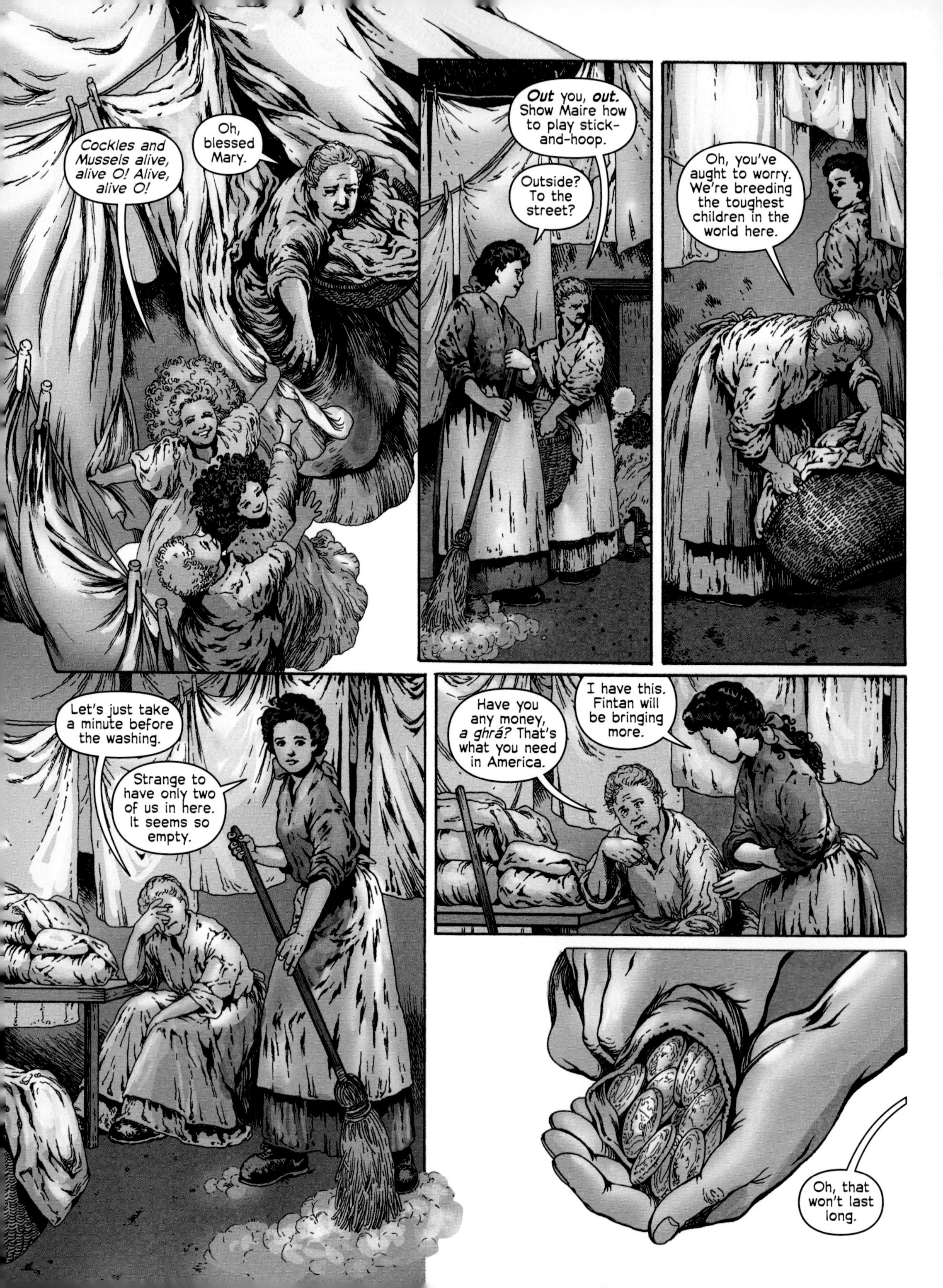
Cockles and Mussels alive, alive O! Alive, alive O!
Oh, blessed Mary.
Out you, out. Show Maire how to play stick-and-hoop.
Outside? To the street?
Oh, you've aught to worry. We're breeding the toughest children in the world here.
Let's just take a minute before the washing.
Strange to have only two of us in here. It seems so empty.
Have you any money, a ghrá? That's what you need in America.
I have this. Fintan will be bringing more.
Oh, that won't last long.

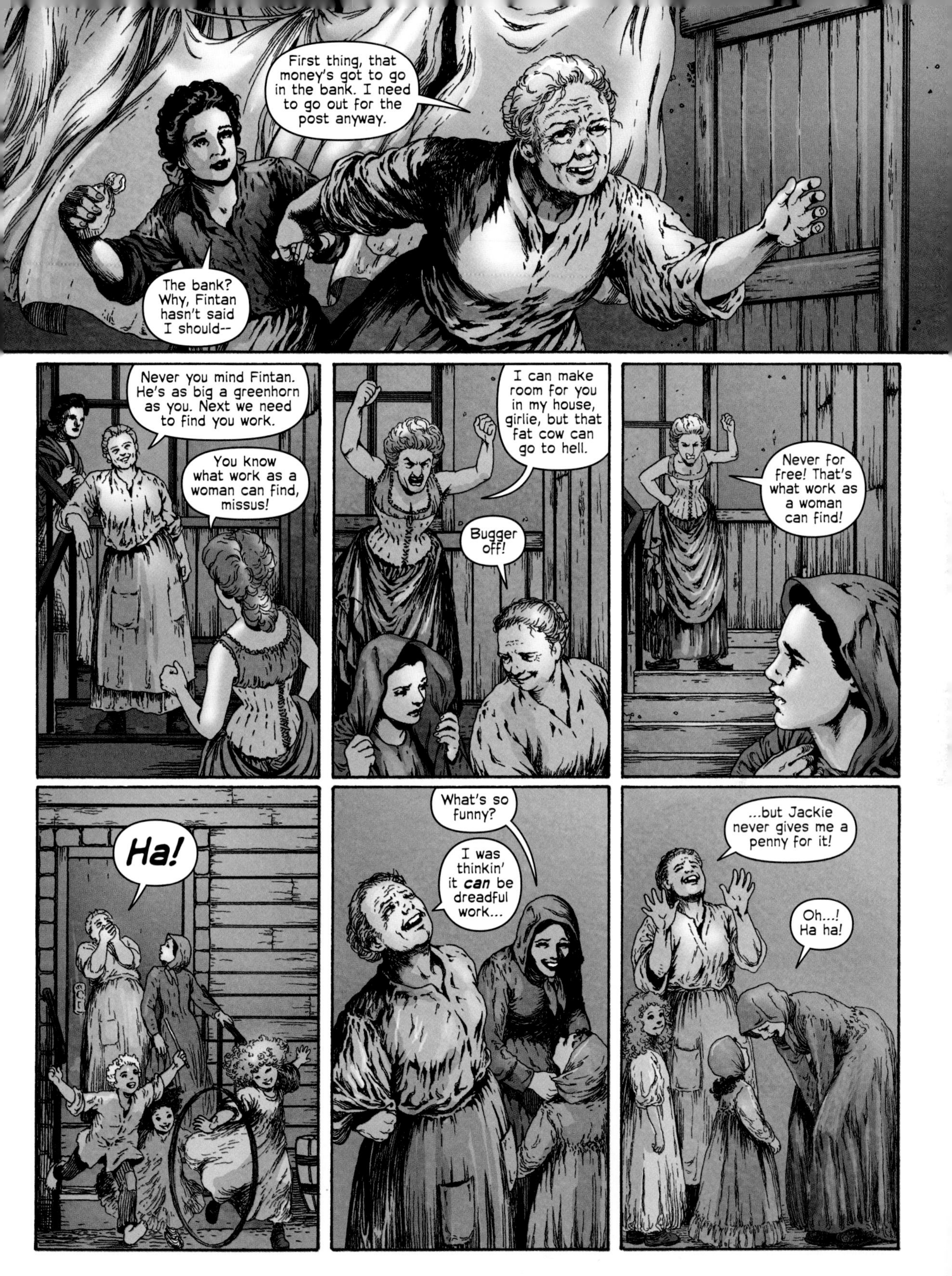
First thing, that money's got to go in the bank. I need to go out for the post anyway.
The bank? Why, Fintan hasn't said I should--
Never you mind Fintan. He's as big a greenhorn as you. Next we need to find you work.
You know what work as a woman can find, missus!
I can make room for you in my house, girlie, but that fat cow can go to hell.
Bugger off!
Never for free! That's what work as a woman can find!
Ha!
What's so funny?
I was thinkin' it can be dreadful work...
...but Jackie never gives me a penny for it!
Oh...! Ha ha!

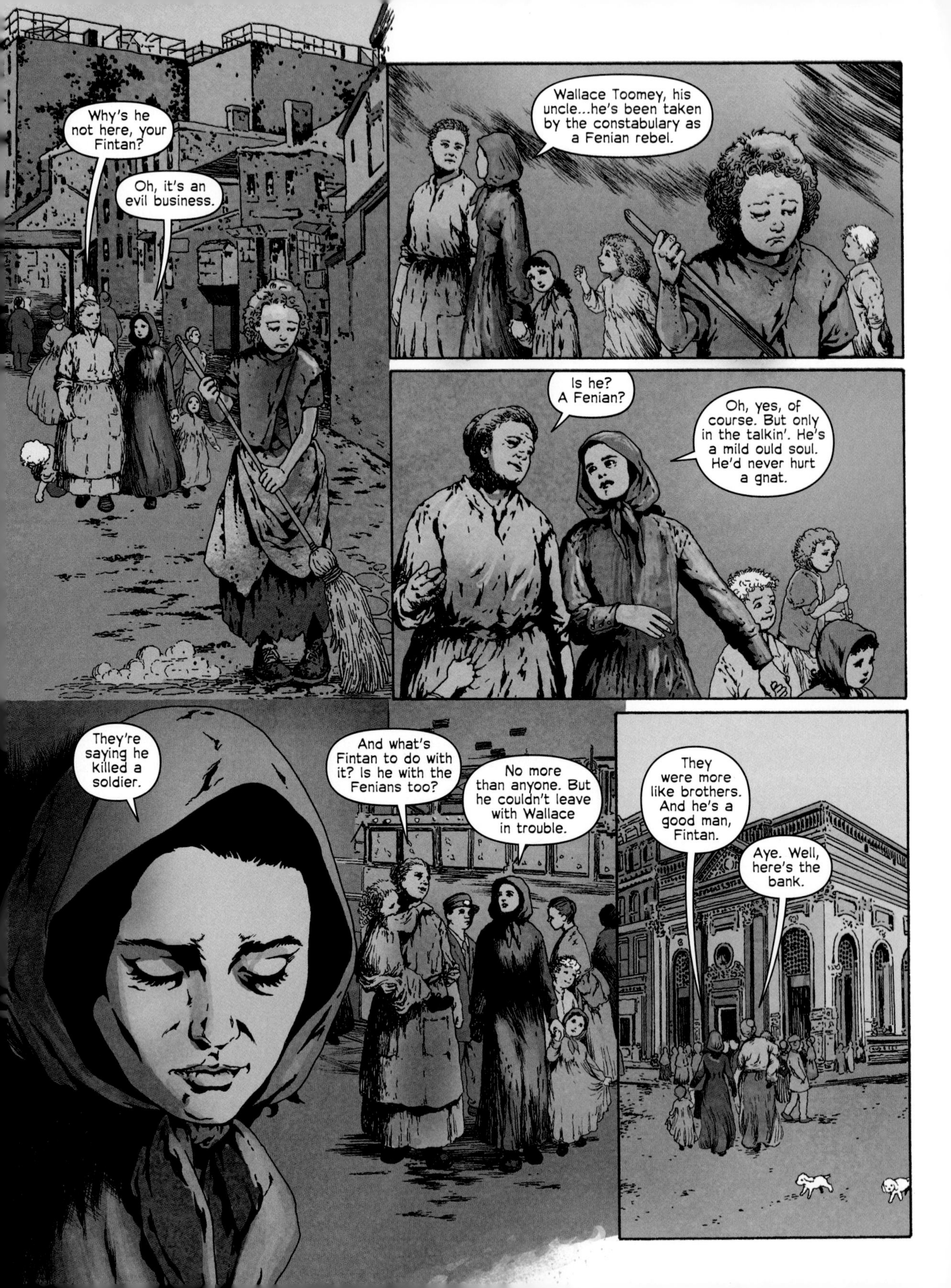

Why's he not here, your Fintan?
Oh, it's an evil business.
Wallace Toomey, his uncle...he's been taken by the constabulary as a Fenian rebel.
Is he? A Fenian?
Oh, yes, of course. But only in the talkin'. He's a mild ould soul. He'd never hurt a gnat.
They're saying he killed a soldier.
And what's Fintan to do with it? Is he with the Fenians too?
No more than anyone. But he couldn't leave with Wallace in trouble.
They were more like brothers. And he's a good man, Fintan.
Aye. Well, here's the bank.

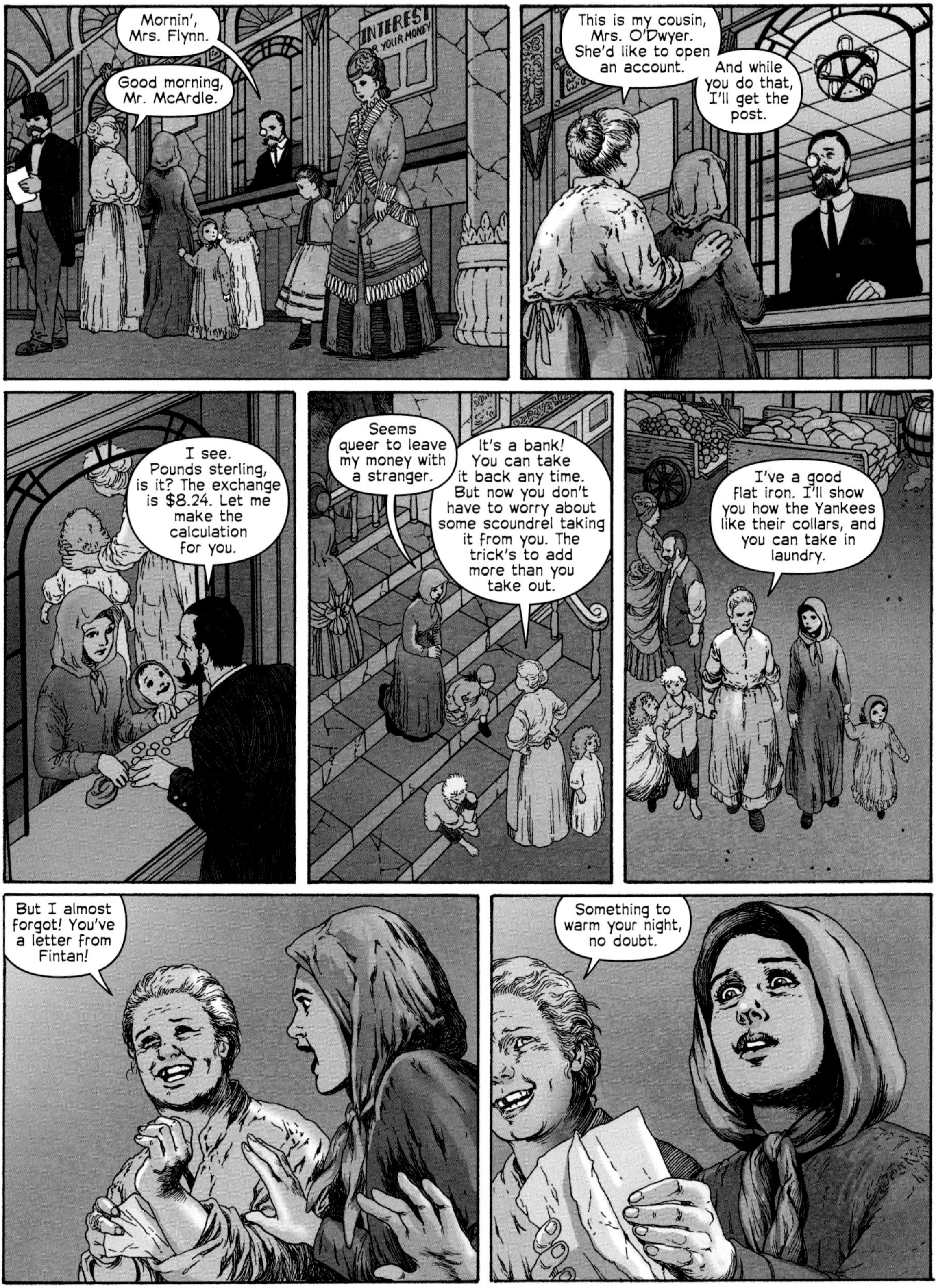
Mornin', Mrs. Flynn.
Good morning, Mr. McArdle.
INTEREST FOR YOUR MONEY
This is my cousin, Mrs. O'Dwyer. She'd like to open an account.
And while you do that, I'll get the post.
I see. Pounds sterling, is it? The exchange is $8.24. Let me make the calculation for you.
Seems queer to leave my money with a stranger.
It's a bank! You can take it back any time. But now you don't have to worry about some scoundrel taking it from you. The trick's to add more than you take out.
I've a good flat iron. I'll show you how the Yankees like their collars, and you can take in laundry.
But I almost forgot! You've a letter from Fintan!
Something to warm your night, no doubt.

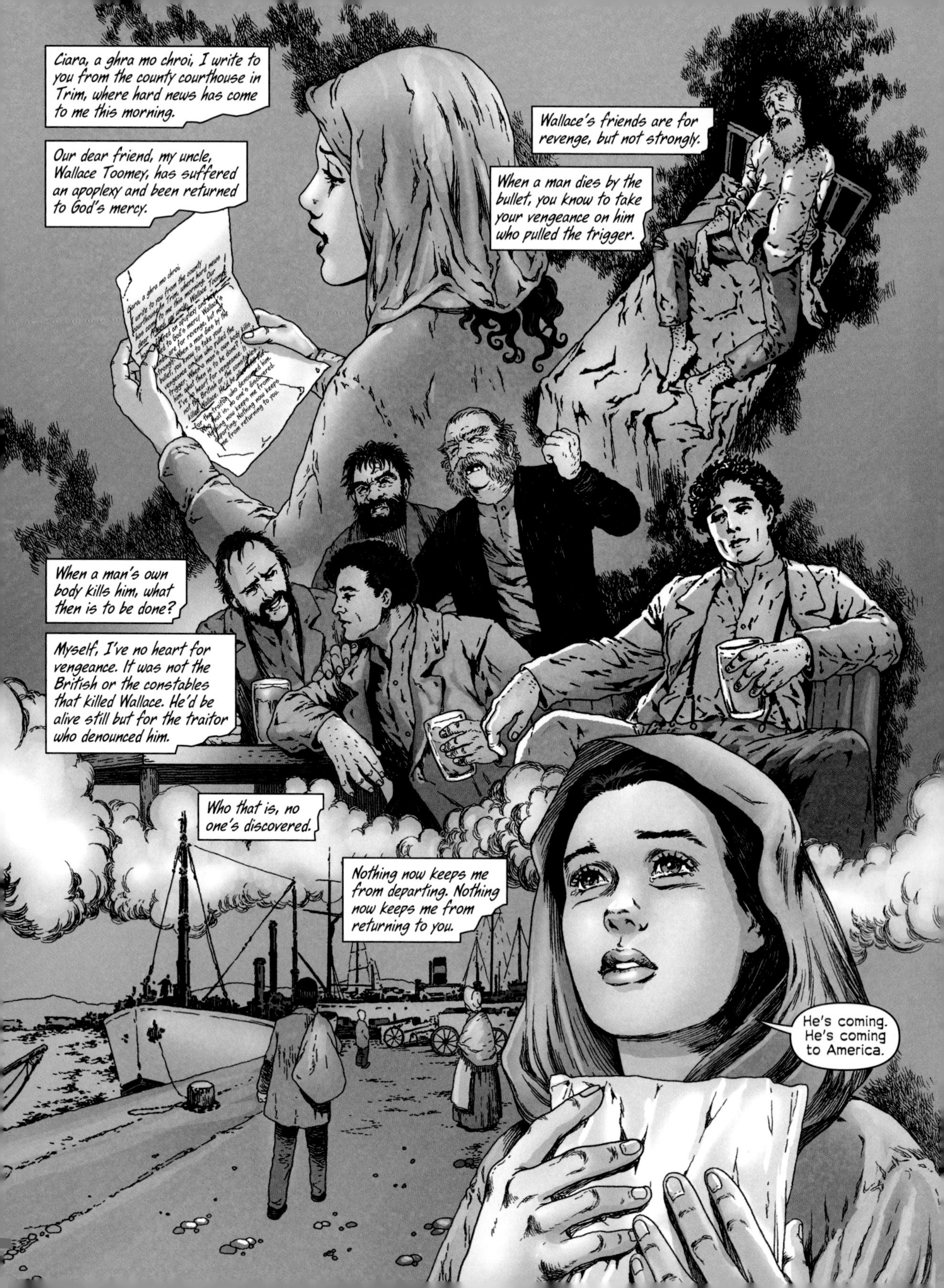
Ciara, a ghra mo chroi, I write to you from the county courthouse in Trim, where hard news has come to me this morning.
Our dear friend, my uncle, Wallace Toomey, has suffered an apoplexy and been returned to God's mercy.
Wallace's friends are for revenge, but not strongly.
When a man dies by the bullet, you know to take your vengeance on him who pulled the trigger.
When a man's own body kills him, what then is to be done?
Myself, I've no heart for vengeance. It was not the British or the constables that killed Wallace. He'd be alive still but for the traitor who denounced him.
Who that is, no one's discovered.
Nothing now keeps me from departing. Nothing now keeps me from returning to you.
He's coming. He's coming to America.

Why *another* production of Julius Caesar? Yes, why indeed?

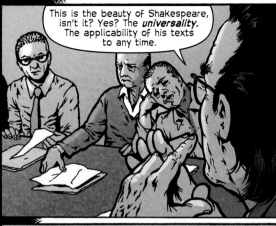

This is the beauty of Shakespeare, isn't it? Yes? The *universality.* The applicability of his texts to any time.

When Antony says "So are they all, all honourable men," does this not ring somehow familiar? Yes?

We're emerging now from a dark decade, children, filled with "honourable men" doing the most scurrilous things. Ruining lives under the guise of patriotism.

Mr. McCarthy. Mr. Rankin. Mr. Nixon.

Our Julius will rip through the pretensions of these honourable men. Each and every one of you will help me do that. Yes? Yes.

Very well, children. Let's get to work.

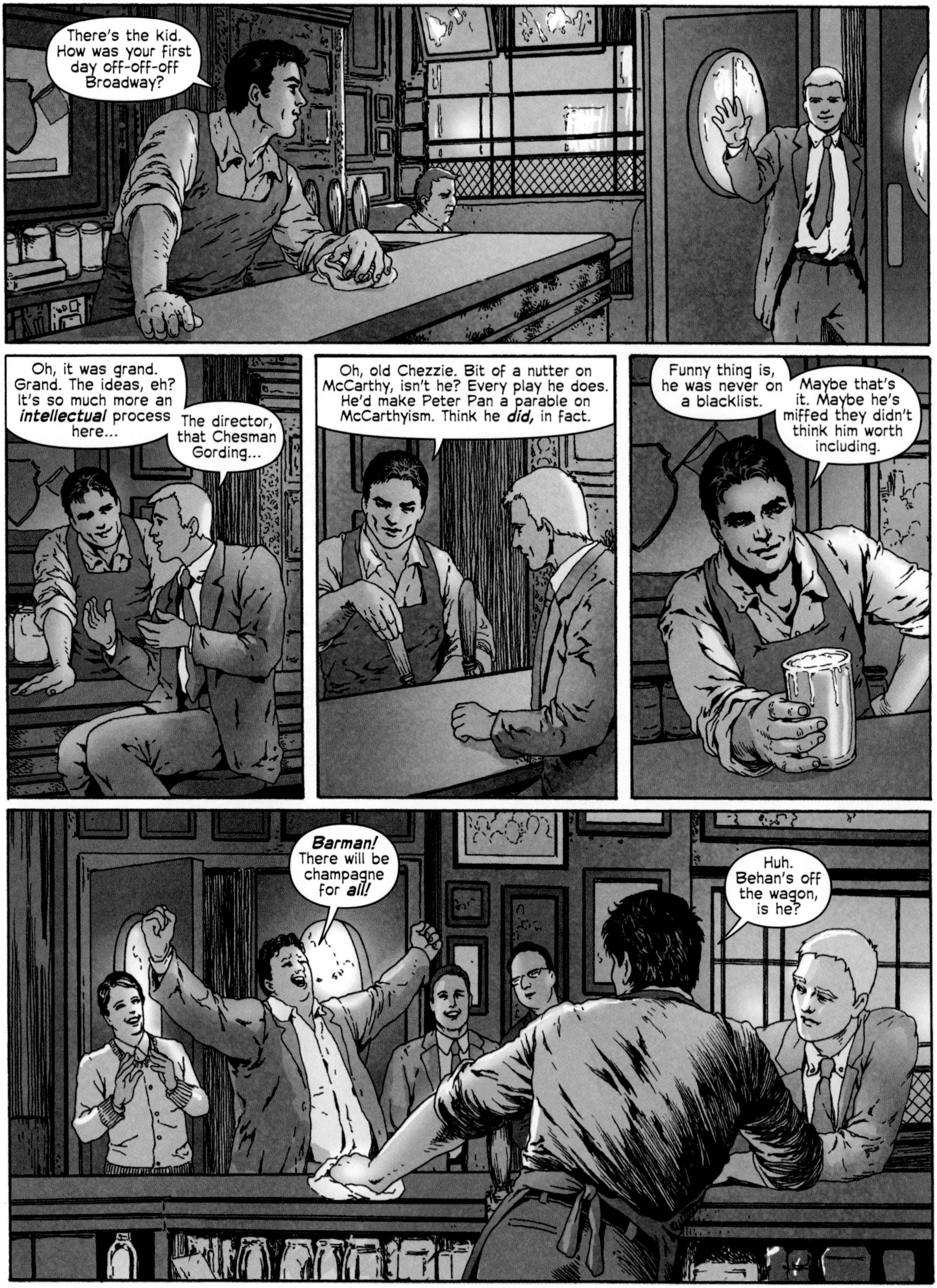
There's the kid. How was your first day off-off-off Broadway?
Oh, it was grand. Grand. The ideas, eh? It's so much more an *intellectual* process here...
The director, that Chesman Gording...
Oh, old Chezzie. Bit of a nutter on McCarthy, isn't he? Every play he does. He'd make Peter Pan a parable on McCarthyism. Think he *did,* in fact.
Funny thing is, he was never on a blacklist.
Maybe that's it. Maybe he's miffed they didn't think him worth including.
Barman! There will be champagne for *all!*
Huh. Behan's off the wagon, is he?

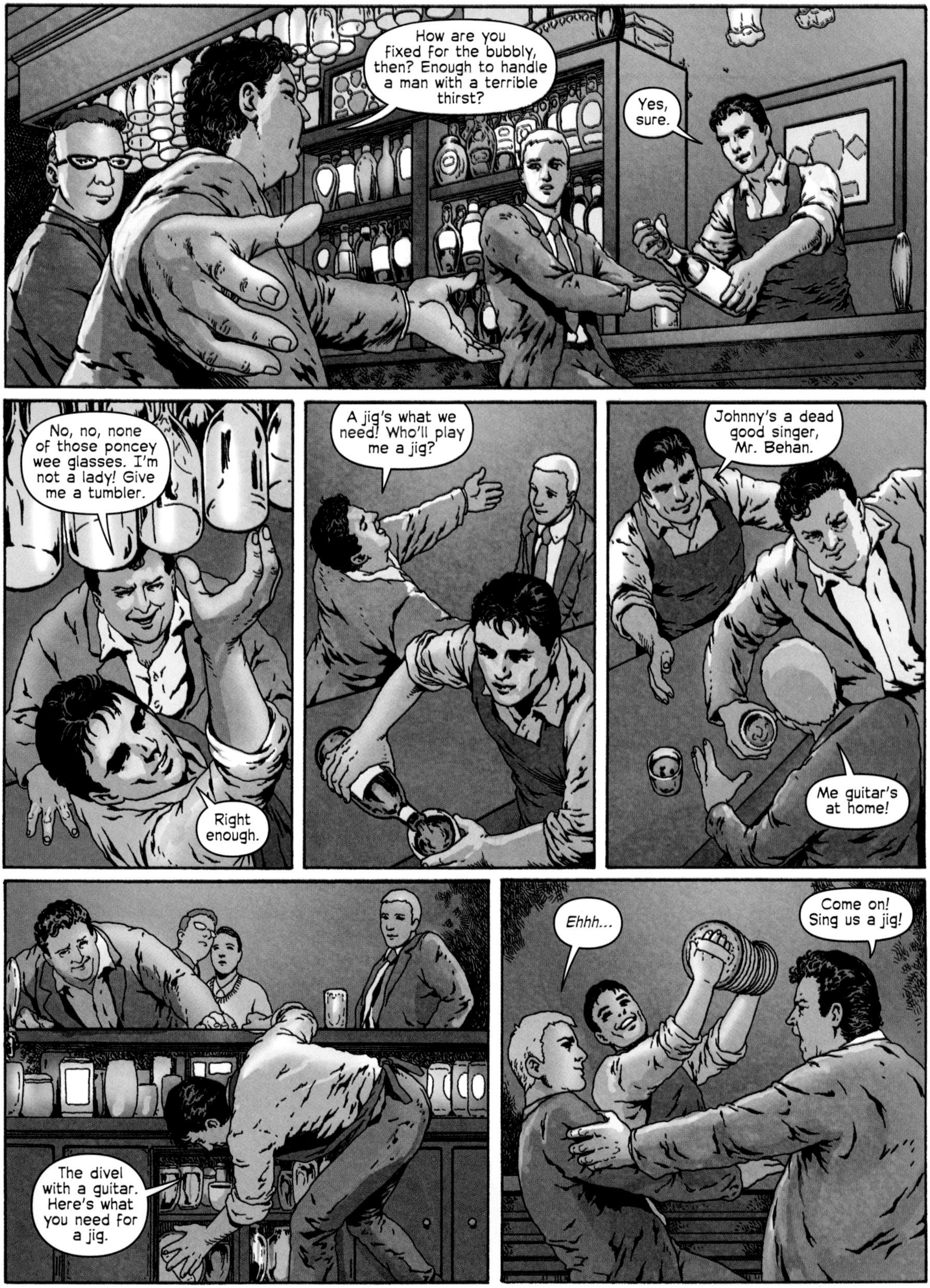
How are you fixed for the bubbly, then? Enough to handle a man with a terrible thirst?
Yes, sure.
No, no, none of those poncey wee glasses. I'm not a lady! Give me a tumbler.
Right enough.
A jig's what we need! Who'll play me a jig?
Johnny's a dead good singer, Mr. Behan.
Me guitar's at home!
The divel with a guitar. Here's what you need for a jig.
Ehhh...
Come on! Sing us a jig!

I....am a little beggarman, a-begging I have been...

...for three score years in this little isle of green. I'm known along the Liffey from the Basin to the Zoo...

And everybody calls me by the name of Johnny Dhu!

I...uh... I *used* to know the words to this one...

Of all the trades a-going, sure the beggin' is the best, for when a man is tired he can sit him down and rest

He can beg for his dinner, he has nothing else to do, but to slip around the corner with his old rigadoo!

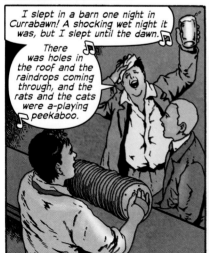

I slept in a barn one night in Currabawn! A shocking wet night it was, but I slept until the dawn.

There was holes in the roof and the raindrops coming through, and the rats and the cats were a-playing peekaboo.

Who did I waken but the woman of the house, with her white spotted apron and her calico blouse. She began to frighten, and I said boo--

Sure, don't be afraid at all--

--it's only Johnny Dhu!

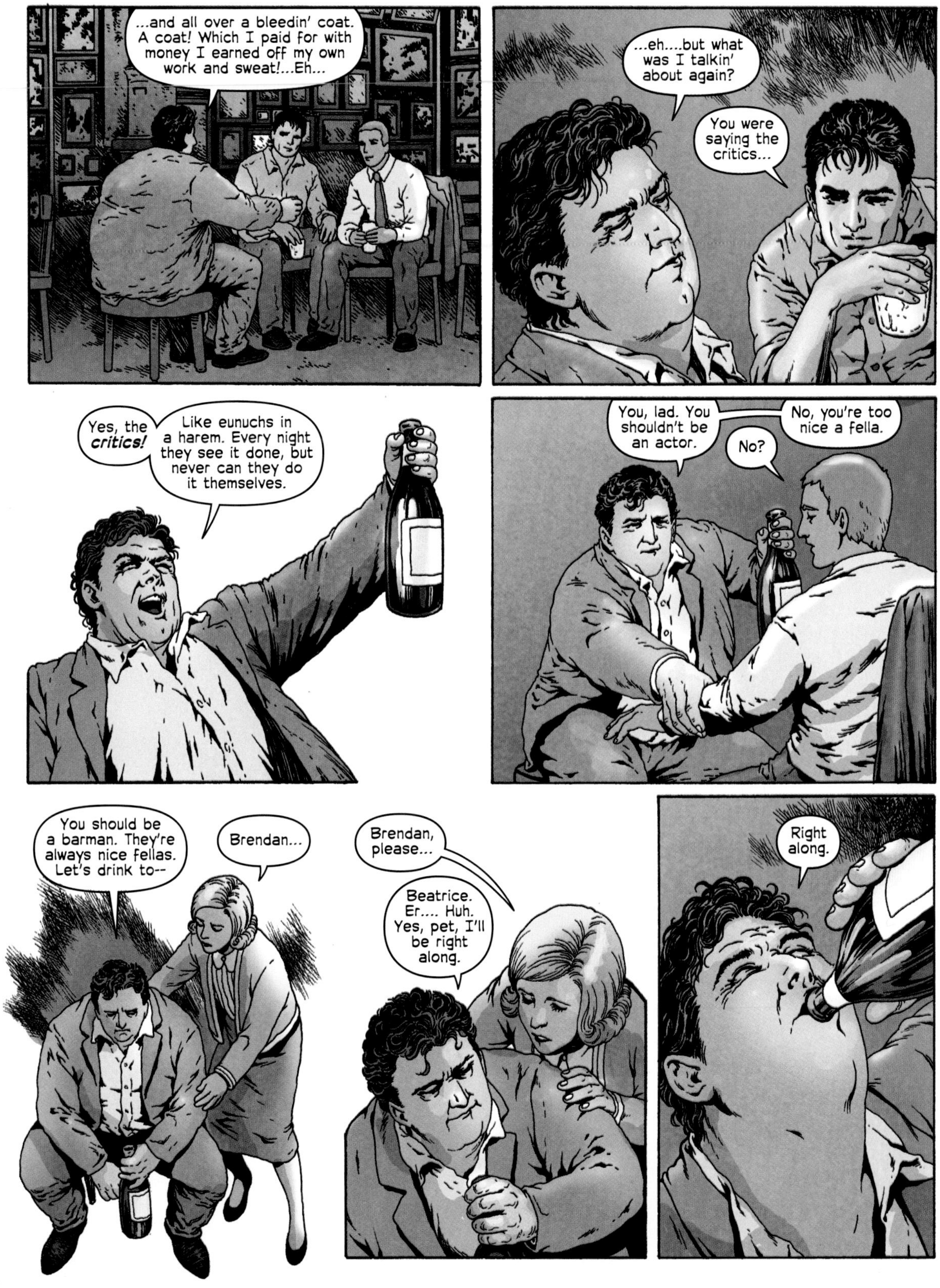
...and all over a bleedin' coat. A coat! Which I paid for with money I earned off my own work and sweat!...Eh...
...eh....but what was I talkin' about again?
You were saying the critics...
Yes, the *critics!*
Like eunuchs in a harem. Every night they see it done, but never can they do it themselves.
You, lad. You shouldn't be an actor.
No?
No, you're too nice a fella.
You should be a barman. They're always nice fellas. Let's drink to--
Brendan...
Brendan, please...
Beatrice. Er.... Huh. Yes, pet, I'll be right along.
Right along.

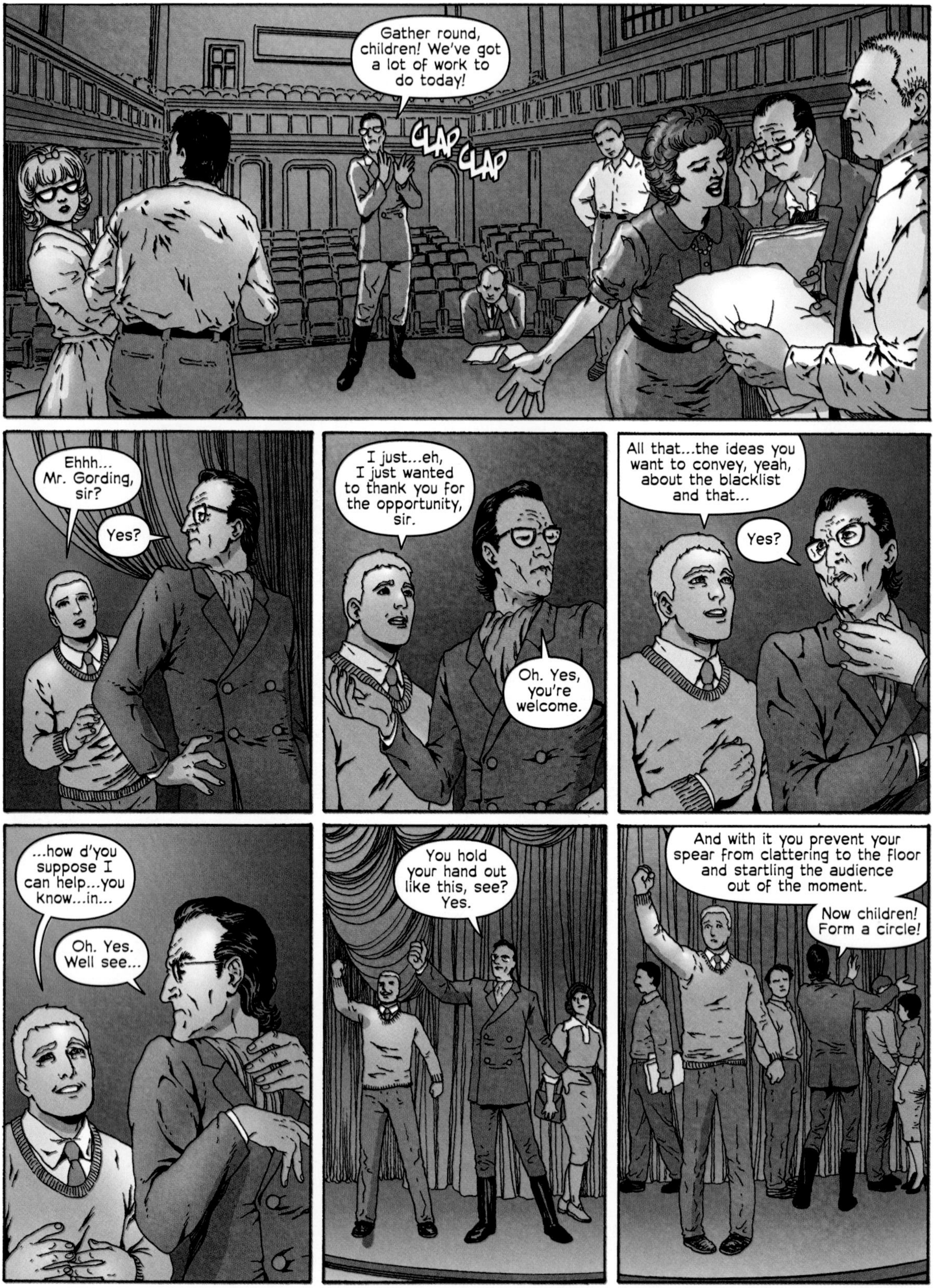
Gather round, children! We've got a lot of work to do today!
CLAP CLAP
Ehhh... Mr. Gording, sir?
Yes?
I just...eh, I just wanted to thank you for the opportunity, sir.
Oh. Yes, you're welcome.
All that...the ideas you want to convey, yeah, about the blacklist and that...
Yes?
...how d'you suppose I can help...you know...in...
Oh. Yes. Well see...
You hold your hand out like this, see? Yes.
And with it you prevent your spear from clattering to the floor and startling the audience out of the moment.
Now children! Form a circle!

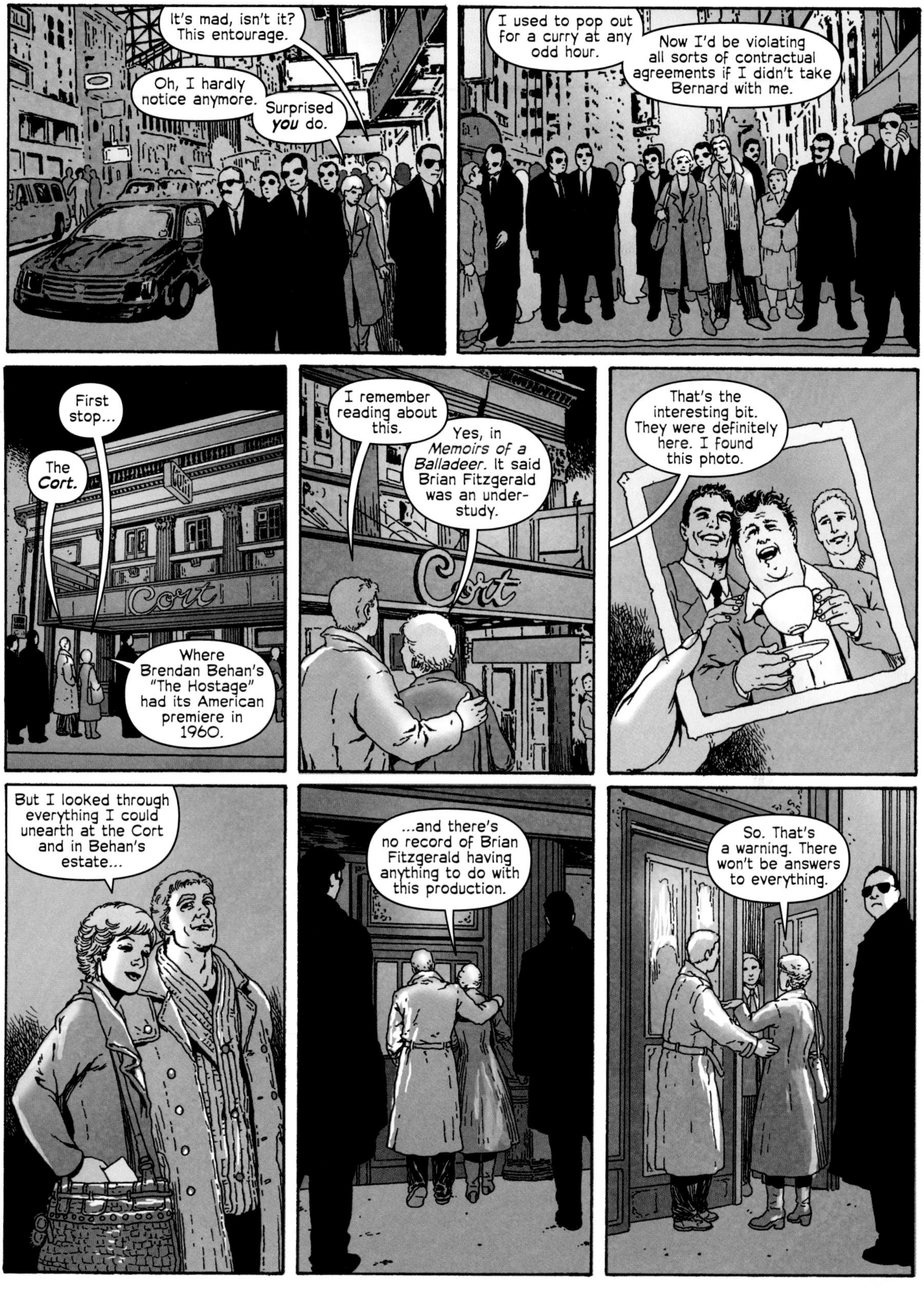
It's mad, isn't it? This entourage.
Oh, I hardly notice anymore.
Surprised *you* do.
I used to pop out for a curry at any odd hour.
Now I'd be violating all sorts of contractual agreements if I didn't take Bernard with me.
First stop...
The *Cort.*
Where Brendan Behan's "The Hostage" had its American premiere in 1960.
I remember reading about this.
Yes, in *Memoirs of a Balladeer.* It said Brian Fitzgerald was an understudy.
That's the interesting bit. They were definitely here. I found this photo.
But I looked through everything I could unearth at the Cort and in Behan's estate...
...and there's no record of Brian Fitzgerald having anything to do with this production.
So. That's a warning. There won't be answers to everything.

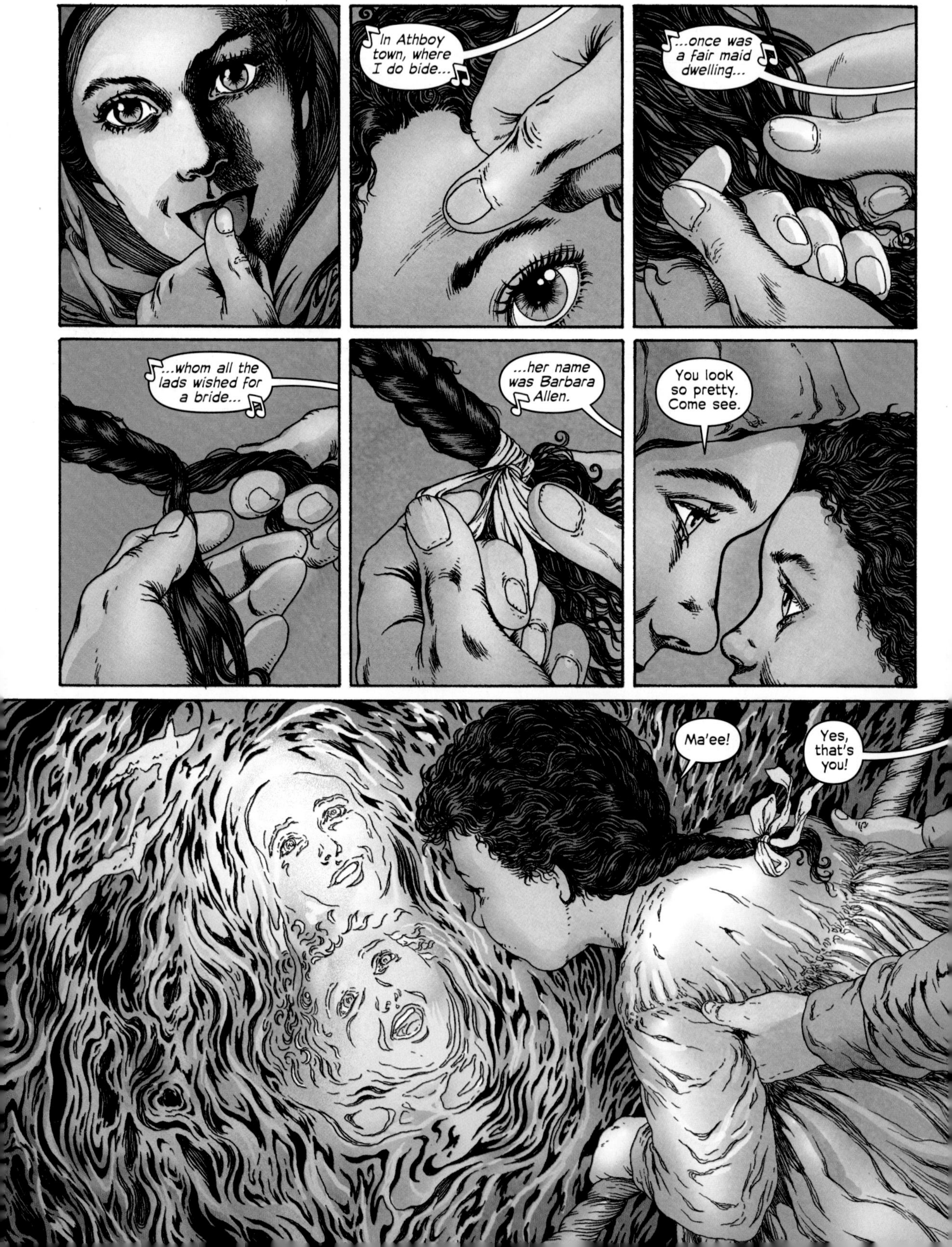
In Athboy town, where I do bide...
...once was a fair maid dwelling...
...whom all the lads wished for a bride...
...her name was Barbara Allen.
You look so pretty. Come see.
Ma'ee!
Yes, that's you!

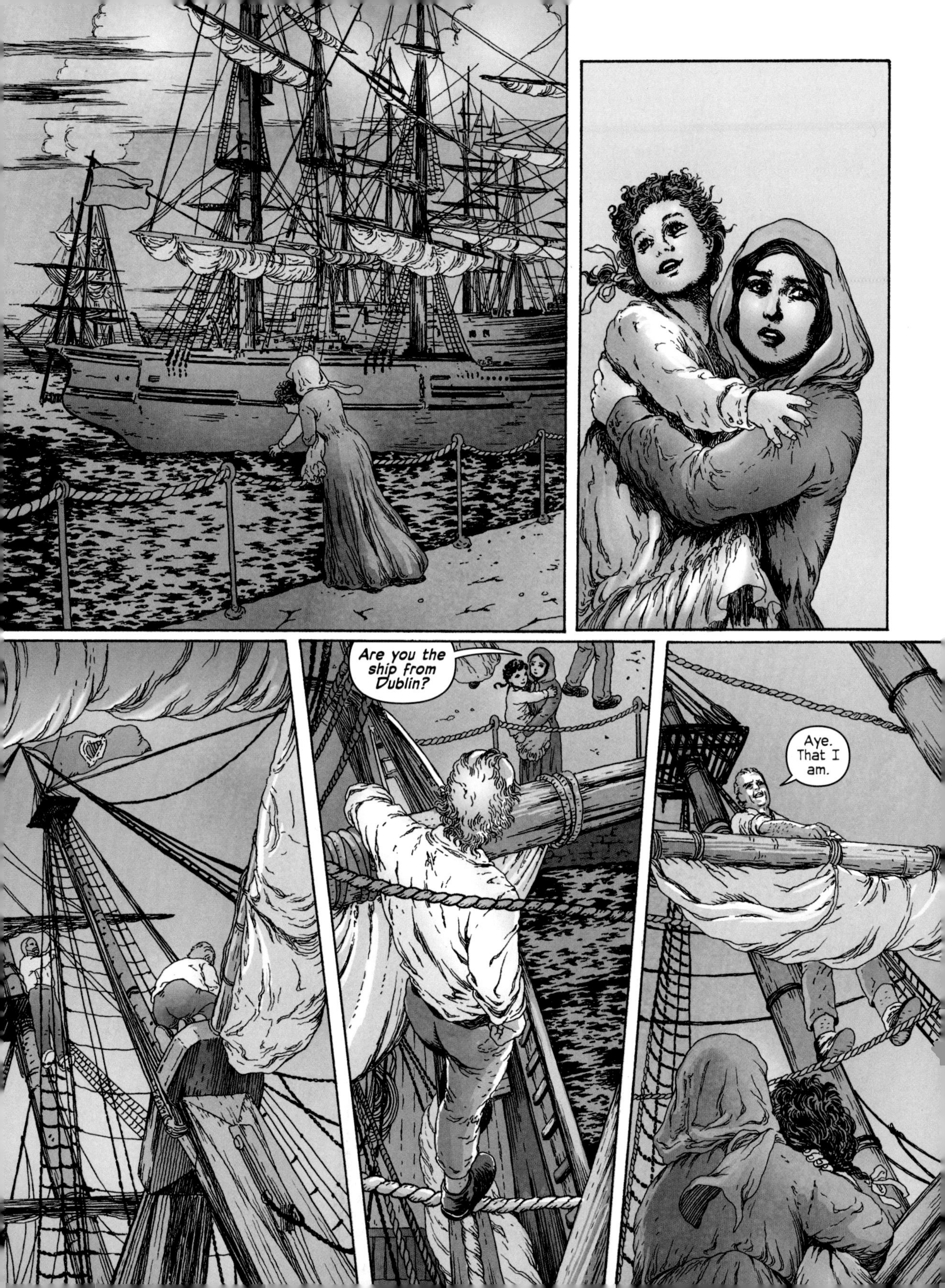
Are you the ship from Dublin?
Aye. That I am.

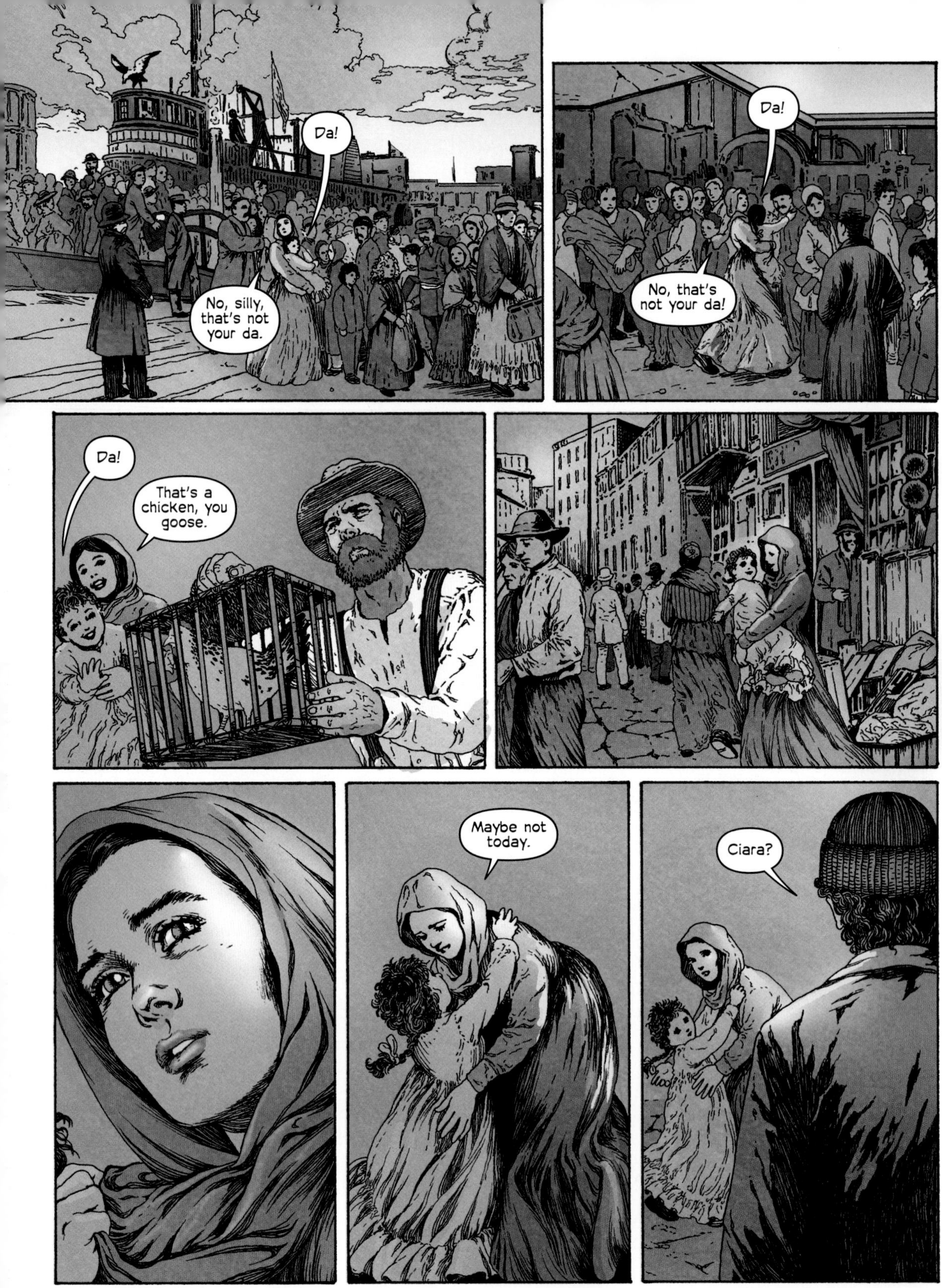
Da!
No, silly, that's not your da.
Da!
No, that's not your da!
Da!
That's a chicken, you goose.
Maybe not today.
Ciara?

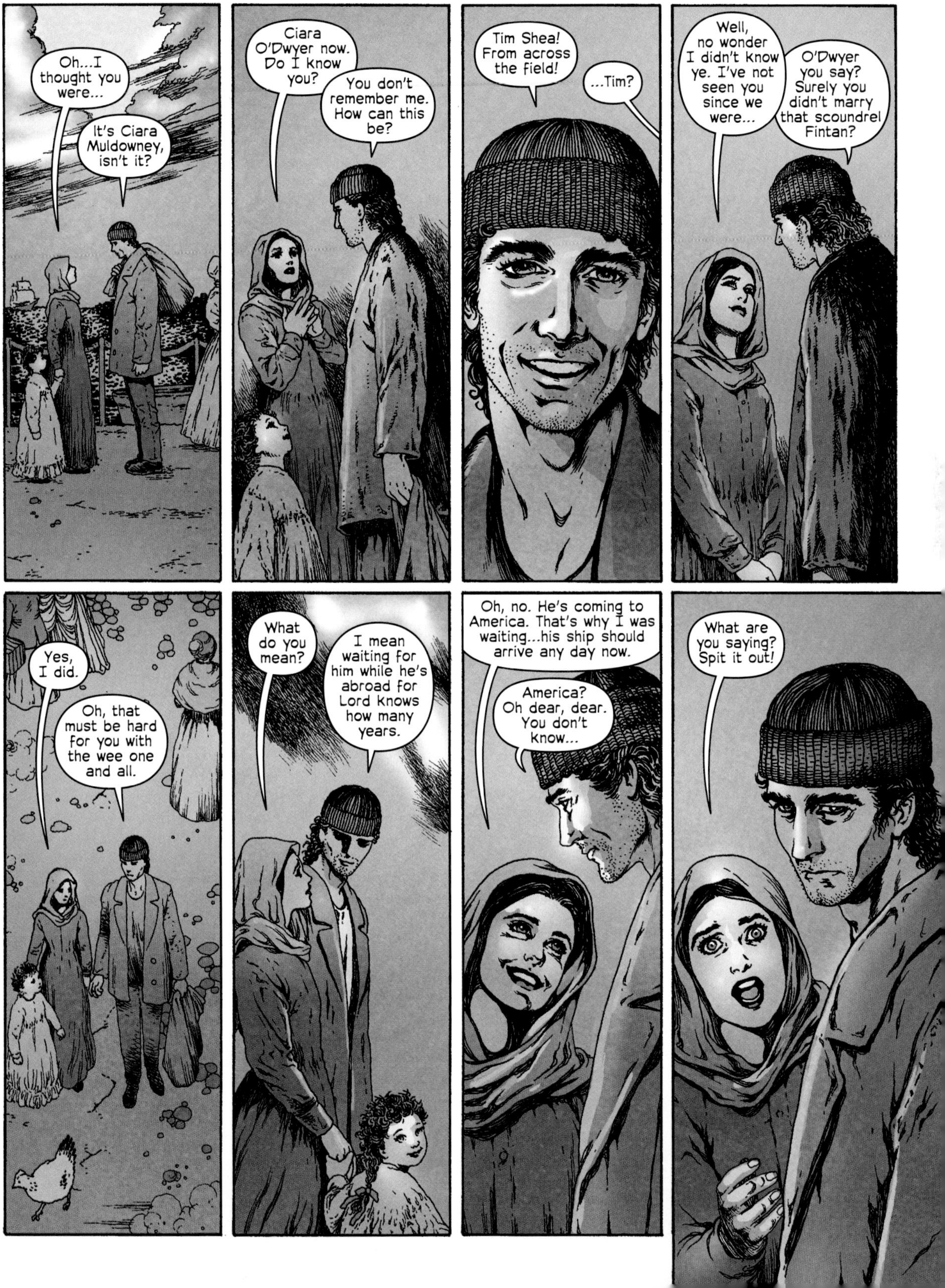
Oh...I thought you were...
It's Ciara Muldowney, isn't it?
Ciara O'Dwyer now. Do I know you?
You don't remember me. How can this be?
Tim Shea! From across the field!
...Tim?
Well, no wonder I didn't know ye. I've not seen you since we were...
O'Dwyer you say? Surely you didn't marry that scoundrel Fintan?
Yes, I did.
Oh, that must be hard for you with the wee one and all.
What do you mean?
I mean waiting for him while he's abroad for Lord knows how many years.
Oh, no. He's coming to America. That's why I was waiting...his ship should arrive any day now.
America? Oh dear, dear. You don't know...
What are you saying? Spit it out!

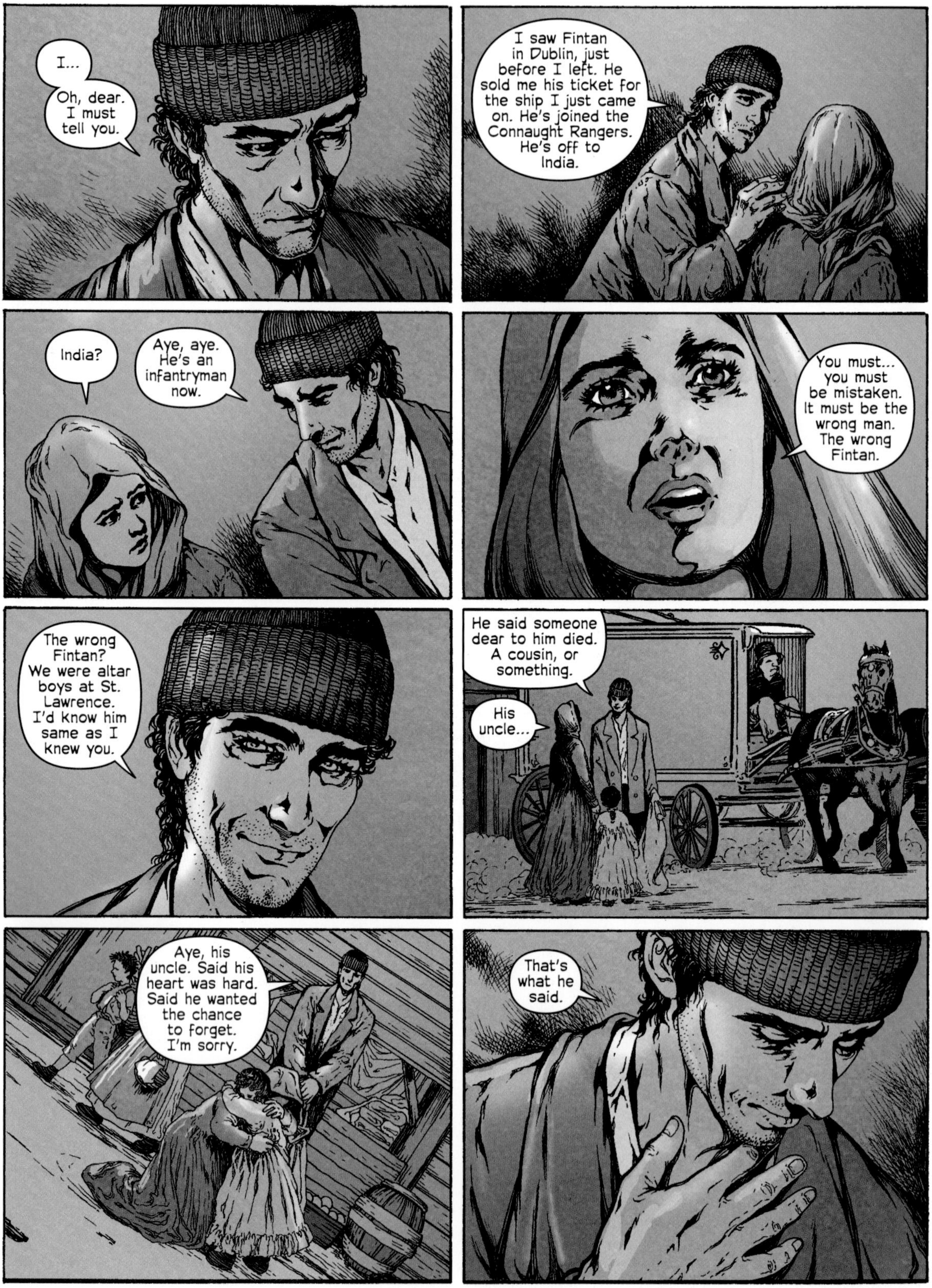
I...
Oh, dear. I must tell you.
I saw Fintan in Dublin, just before I left. He sold me his ticket for the ship I just came on. He's joined the Connaught Rangers. He's off to India.
India?
Aye, aye. He's an infantryman now.
You must... you must be mistaken. It must be the wrong man. The wrong Fintan.
The wrong Fintan? We were altar boys at St. Lawrence. I'd know him same as I knew you.
He said someone dear to him died. A cousin, or something.
His uncle...
Aye, his uncle. Said his heart was hard. Said he wanted the chance to forget. I'm sorry.
That's what he said.

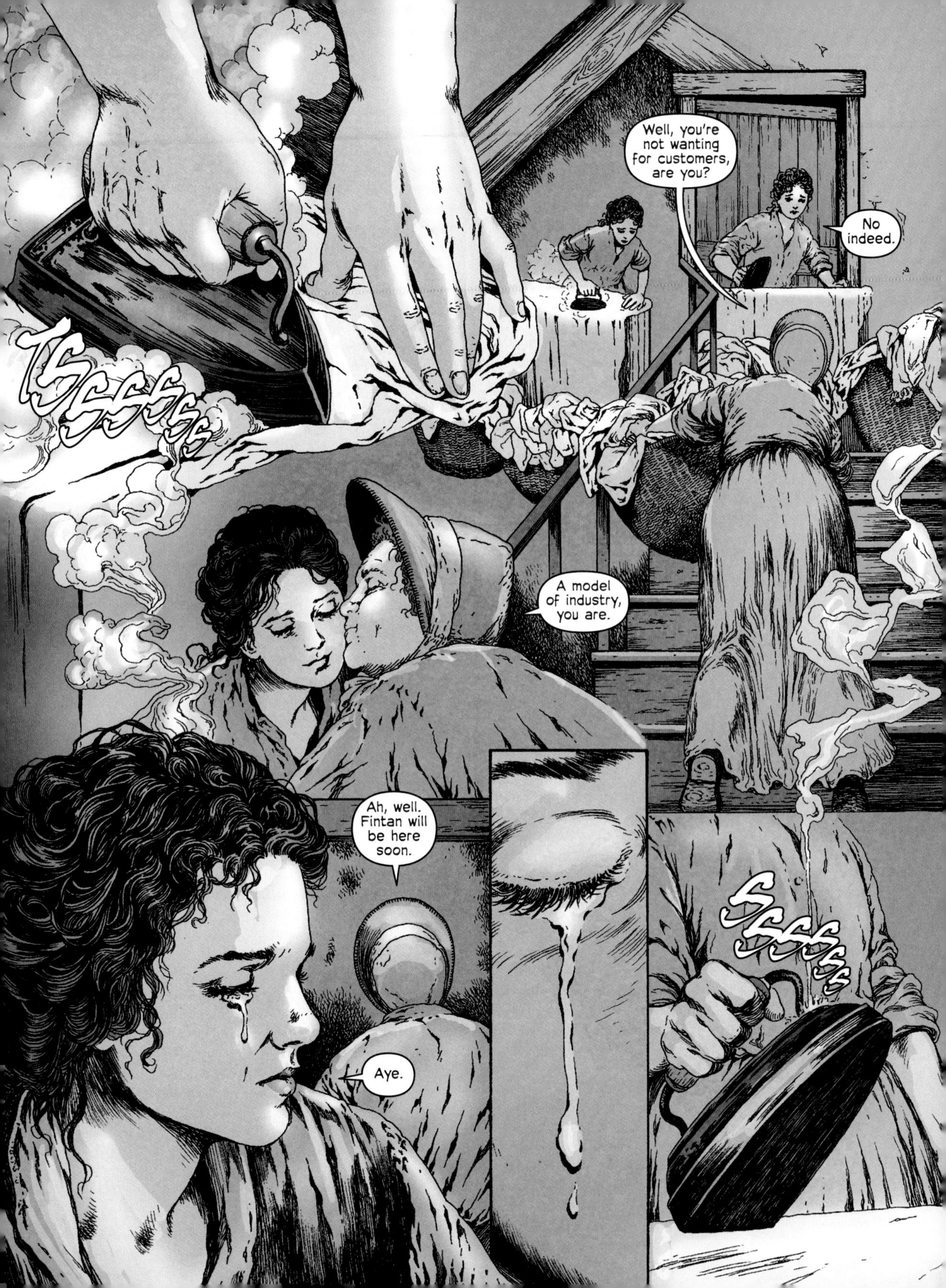

TSSSSSS
Well, you're not wanting for customers, are you?
No indeed.
A model of industry, you are.
Ah, well. Fintan will be here soon.
Aye.
SSSSSS

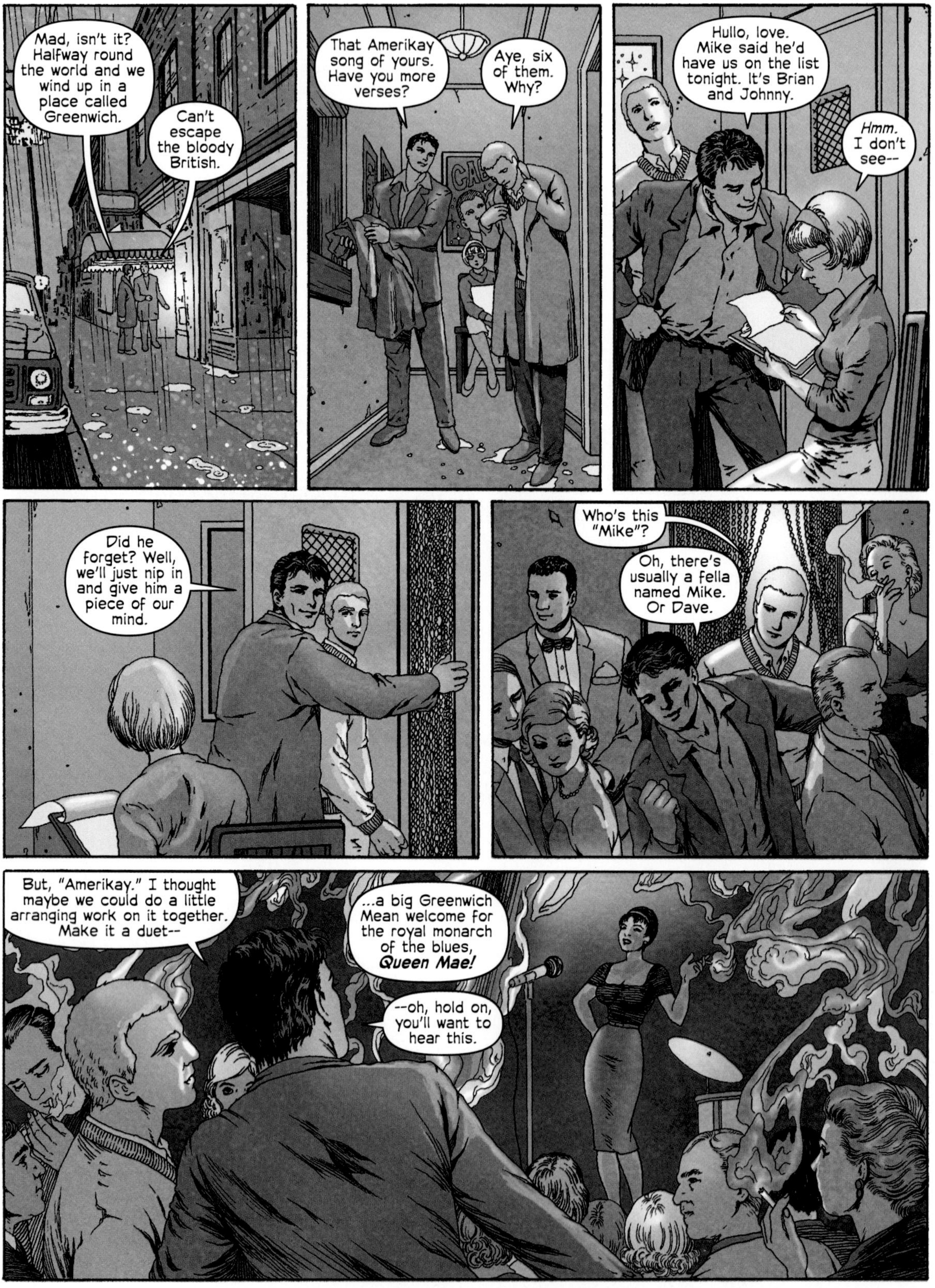
Mad, isn't it? Halfway round the world and we wind up in a place called Greenwich.
Can't escape the bloody British.
That Amerikay song of yours. Have you more verses?
Aye, six of them. Why?
Hullo, love. Mike said he'd have us on the list tonight. It's Brian and Johnny.
Hmm. I don't see--
Did he forget? Well, we'll just nip in and give him a piece of our mind.
Who's this "Mike"?
Oh, there's usually a fella named Mike. Or Dave.
But, "Amerikay." I thought maybe we could do a little arranging work on it together. Make it a duet--
...a big Greenwich Mean welcome for the royal monarch of the blues, ***Queen Mae!***
--oh, hold on, you'll want to hear this.

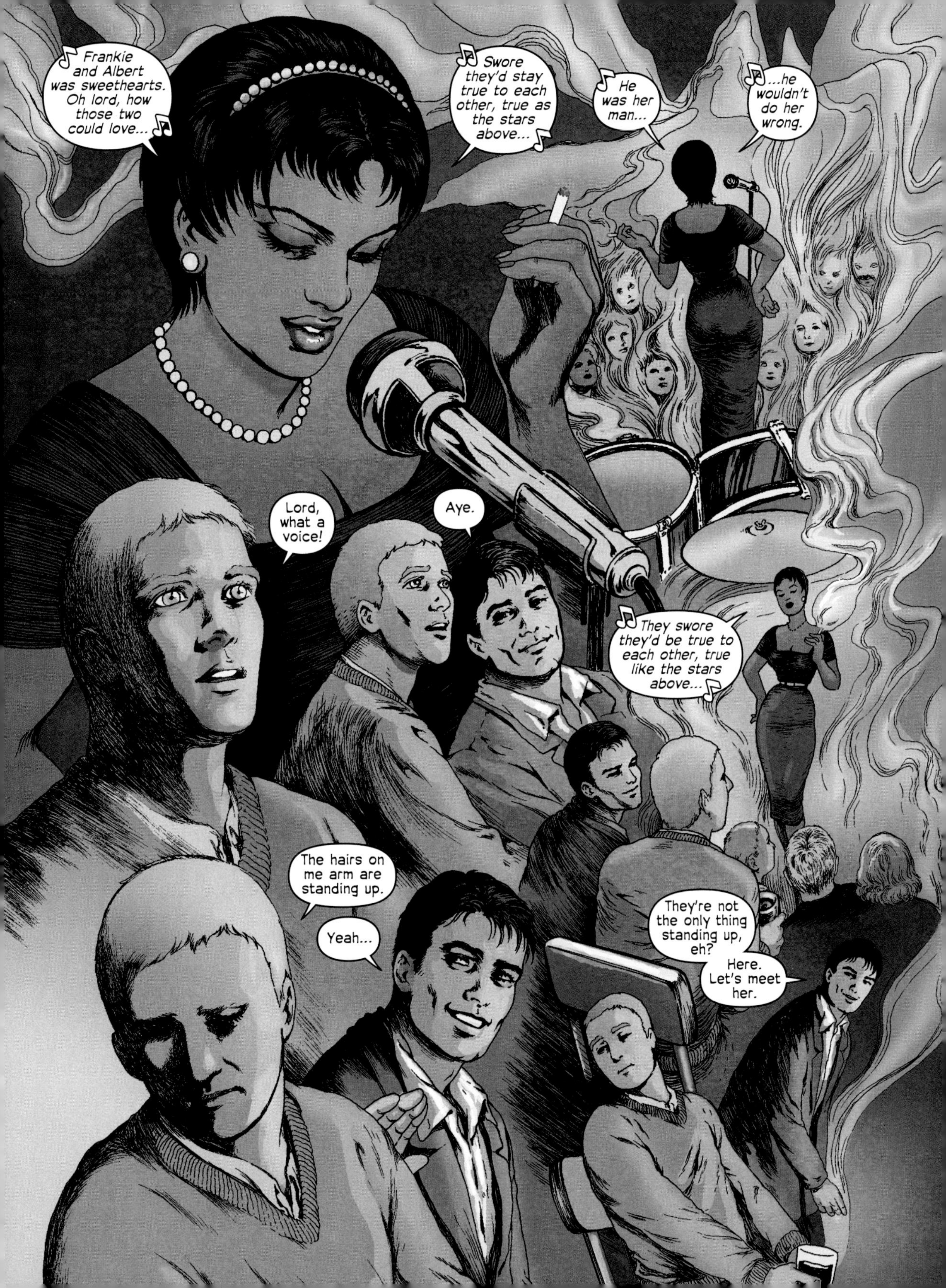
Frankie and Albert was sweethearts. Oh lord, how those two could love...
Swore they'd stay true to each other, true as the stars above...
He was her man...
...he wouldn't do her wrong.
Lord, what a voice!
Aye.
They swore they'd be true to each other, true like the stars above...
The hairs on me arm are standing up.
Yeah...
They're not the only thing standing up, eh?
Here. Let's meet her.

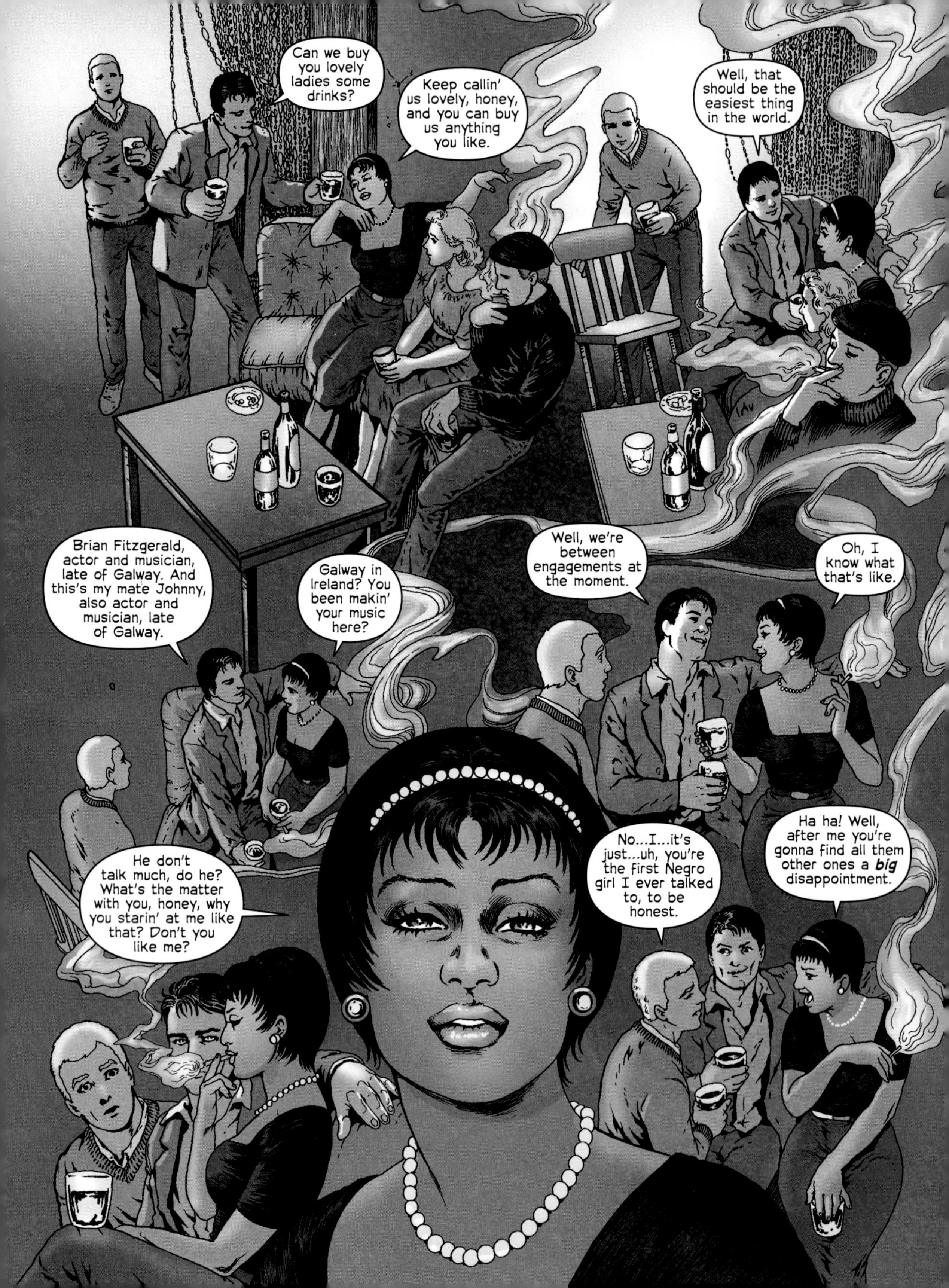
Can we buy you lovely ladies some drinks?
Keep callin' us lovely, honey, and you can buy us anything you like.
Well, that should be the easiest thing in the world.
Brian Fitzgerald, actor and musician, late of Galway. And this's my mate Johnny, also actor and musician, late of Galway.
Galway in Ireland? You been makin' your music here?
Well, we're between engagements at the moment.
Oh, I know what that's like.
He don't talk much, do he? What's the matter with you, honey, why you starin' at me like that? Don't you like me?
No...I...it's just...uh, you're the first Negro girl I ever talked to, to be honest.
Ha ha! Well, after me you're gonna find all them other ones a *big* disappointment.

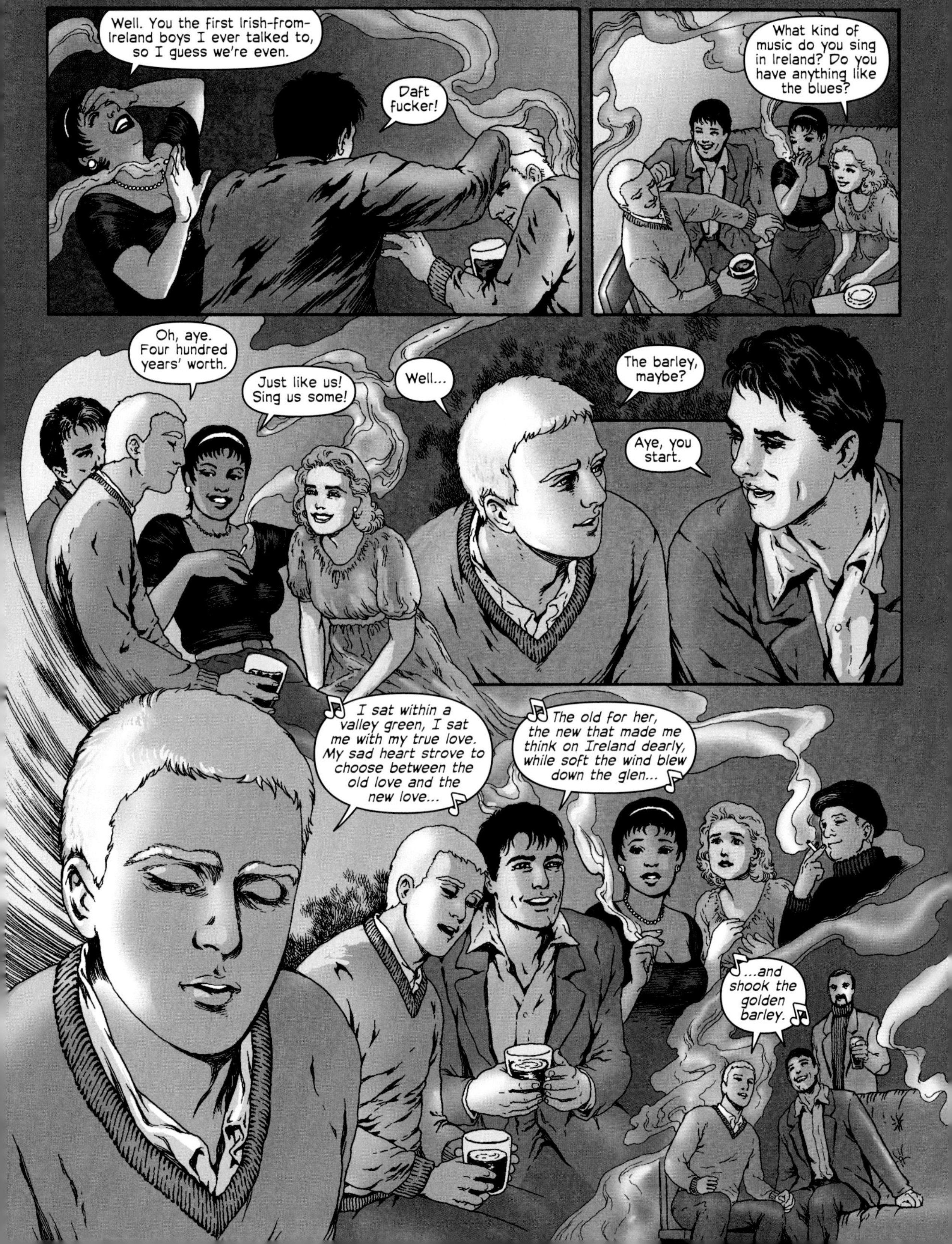
Well. You the first Irish-from-Ireland boys I ever talked to, so I guess we're even.
Daft fucker!
What kind of music do you sing in Ireland? Do you have anything like the blues?
Oh, aye. Four hundred years' worth.
Just like us! Sing us some!
Well...
The barley, maybe?
Aye, you start.
I sat within a valley green, I sat me with my true love. My sad heart strove to choose between the old love and the new love...
The old for her, the new that made me think on Ireland dearly, while soft the wind blew down the glen...
...and shook the golden barley.

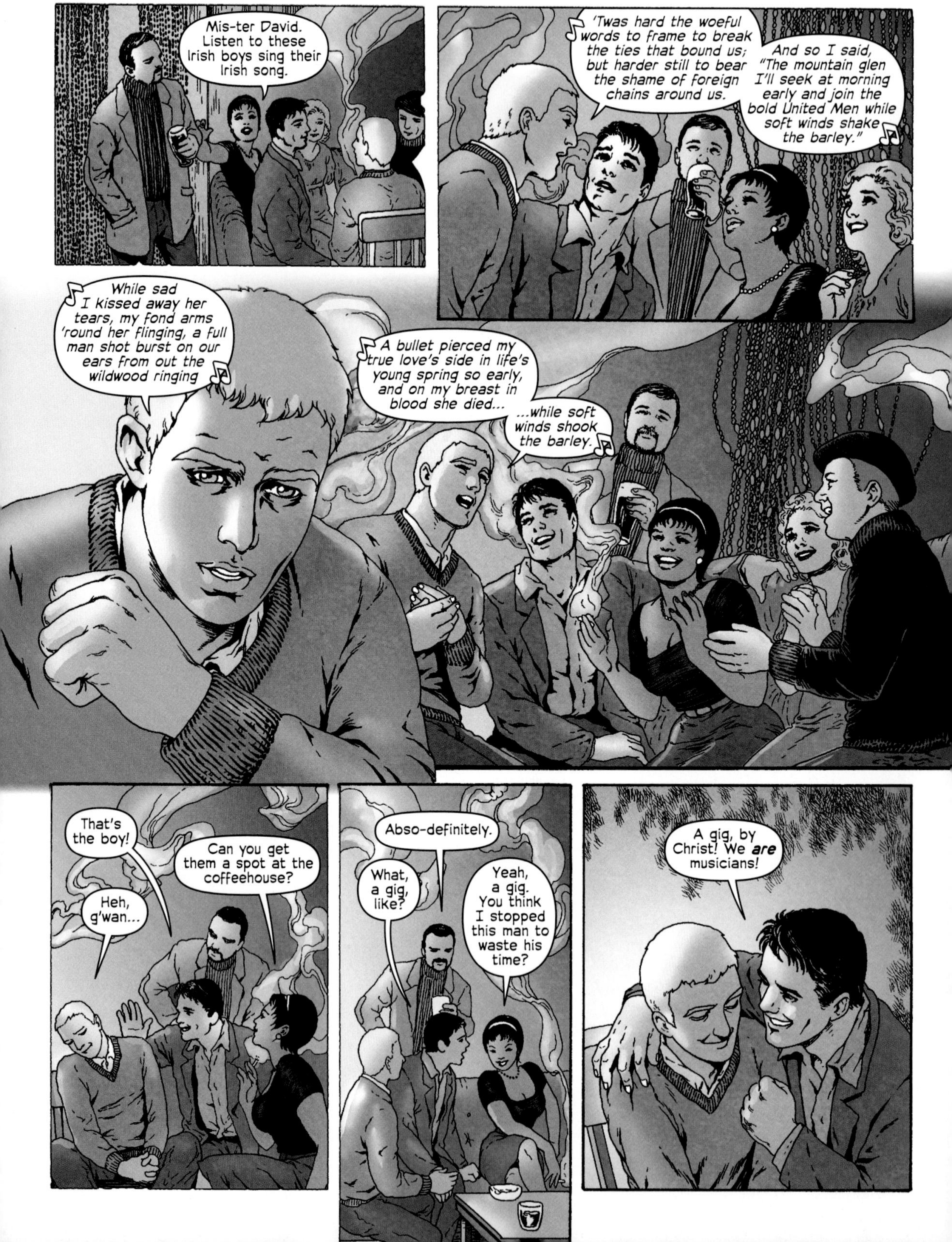

Mis-ter David. Listen to these Irish boys sing their Irish song.
'Twas hard the woeful words to frame to break the ties that bound us; but harder still to bear the shame of foreign chains around us.
And so I said, "The mountain glen I'll seek at morning early and join the bold United Men while soft winds shake the barley."
While sad I kissed away her tears, my fond arms 'round her flinging, a full man shot burst on our ears from out the wildwood ringing
A bullet pierced my true love's side in life's young spring so early, and on my breast in blood she died...
...while soft winds shook the barley.
That's the boy!
Heh, g'wan...
Can you get them a spot at the coffeehouse?
Abso-definitely.
What, a gig, like?
Yeah, a gig. You think I stopped this man to waste his time?
A gig, by Christ! We ***are*** musicians!

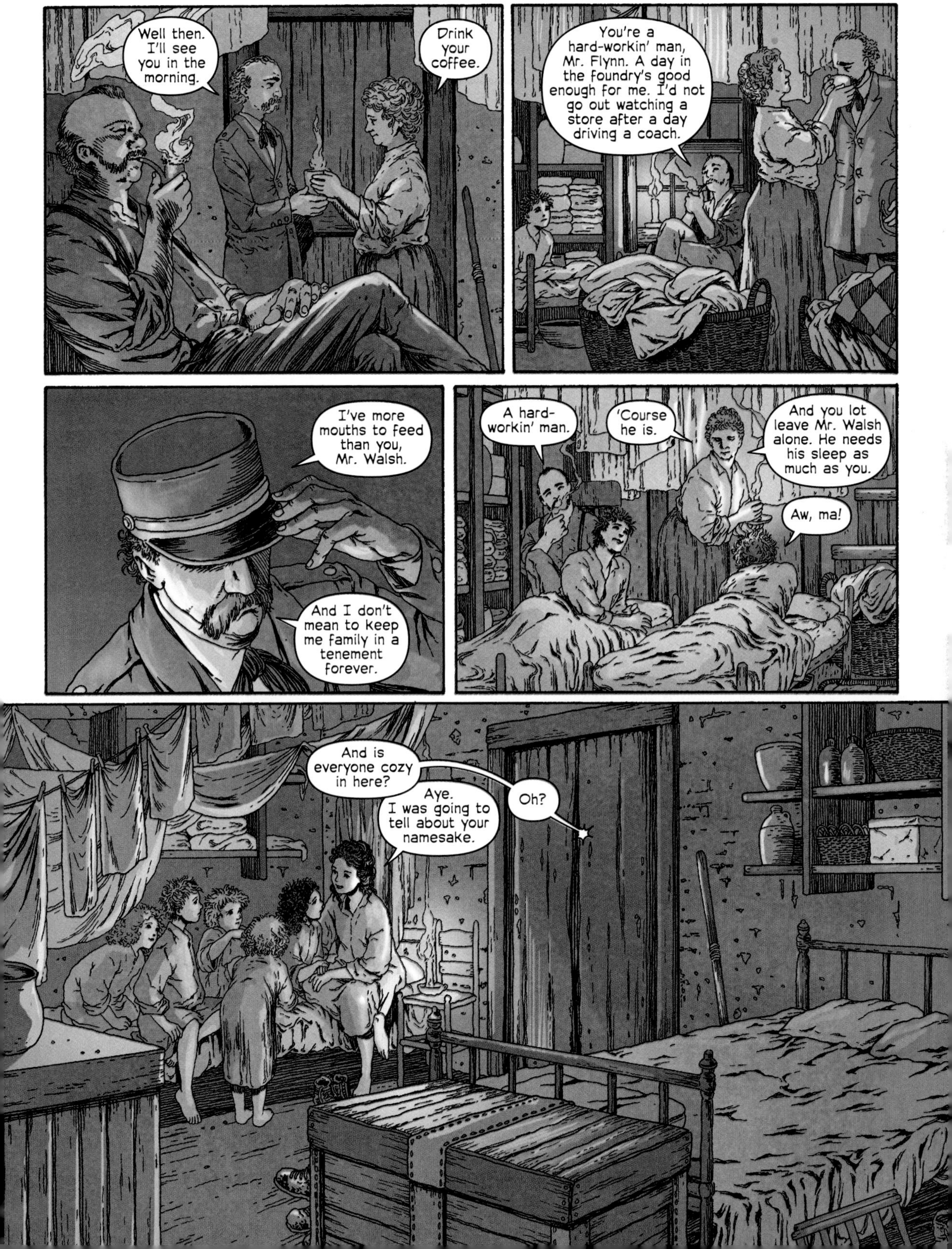
Well then. I'll see you in the morning.
Drink your coffee.
You're a hard-workin' man, Mr. Flynn. A day in the foundry's good enough for me. I'd not go out watching a store after a day driving a coach.
I've more mouths to feed than you, Mr. Walsh.
And I don't mean to keep me family in a tenement forever.
A hard-workin' man.
'Course he is.
And you lot leave Mr. Walsh alone. He needs his sleep as much as you.
Aw, ma!
And is everyone cozy in here?
Aye. I was going to tell about your namesake.
Oh?

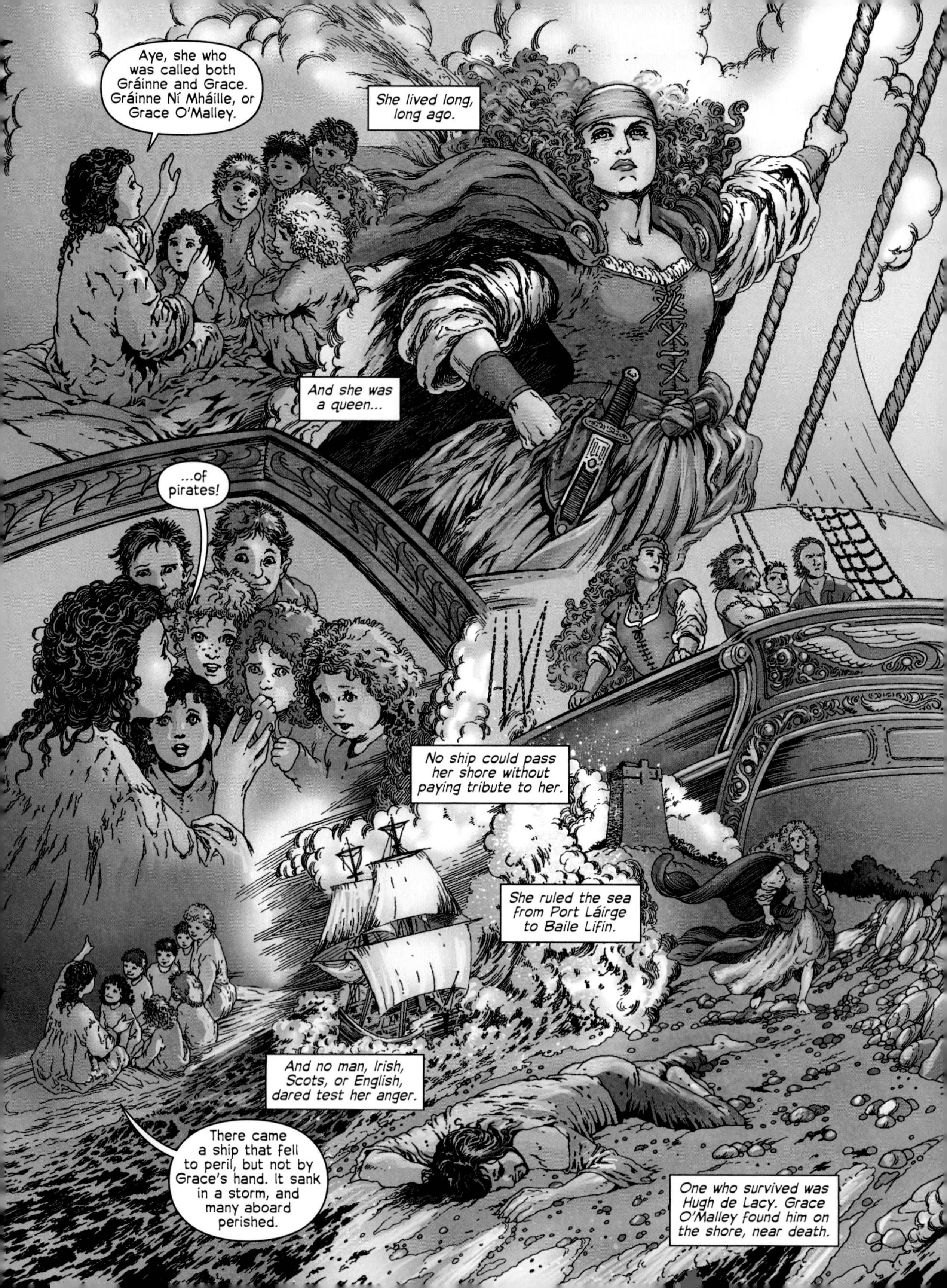
Aye, she who was called both Gráinne and Grace. Gráinne Ní Mháille, or Grace O'Malley.
She lived long, long ago.
And she was a queen...
...of pirates!
No ship could pass her shore without paying tribute to her.
She ruled the sea from Port Láirge to Baile Lifin.
And no man, Irish, Scots, or English, dared test her anger.
There came a ship that fell to peril, but not by Grace's hand. It sank in a storm, and many aboard perished.
One who survived was Hugh de Lacy. Grace O'Malley found him on the shore, near death.

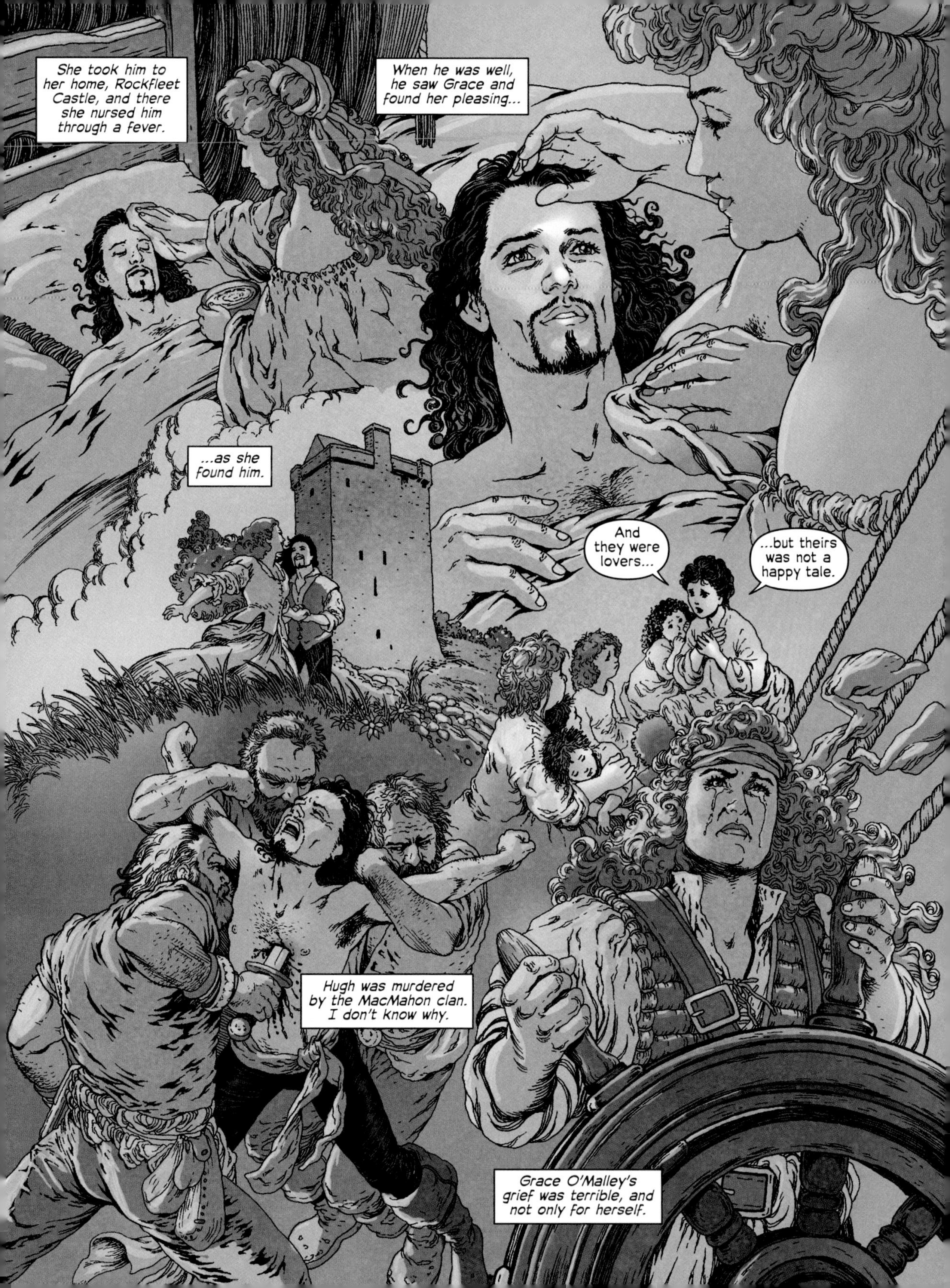
She took him to her home, Rockfleet Castle, and there she nursed him through a fever.
When he was well, he saw Grace and found her pleasing...
...as she found him.
And they were lovers...
...but theirs was not a happy tale.
Hugh was murdered by the MacMahon clan. I don't know why.
Grace O'Malley's grief was terrible, and not only for herself.

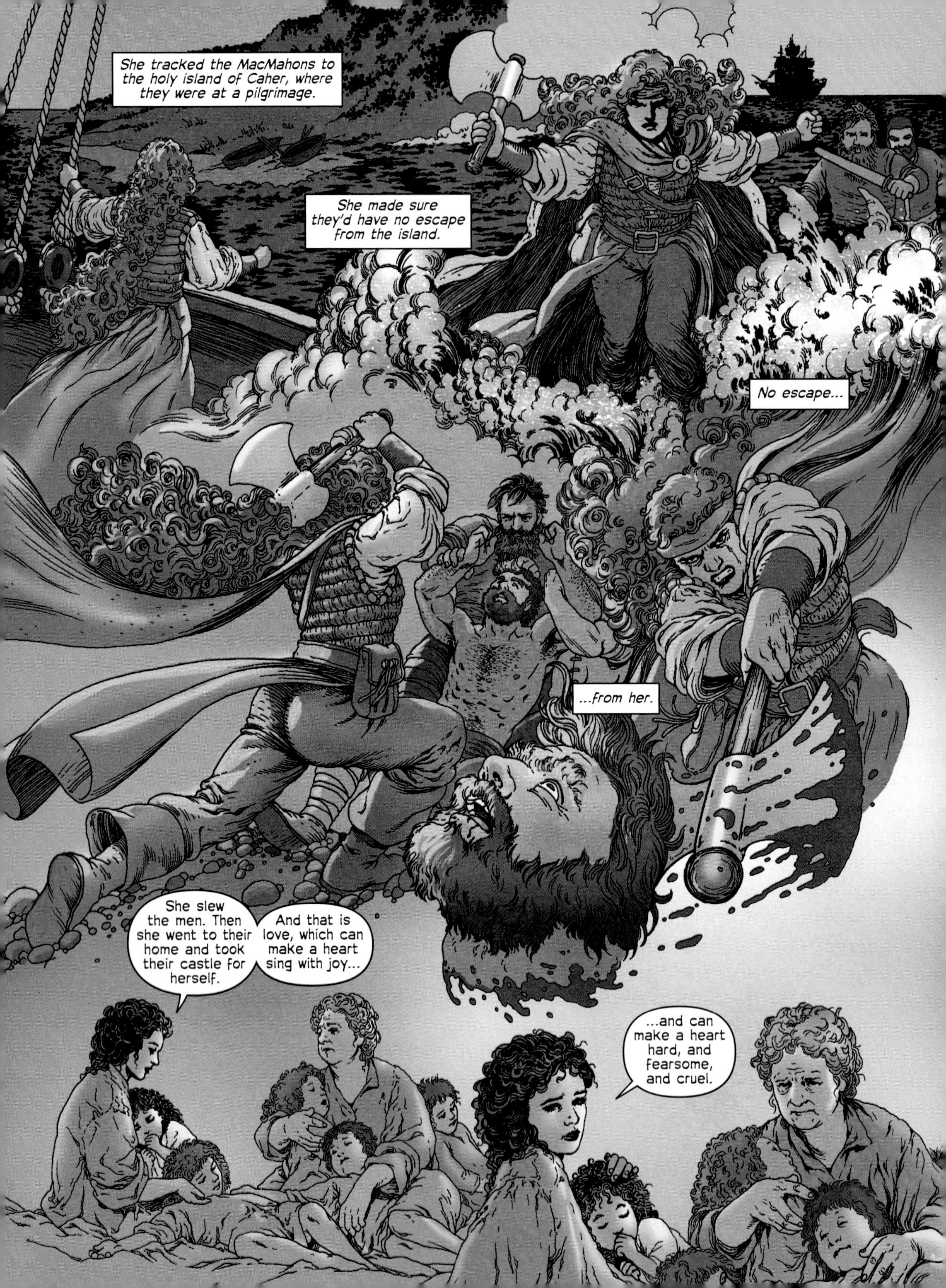
She tracked the MacMahons to the holy island of Caher, where they were at a pilgrimage.
She made sure they'd have no escape from the island.
No escape...
...from her.
She slew the men. Then she went to their home and took their castle for herself.
And that is love, which can make a heart sing with joy...
...and can make a heart hard, and fearsome, and cruel.

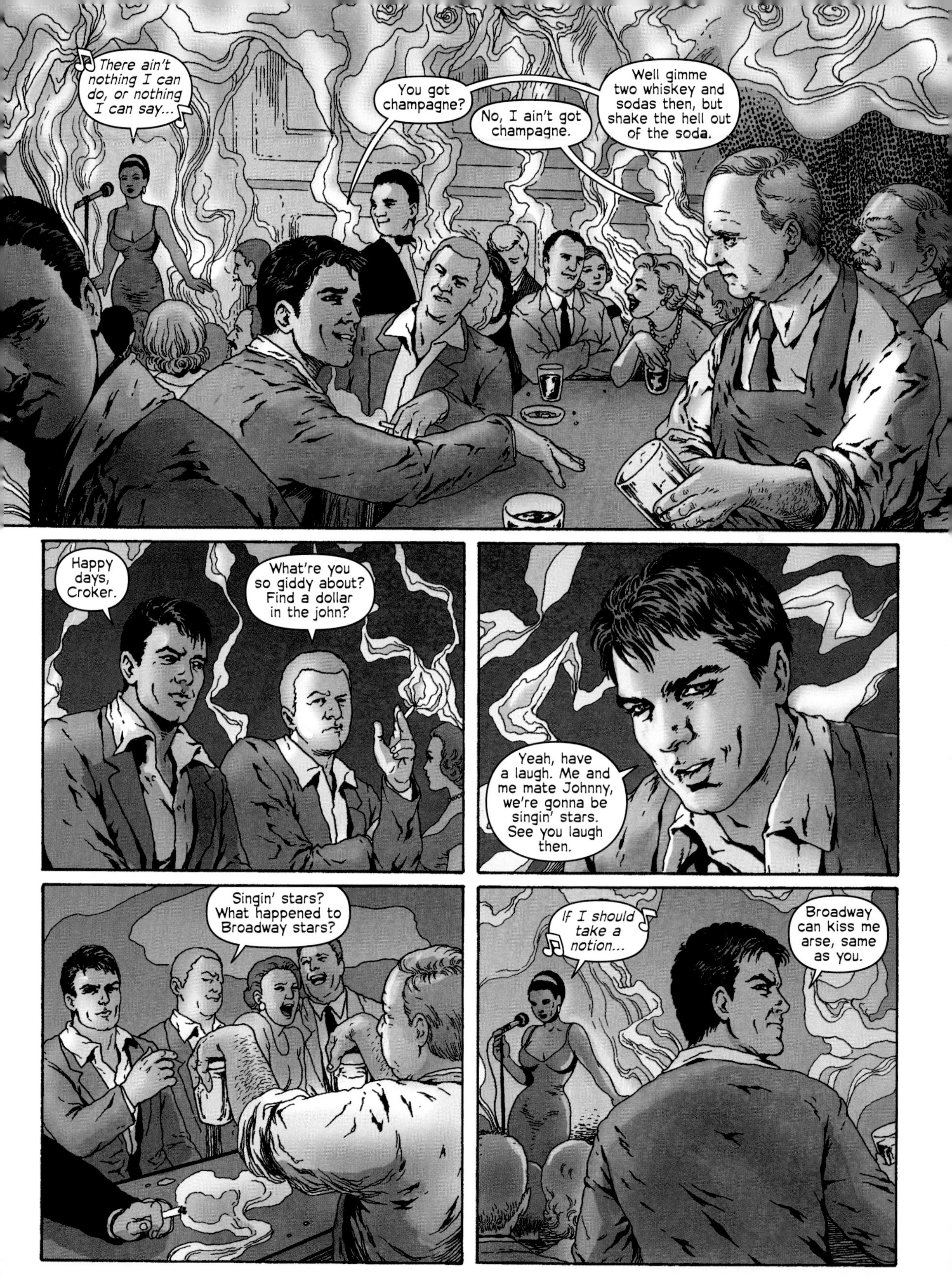
There ain't nothing I can do, or nothing I can say...
You got champagne?
No, I ain't got champagne.
Well gimme two whiskey and sodas then, but shake the hell out of the soda.
Happy days, Croker.
What're you so giddy about? Find a dollar in the john?
Yeah, have a laugh. Me and me mate Johnny, we're gonna be singin' stars. See you laugh then.
Singin' stars? What happened to Broadway stars?
If I should take a notion...
Broadway can kiss me arse, same as you.

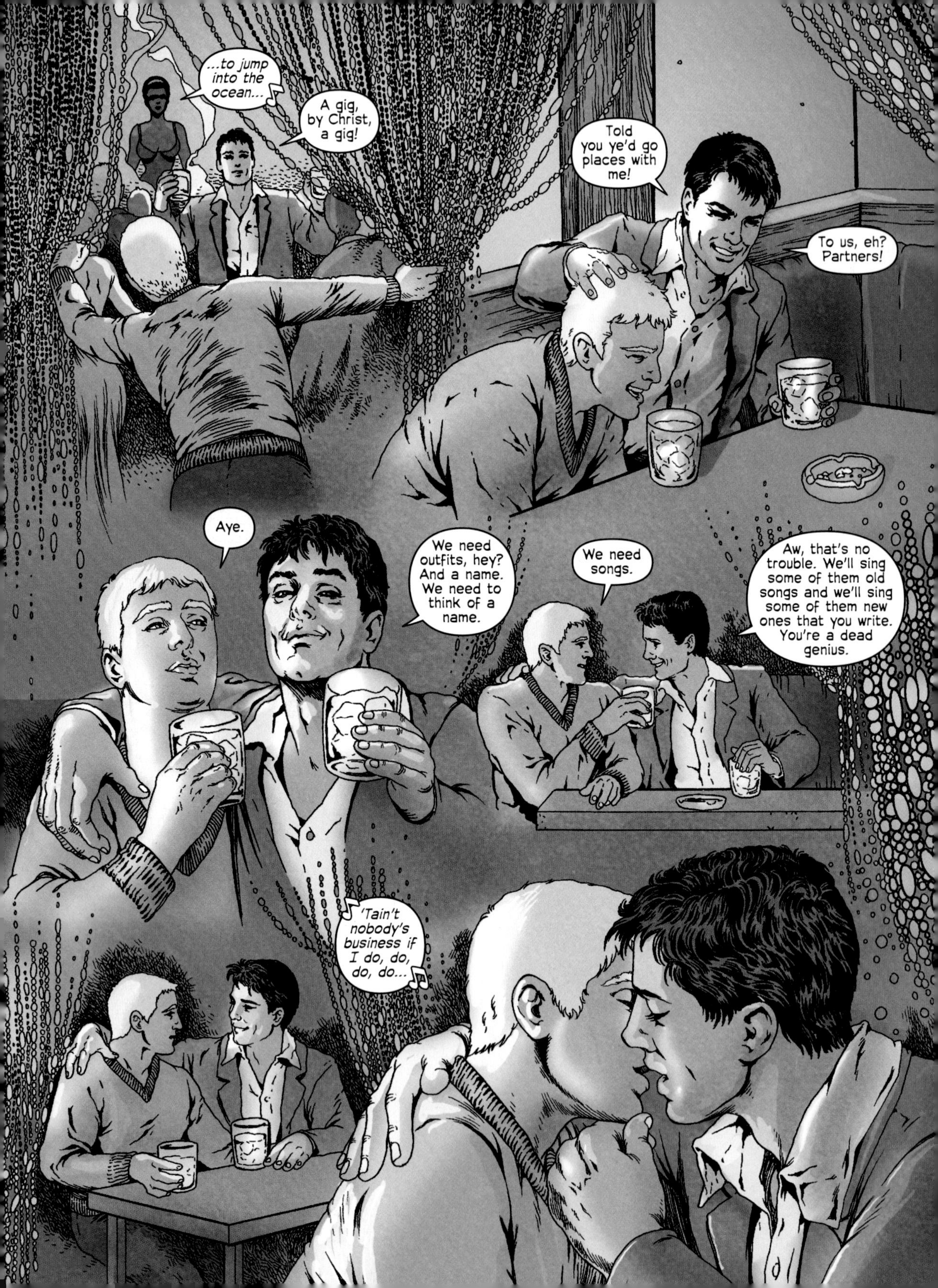
...to jump into the ocean...
A gig, by Christ, a gig!
Told you ye'd go places with me!
To us, eh? Partners!
Aye.
We need outfits, hey? And a name. We need to think of a name.
We need songs.
Aw, that's no trouble. We'll sing some of them old songs and we'll sing some of them new ones that you write. You're a dead genius.
'Tain't nobody's business if I do, do, do, do...

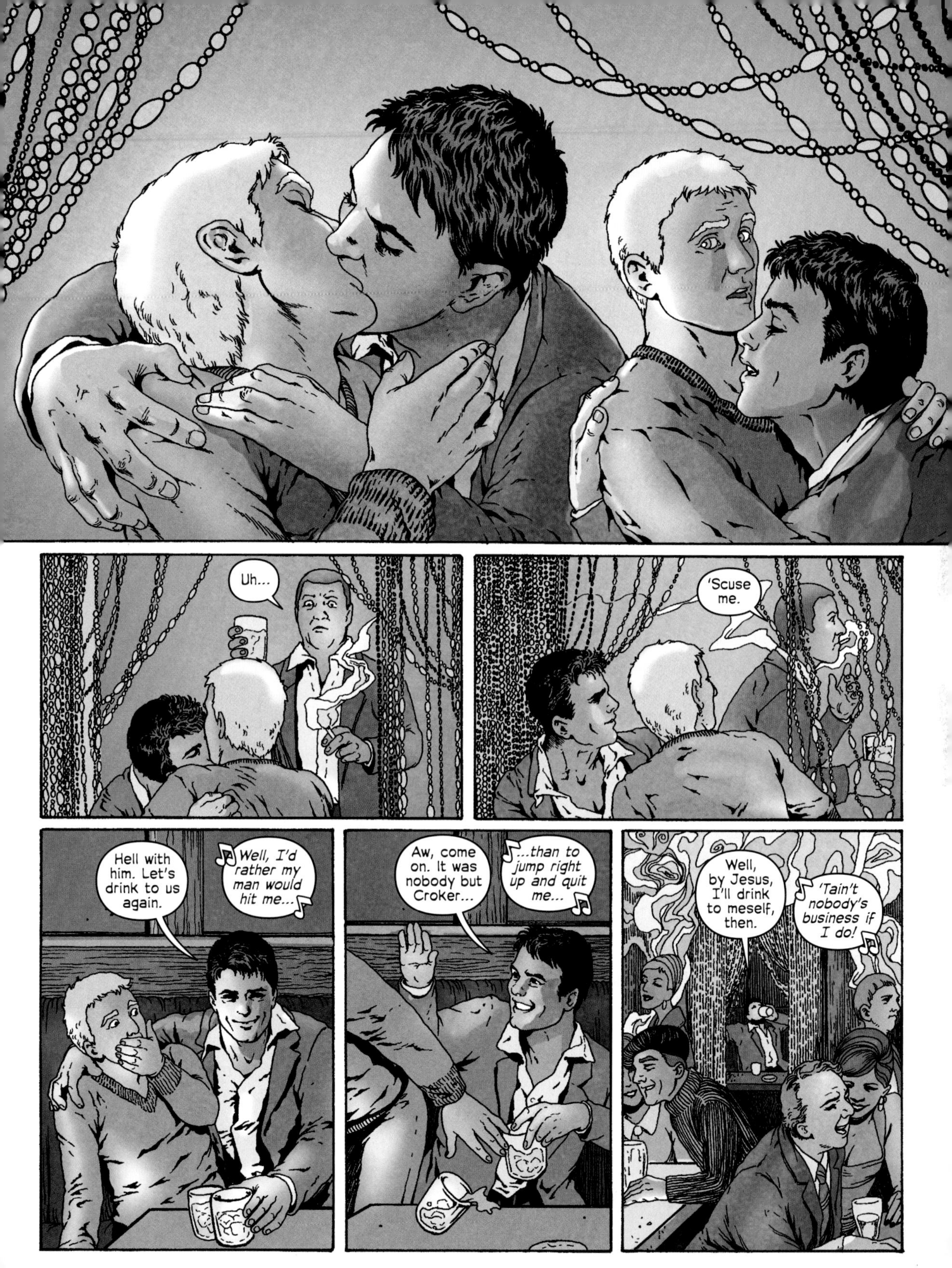
Uh...
'Scuse me.
Hell with him. Let's drink to us again.
Well, I'd rather my man would hit me...
Aw, come on. It was nobody but Croker...
...than to jump right up and quit me...
Well, by Jesus, I'll drink to meself, then.
'Tain't nobody's business if I do!

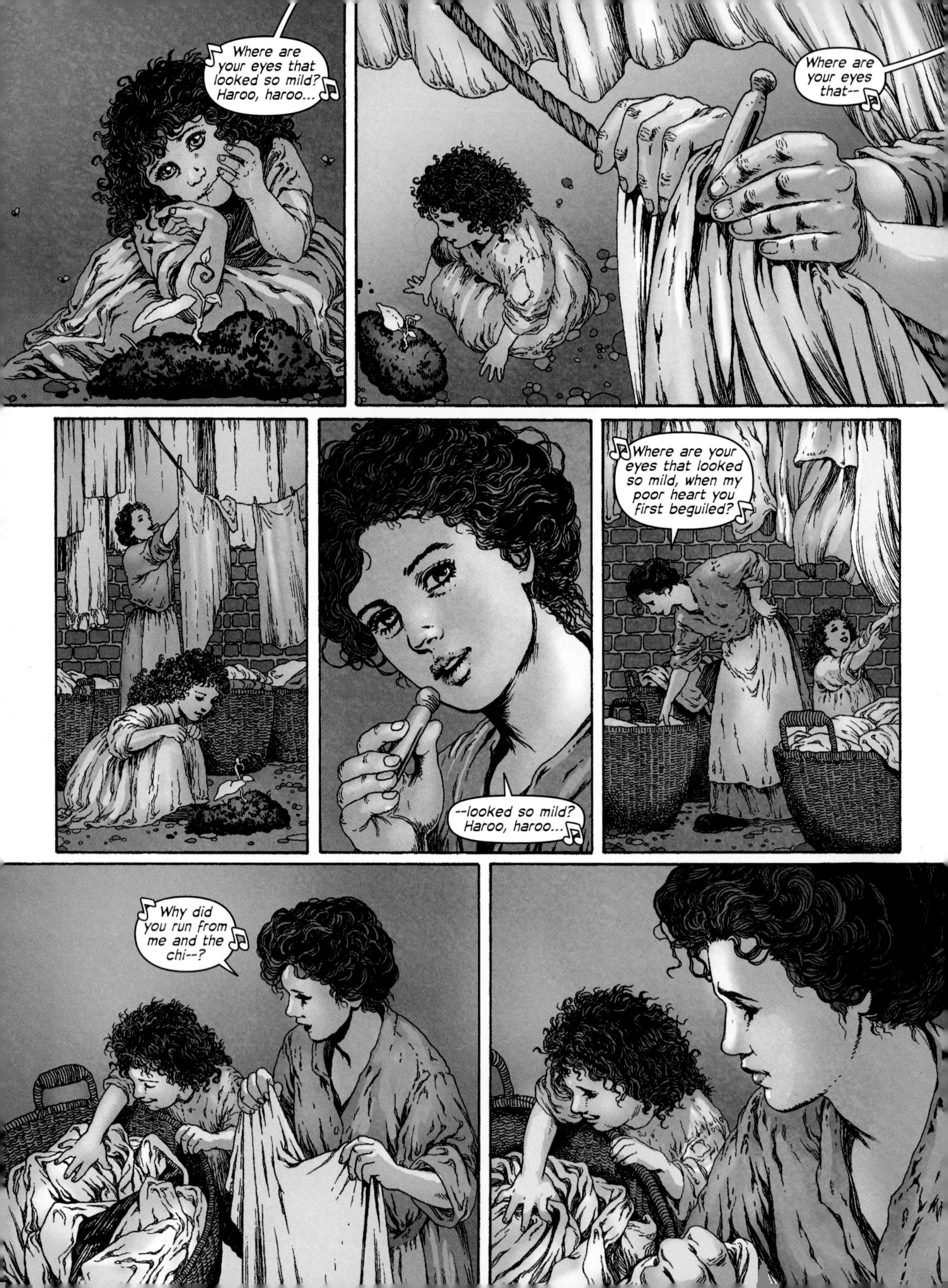
Where are your eyes that looked so mild? Haroo, haroo...
Where are your eyes that--
Where are your eyes that looked so mild, when my poor heart you first beguiled?
--looked so mild? Haroo, haroo...
Why did you run from me and the chi--?

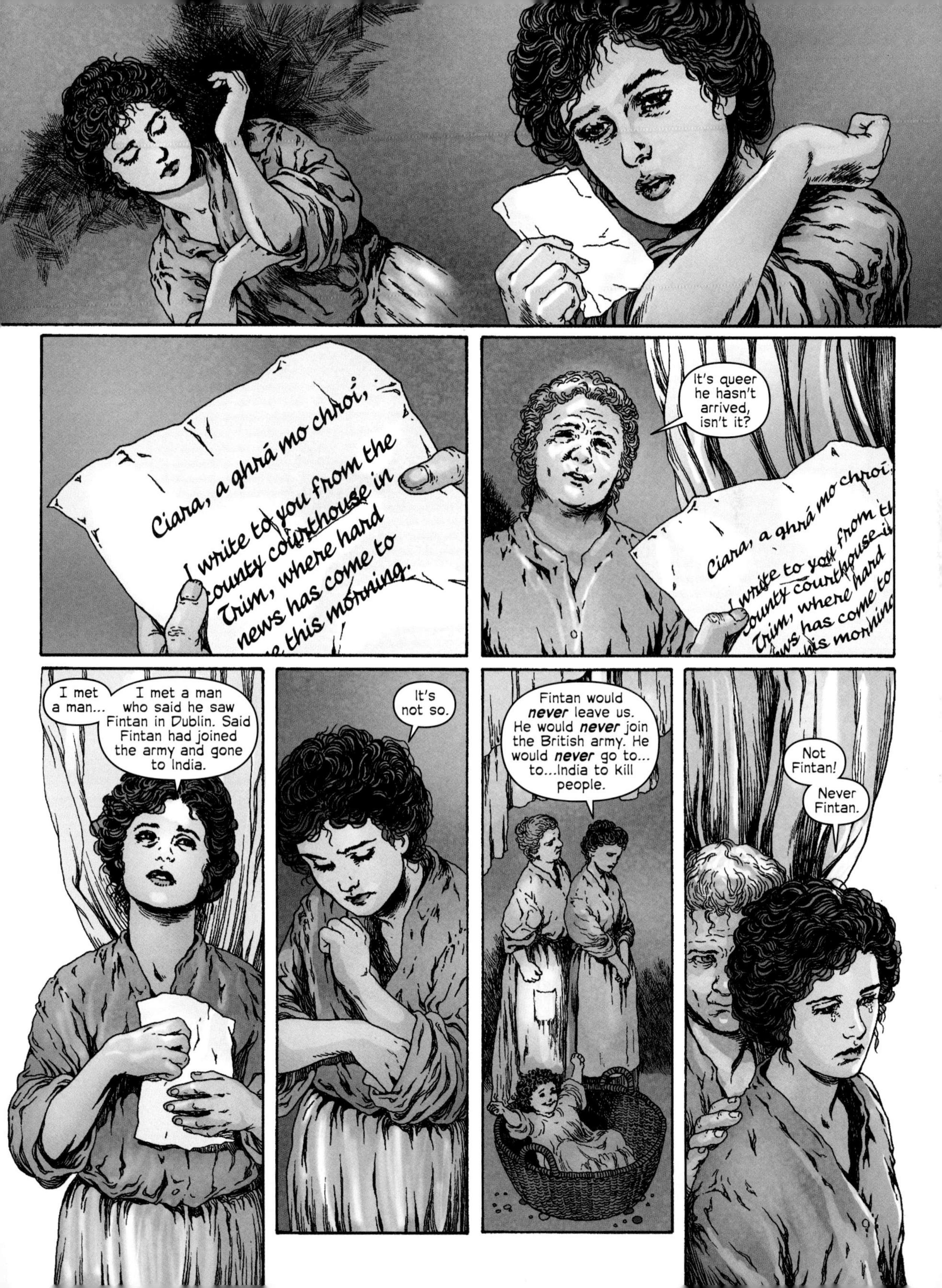
Ciara, a ghrá mo chroí,
I write to you from the county courthouse in Trim, where hard news has come to me this morning.
It's queer he hasn't arrived, isn't it?
Ciara, a ghrá mo chroí,
I write to you from the county courthouse in Trim, where hard news has come to
I met a man...
I met a man who said he saw Fintan in Dublin. Said Fintan had joined the army and gone to India.
It's not so.
Fintan would *never* leave us. He would *never* join the British army. He would *never* go to... to...India to kill people.
Not Fintan!
Never Fintan.

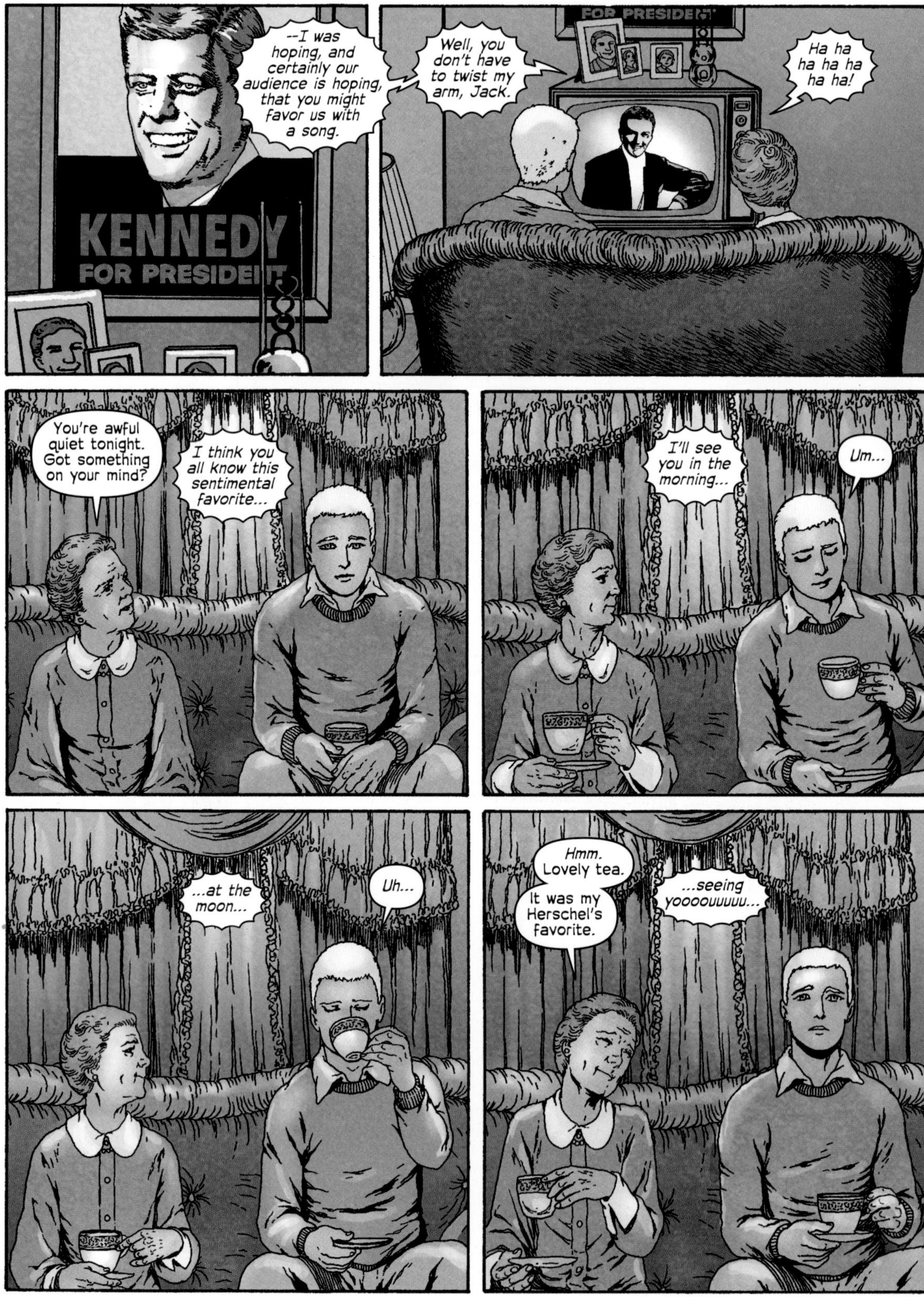
KENNEDY
FOR PRESIDENT
--I was hoping, and certainly our audience is hoping, that you might favor us with a song.
Well, you don't have to twist my arm, Jack.
Ha ha ha ha ha ha ha!
You're awful quiet tonight. Got something on your mind?
I think you all know this sentimental favorite...
I'll see you in the morning...
Um...
...at the moon...
Uh...
Hmm. Lovely tea.
It was my Herschel's favorite.
...seeing yooooUUUUU...

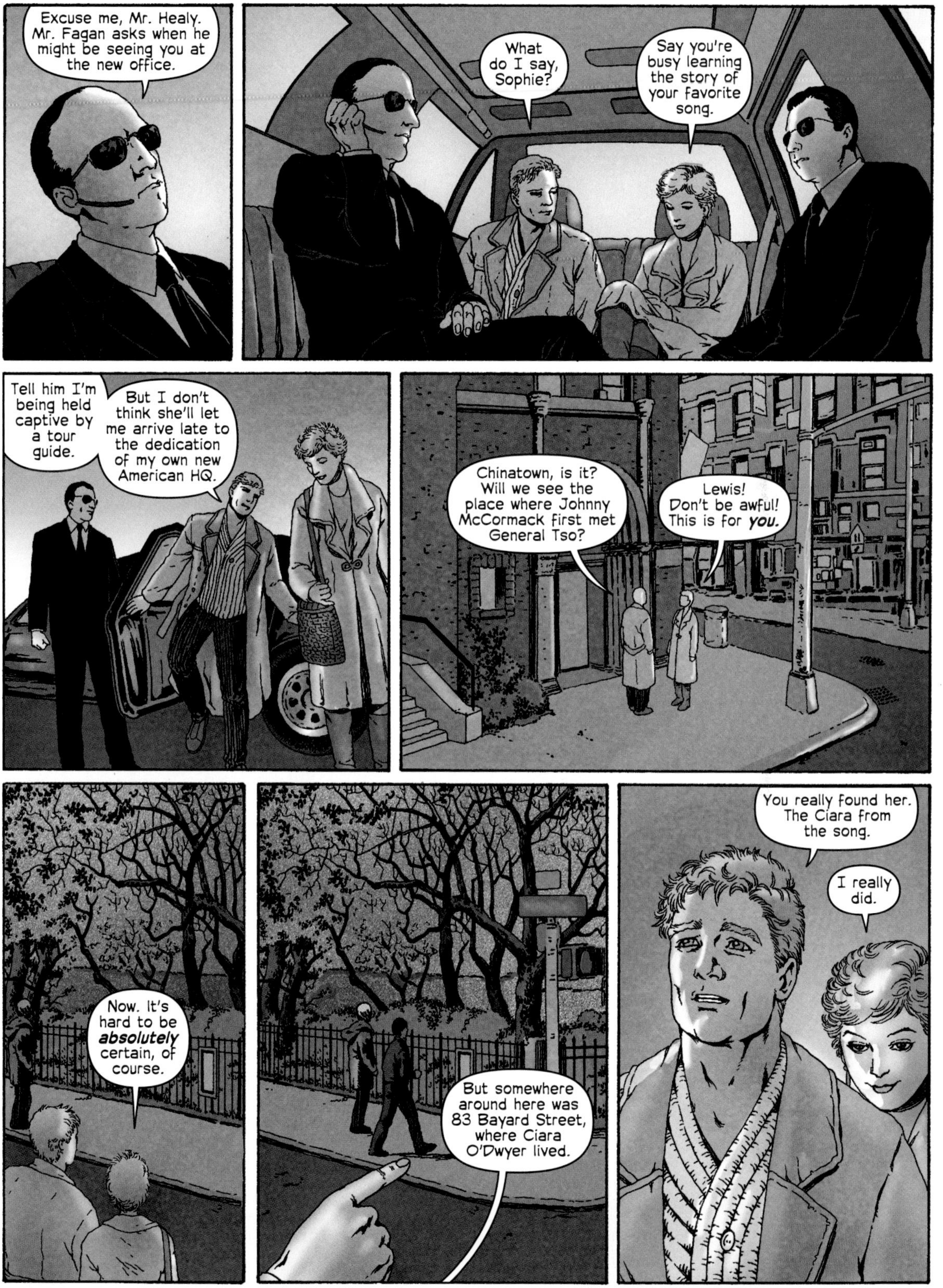
Excuse me, Mr. Healy. Mr. Fagan asks when he might be seeing you at the new office.
What do I say, Sophie?
Say you're busy learning the story of your favorite song.
Tell him I'm being held captive by a tour guide.
But I don't think she'll let me arrive late to the dedication of my own new American HQ.
Chinatown, is it? Will we see the place where Johnny McCormack first met General Tso?
Lewis! Don't be awful! This is for *you.*
Now. It's hard to be ***absolutely*** certain, of course.
But somewhere around here was 83 Bayard Street, where Ciara O'Dwyer lived.
You really found her. The Ciara from the song.
I really did.

BANG!

Watch where you're goin'!

Sorry!

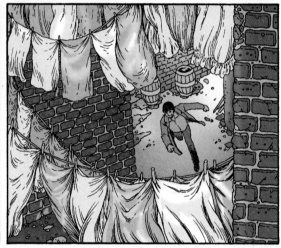

Where'd he go?

Damn!

This way!

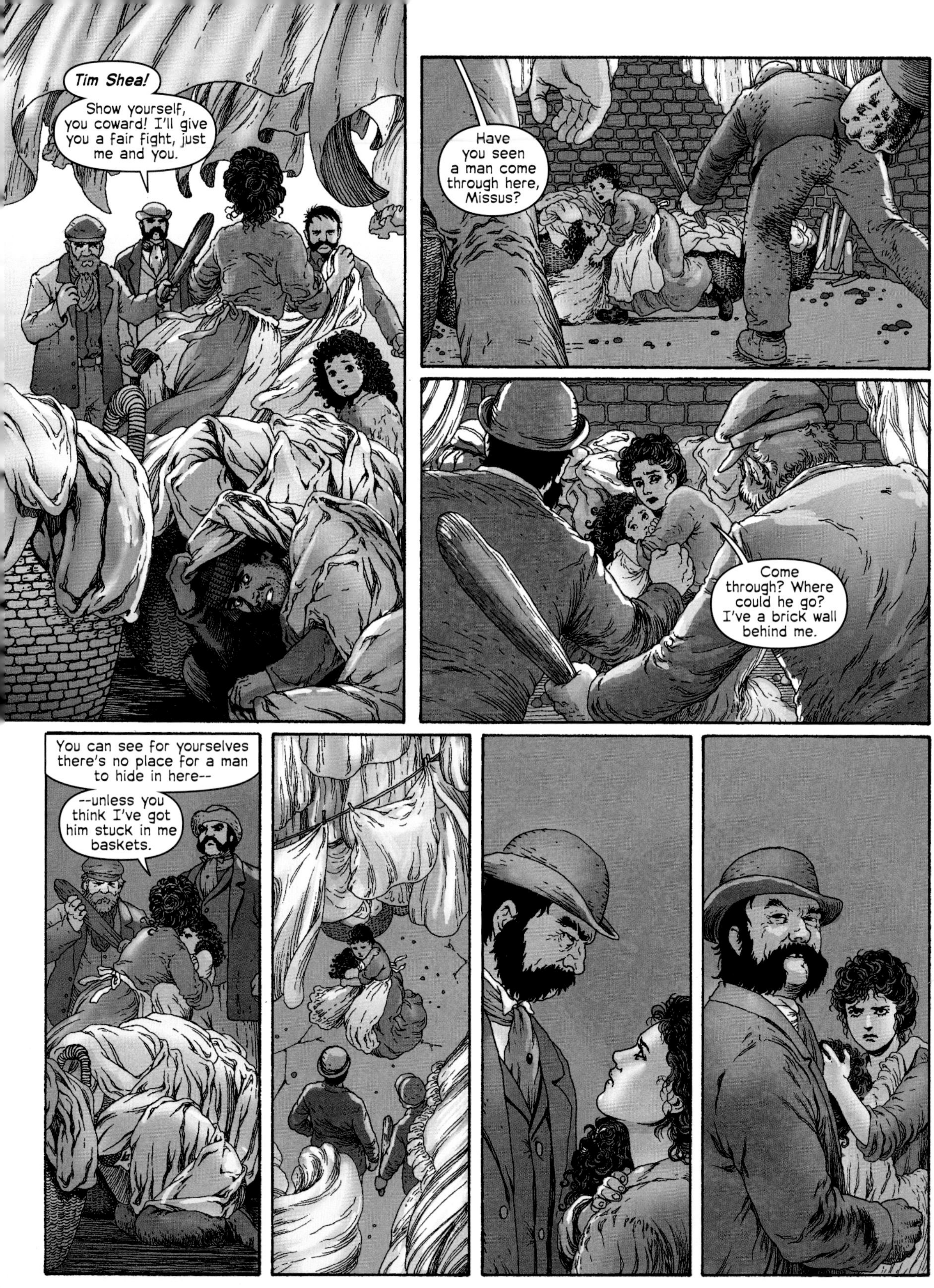
Tim Shea!
Show yourself, you coward! I'll give you a fair fight, just me and you.
Have you seen a man come through here, Missus?
Come through? Where could he go? I've a brick wall behind me.
You can see for yourselves there's no place for a man to hide in here--
--unless you think I've got him stuck in me baskets.

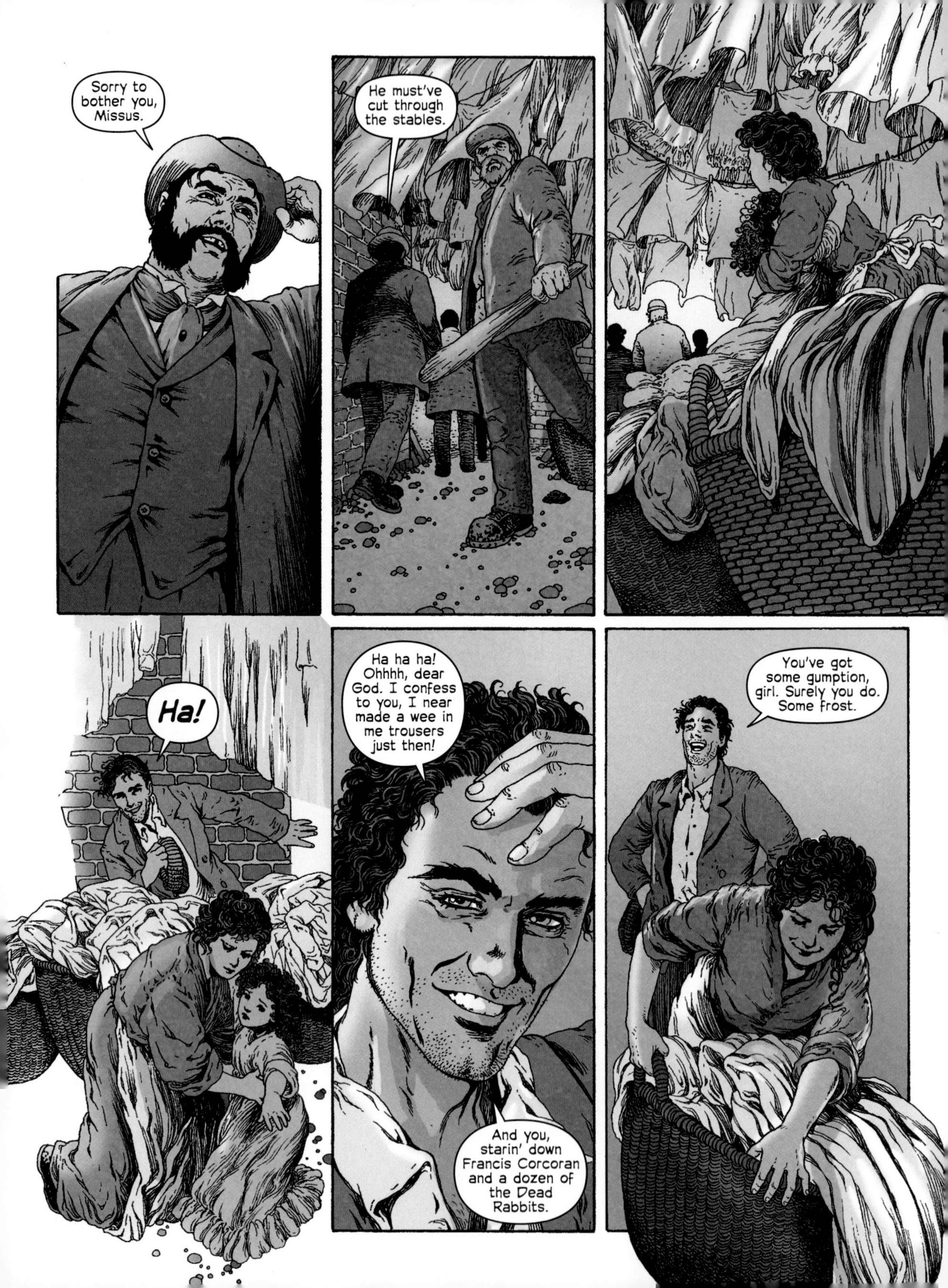
Sorry to bother you, Missus.
He must've cut through the stables.
Ha!
Ha ha ha! Ohhhh, dear God. I confess to you, I near made a wee in me trousers just then!
And you, starin' down Francis Corcoran and a dozen of the Dead Rabbits.
You've got some gumption, girl. Surely you do. Some frost.

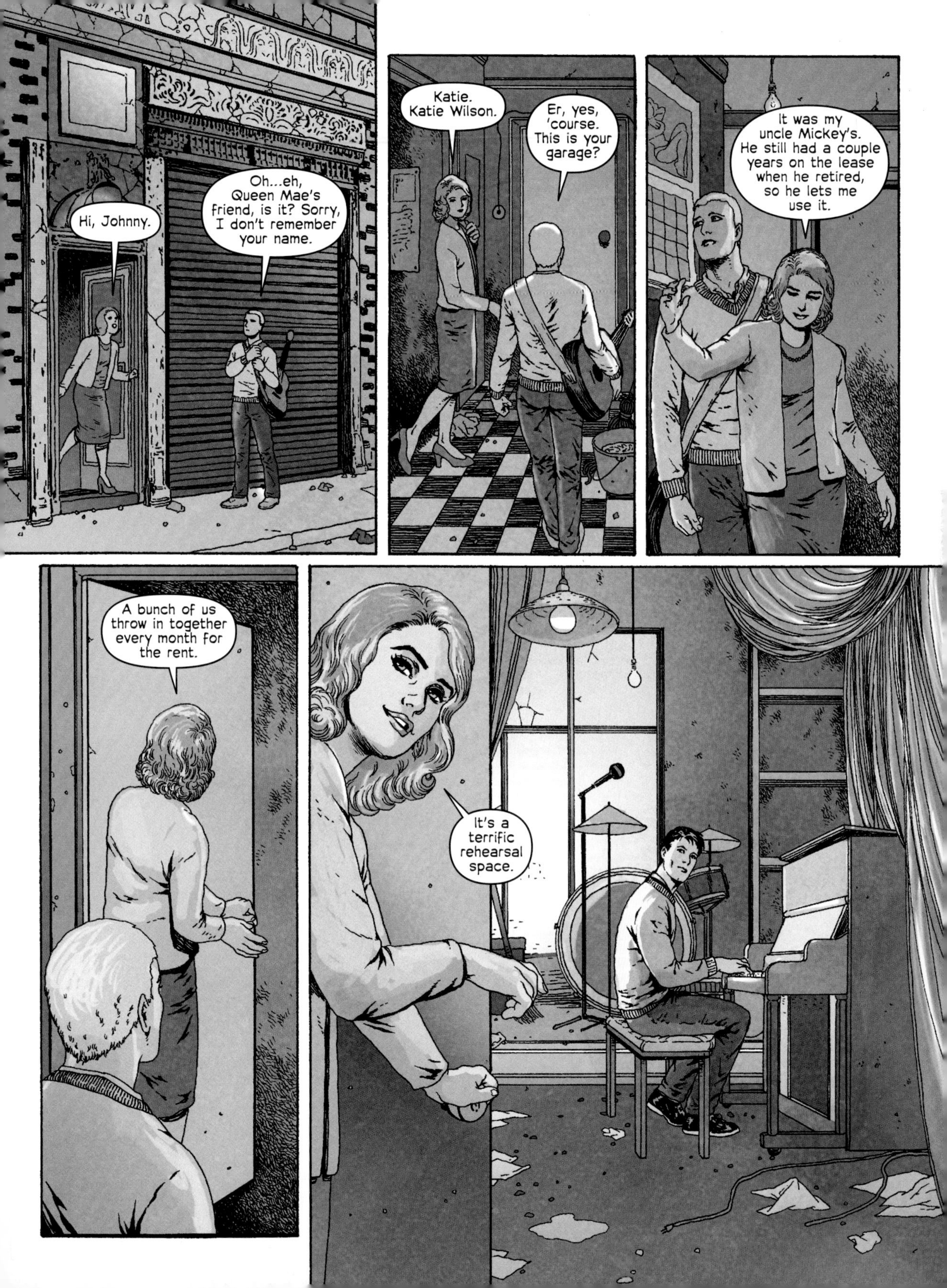
Hi, Johnny.
Oh...eh, Queen Mae's friend, is it? Sorry, I don't remember your name.
Katie. Katie Wilson.
Er, yes, 'course. This is your garage?
It was my uncle Mickey's. He still had a couple years on the lease when he retired, so he lets me use it.
A bunch of us throw in together every month for the rent.
It's a terrific rehearsal space.

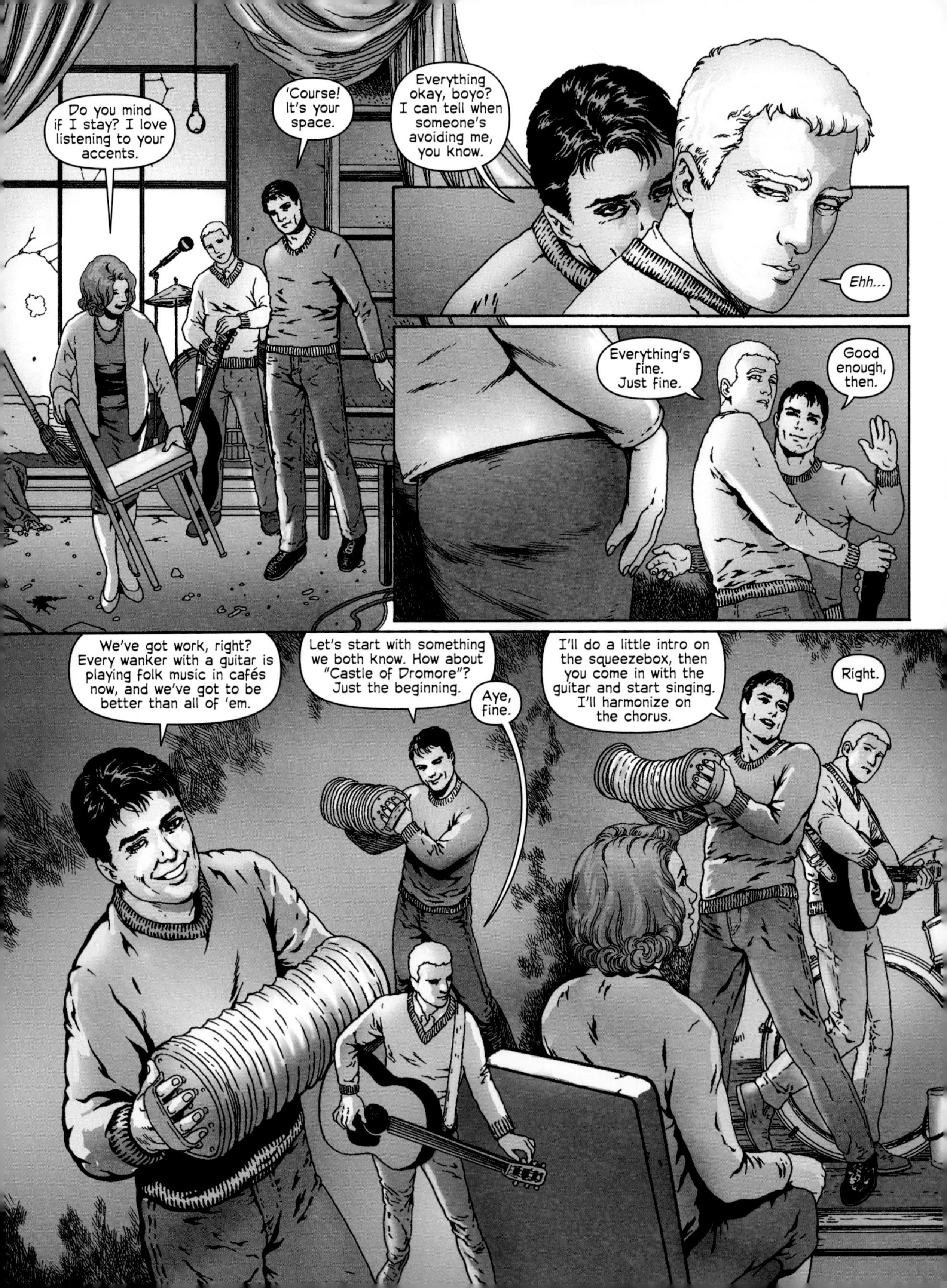

Do you mind if I stay? I love listening to your accents.
'Course! It's your space.
Everything okay, boyo? I can tell when someone's avoiding me, you know.
Ehh...
Everything's fine. Just fine.
Good enough, then.
We've got work, right? Every wanker with a guitar is playing folk music in cafés now, and we've got to be better than all of 'em.
Let's start with something we both know. How about "Castle of Dromore"? Just the beginning.
Aye, fine.
I'll do a little intro on the squeezebox, then you come in with the guitar and start singing. I'll harmonize on the chorus.
Right.

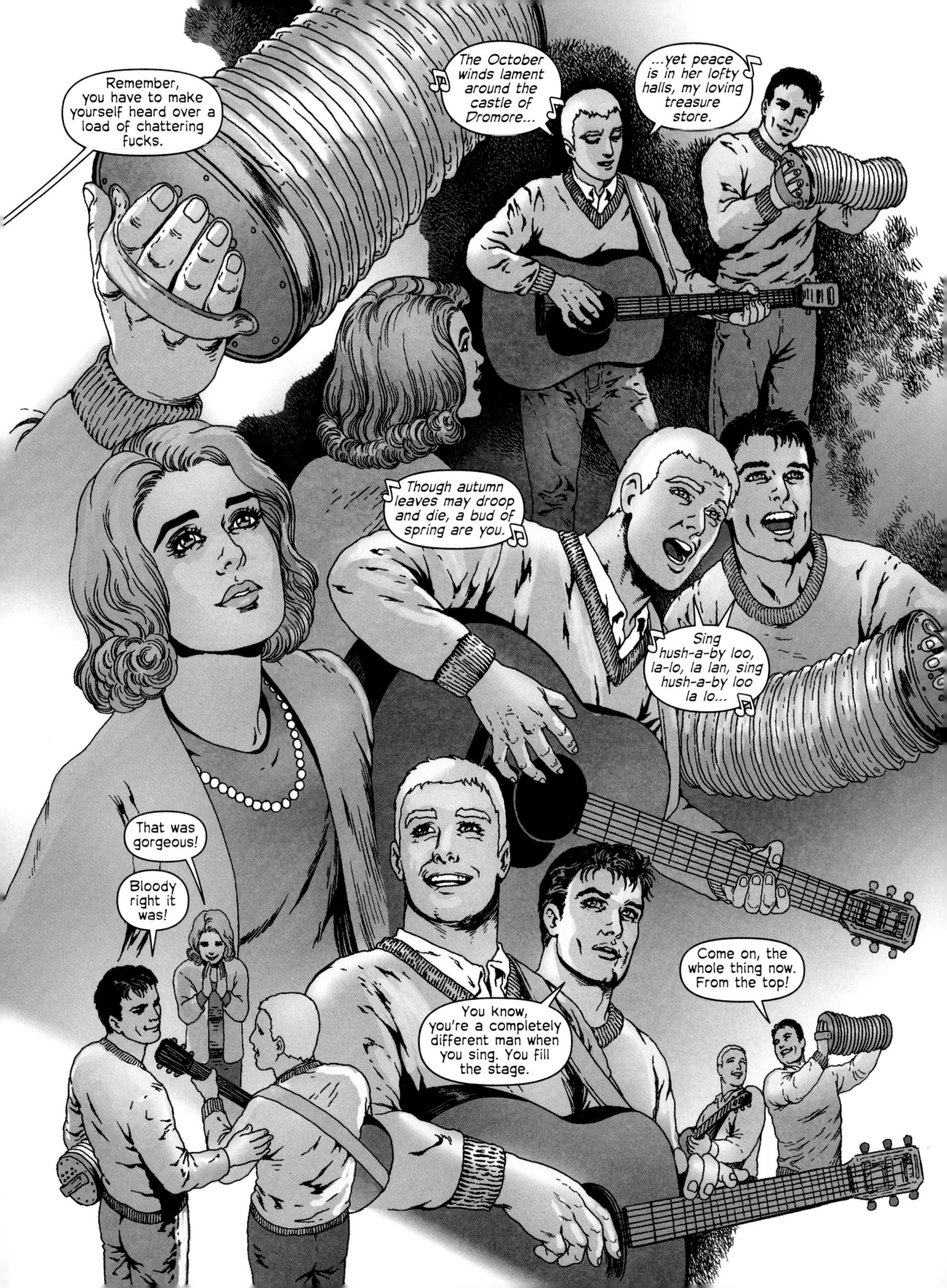

Remember, you have to make yourself heard over a load of chattering fucks.
The October winds lament around the castle of Dromore...
...yet peace is in her lofty halls, my loving treasure store.
Though autumn leaves may droop and die, a bud of spring are you.
Sing hush-a-by loo, la-lo, la lan, sing hush-a-by loo la lo...
That was gorgeous!
Bloody right it was!
You know, you're a completely different man when you sing. You fill the stage.
Come on, the whole thing now. From the top!

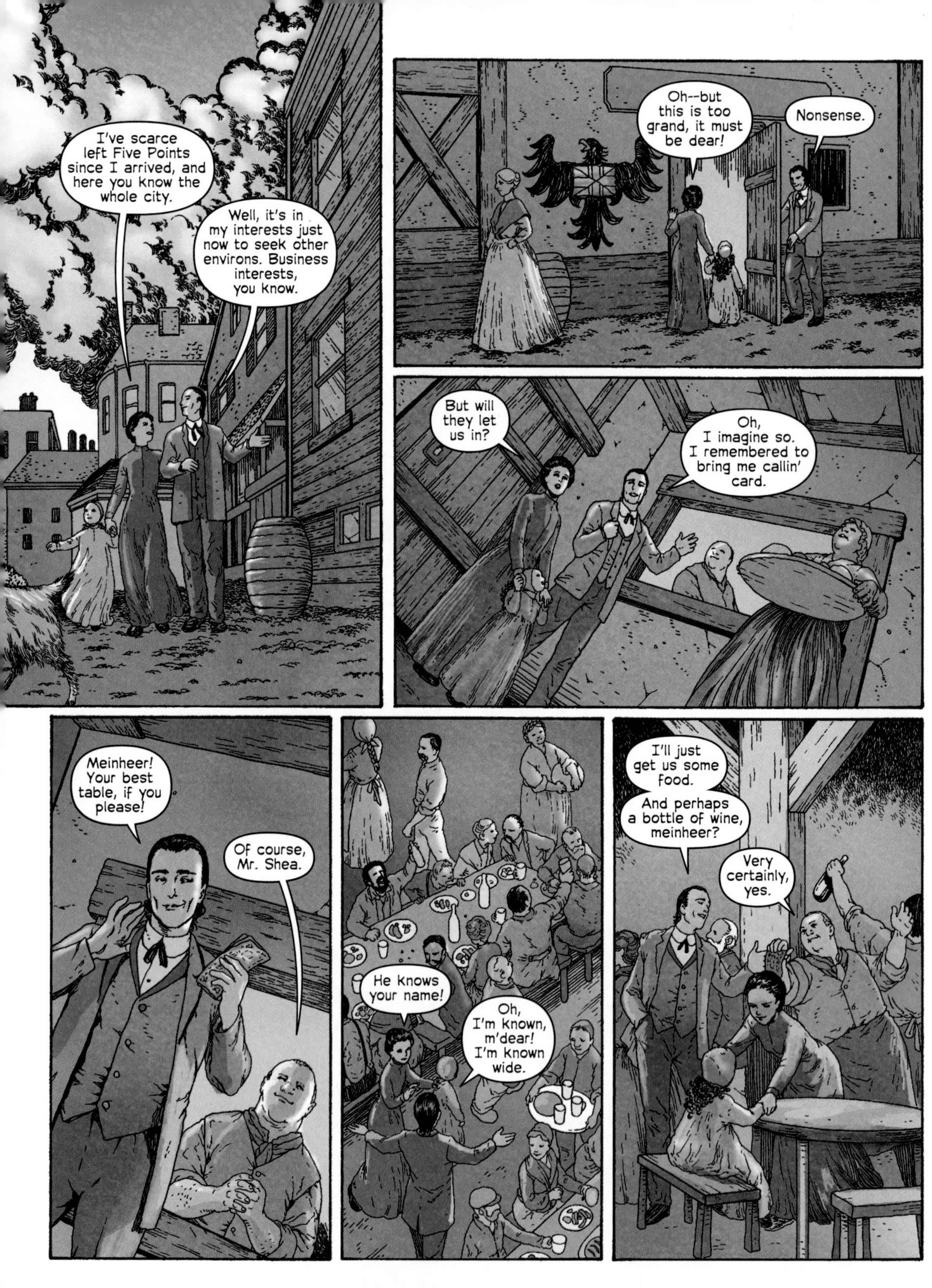
I've scarce left Five Points since I arrived, and here you know the whole city.
Well, it's in my interests just now to seek other environs. Business interests, you know.
Oh--but this is too grand, it must be dear!
Nonsense.
But will they let us in?
Oh, I imagine so. I remembered to bring me callin' card.
Meinheer! Your best table, if you please!
Of course, Mr. Shea.
He knows your name!
Oh, I'm known, m'dear! I'm known wide.
I'll just get us some food.
And perhaps a bottle of wine, meinheer?
Very certainly, yes.

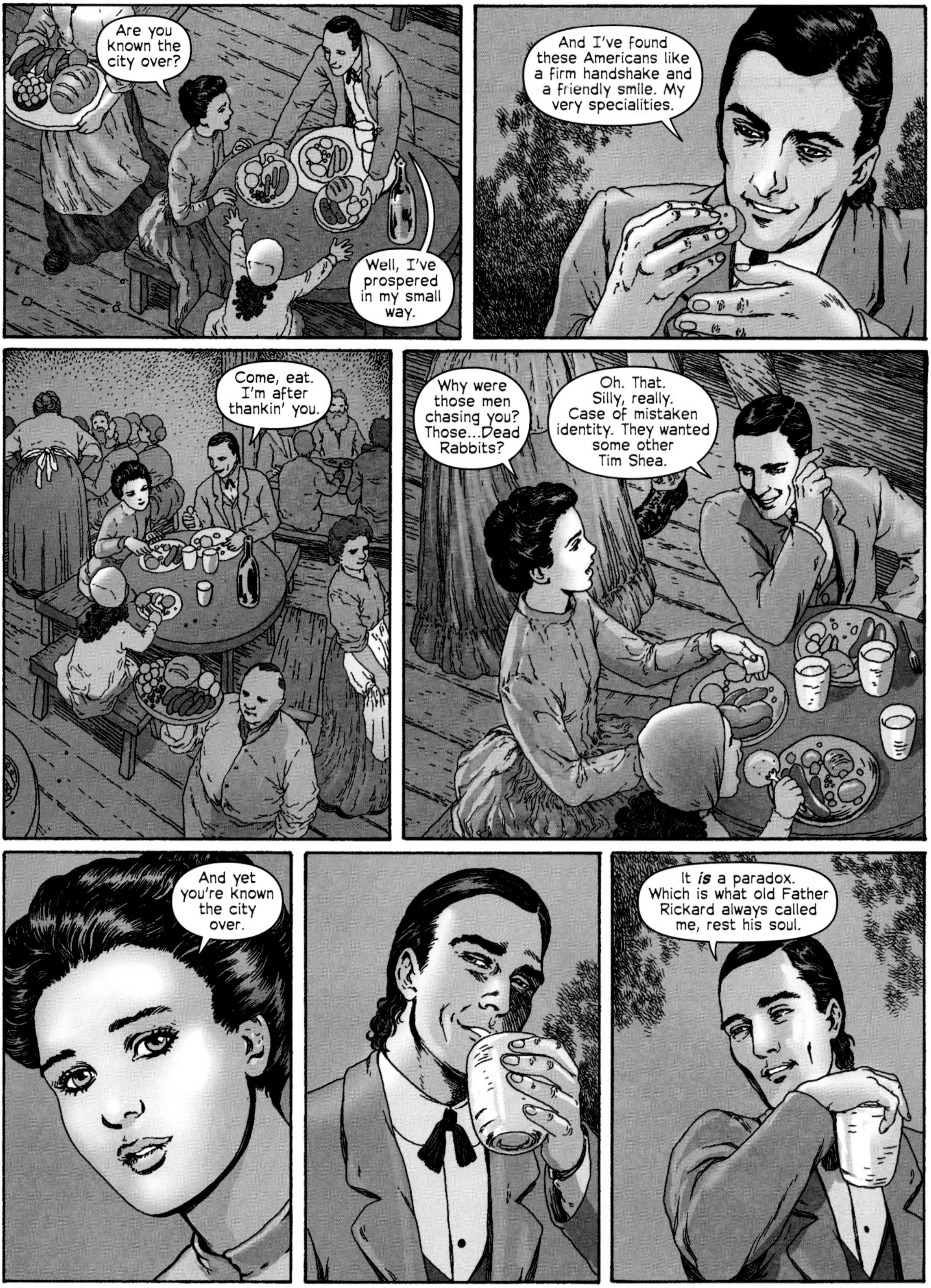
Are you known the city over?
Well, I've prospered in my small way.
And I've found these Americans like a firm handshake and a friendly smile. My very specialities.
Come, eat. I'm after thankin' you.
Why were those men chasing you? Those...Dead Rabbits?
Oh. That. Silly, really. Case of mistaken identity. They wanted some other Tim Shea.
And yet you're known the city over.
It *is* a paradox. Which is what old Father Rickard always called me, rest his soul.

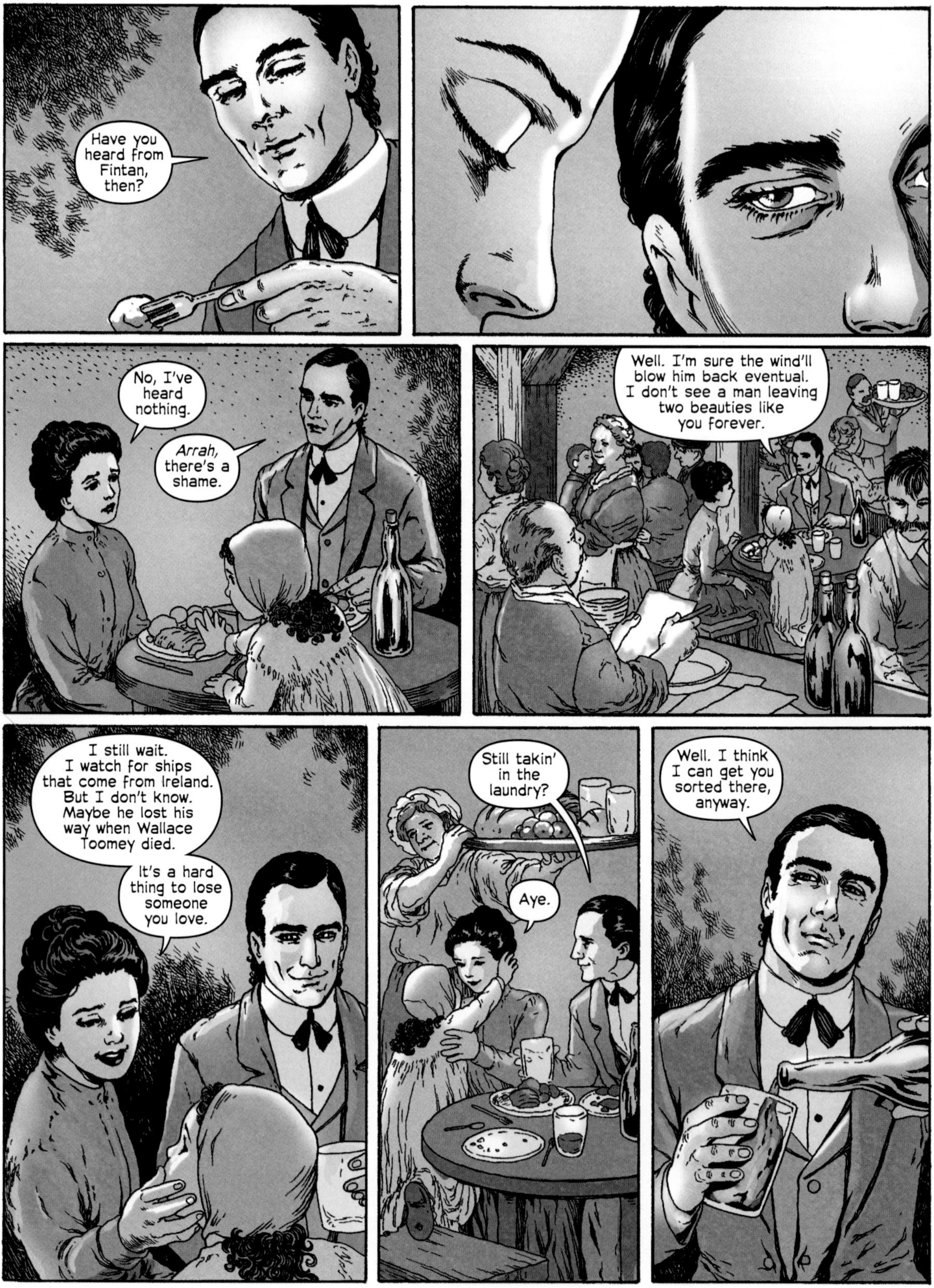
Have you heard from Fintan, then?
No, I've heard nothing.
Arrah, there's a shame.
Well. I'm sure the wind'll blow him back eventual. I don't see a man leaving two beauties like you forever.
I still wait. I watch for ships that come from Ireland. But I don't know. Maybe he lost his way when Wallace Toomey died.
It's a hard thing to lose someone you love.
Still takin' in the laundry?
Aye.
Well. I think I can get you sorted there, anyway.

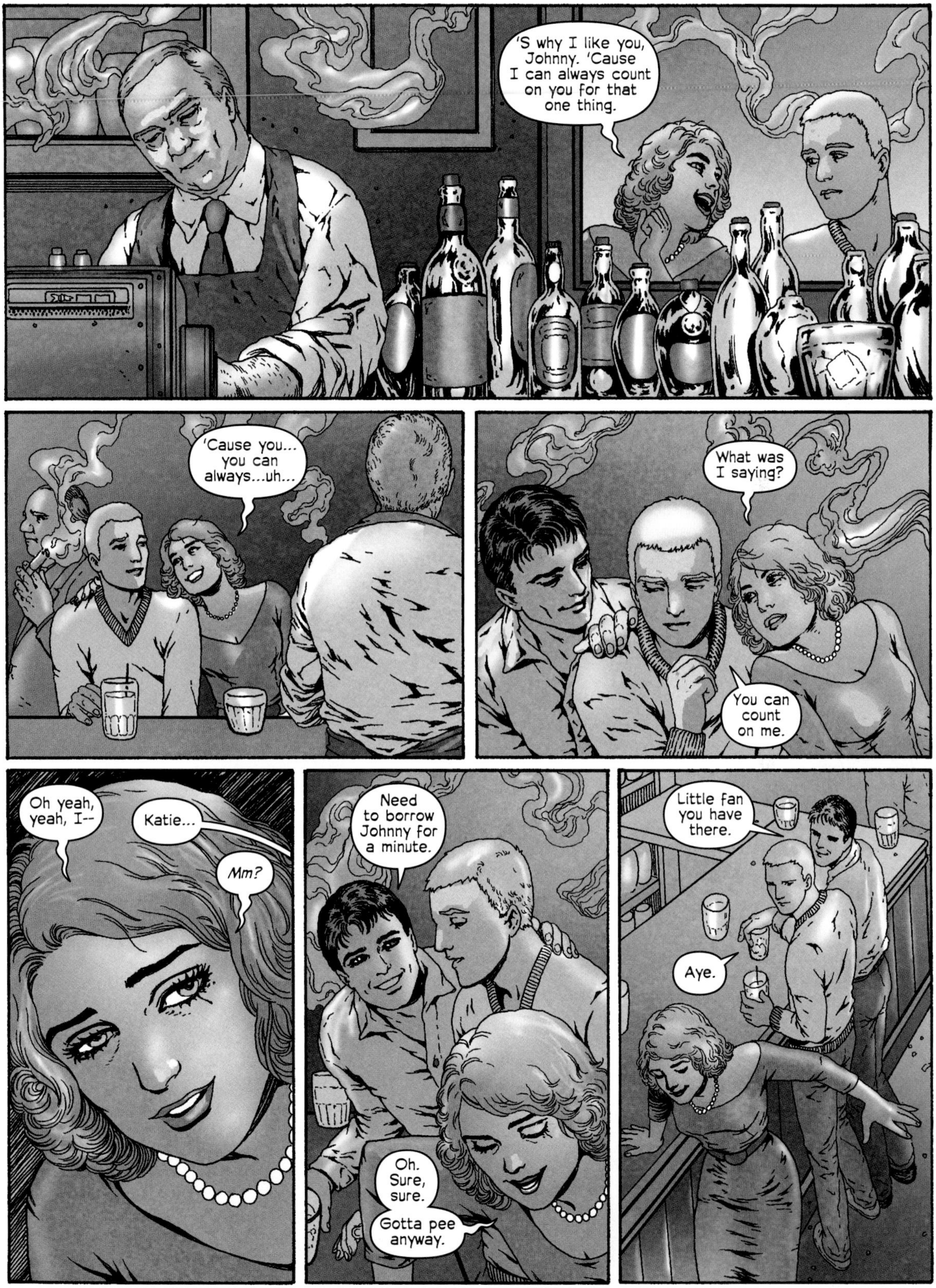
'S why I like you, Johnny. 'Cause I can always count on you for that one thing.
'Cause you... you can always...uh...
What was I saying?
You can count on me.
Oh yeah, yeah, I--
Katie...
Mm?
Need to borrow Johnny for a minute.
Oh. Sure, sure.
Gotta pee anyway.
Little fan you have there.
Aye.

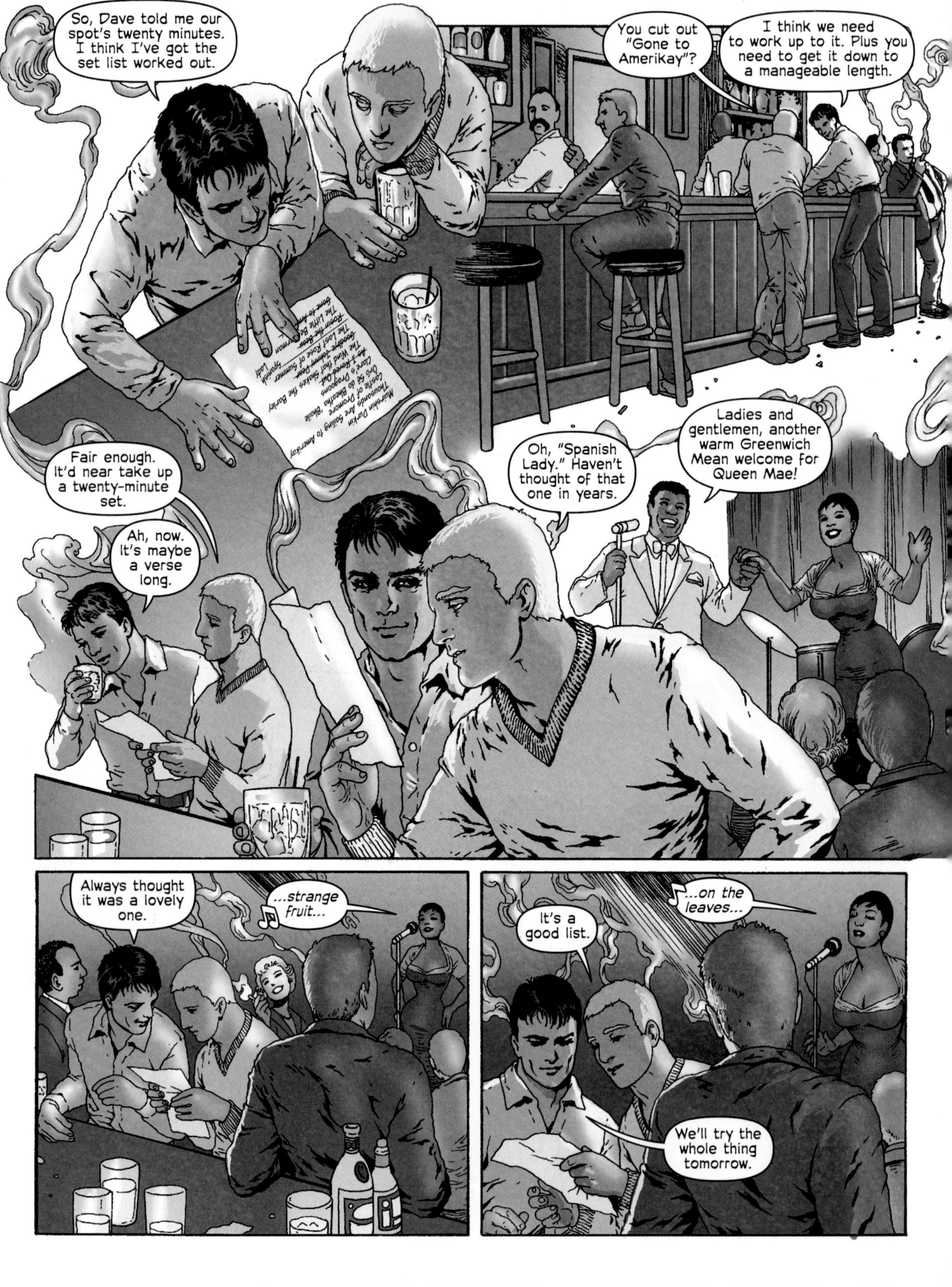
So, Dave told me our spot's twenty minutes. I think I've got the set list worked out.
You cut out "Gone to Amerikay"?
I think we need to work up to it. Plus you need to get it down to a manageable length.
Fair enough. It'd near take up a twenty-minute set.
Ah, now. It's maybe a verse long.
Oh, "Spanish Lady." Haven't thought of that one in years.
Ladies and gentlemen, another warm Greenwich Mean welcome for Queen Mae!
Always thought it was a lovely one.
...strange fruit...
It's a good list.
...on the leaves...
We'll try the whole thing tomorrow.

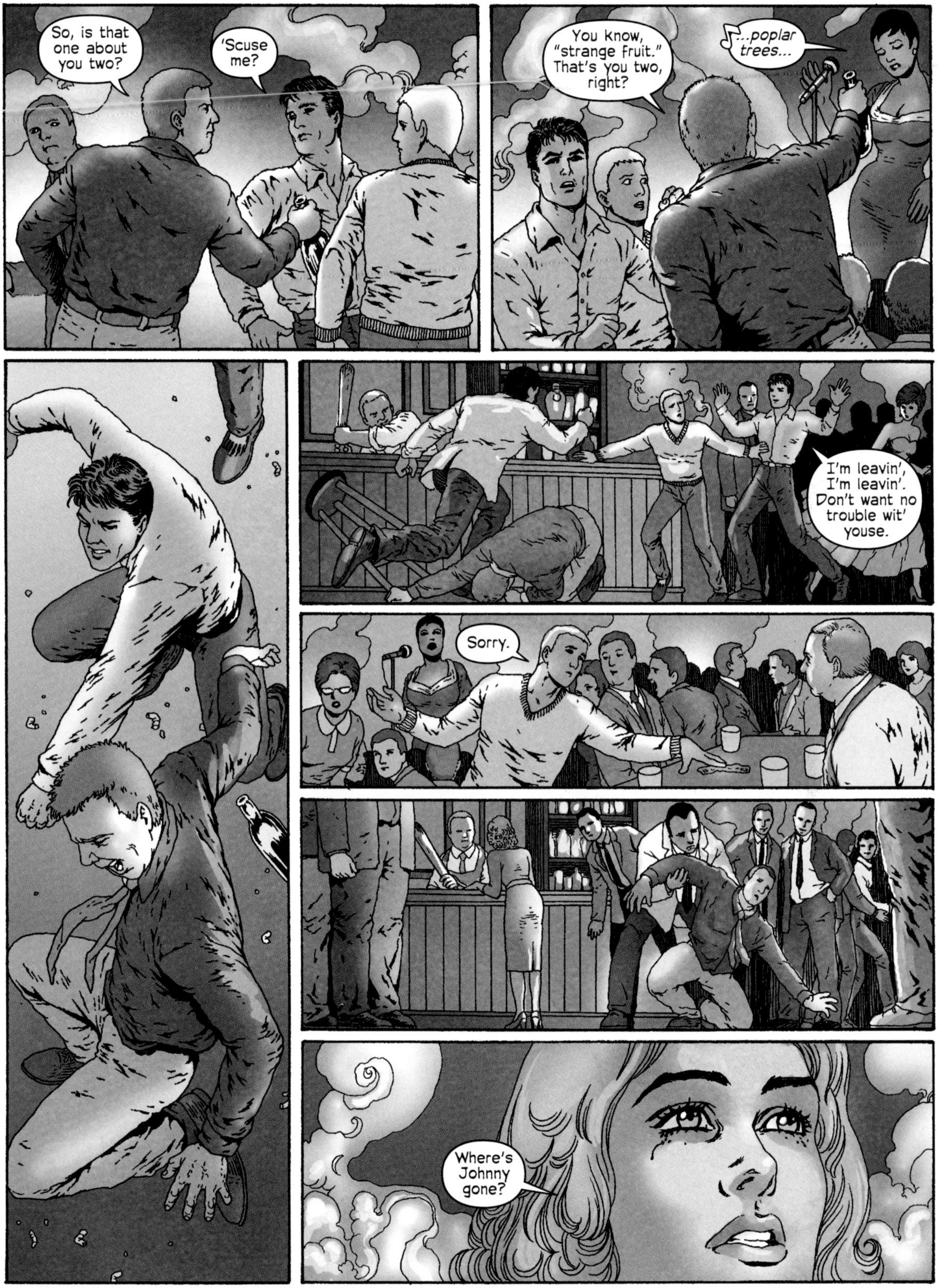
So, is that one about you two?
'Scuse me?
You know, "strange fruit." That's you two, right?
...poplar trees...
I'm leavin', I'm leavin'. Don't want no trouble wit' youse.
Sorry.
Where's Johnny gone?

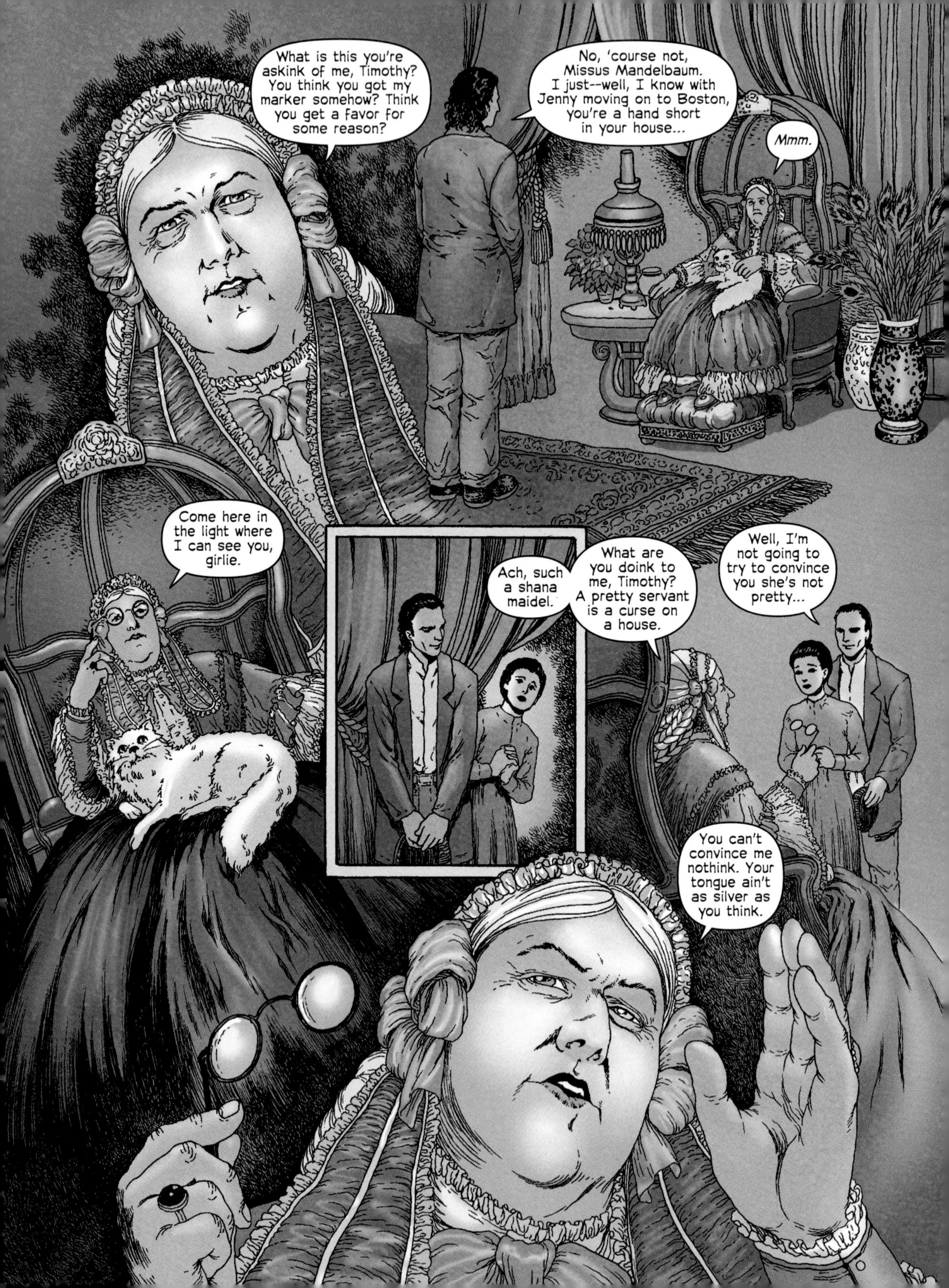
What is this you're askink of me, Timothy? You think you got my marker somehow? Think you get a favor for some reason?
No, 'course not, Missus Mandelbaum. I just--well, I know with Jenny moving on to Boston, you're a hand short in your house...
Mmm.
Come here in the light where I can see you, girlie.
Ach, such a shana maidel.
What are you doink to me, Timothy? A pretty servant is a curse on a house.
Well, I'm not going to try to convince you she's not pretty...
You can't convince me nothink. Your tongue ain't as silver as you think.

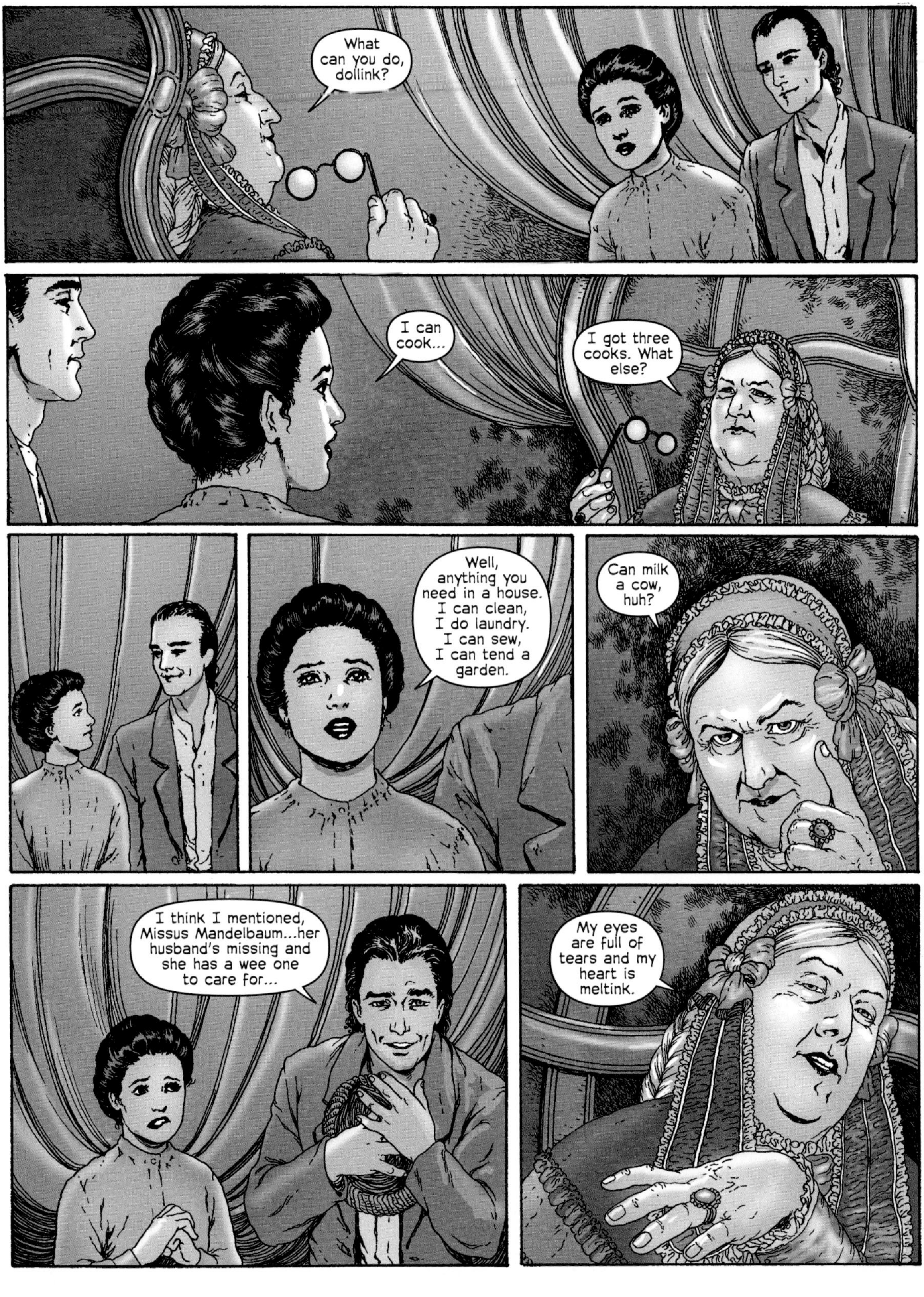
What can you do, dollink?
I can cook...
I got three cooks. What else?
Well, anything you need in a house. I can clean, I do laundry. I can sew, I can tend a garden.
Can milk a cow, huh?
I think I mentioned, Missus Mandelbaum...her husband's missing and she has a wee one to care for...
My eyes are full of tears and my heart is meltink.

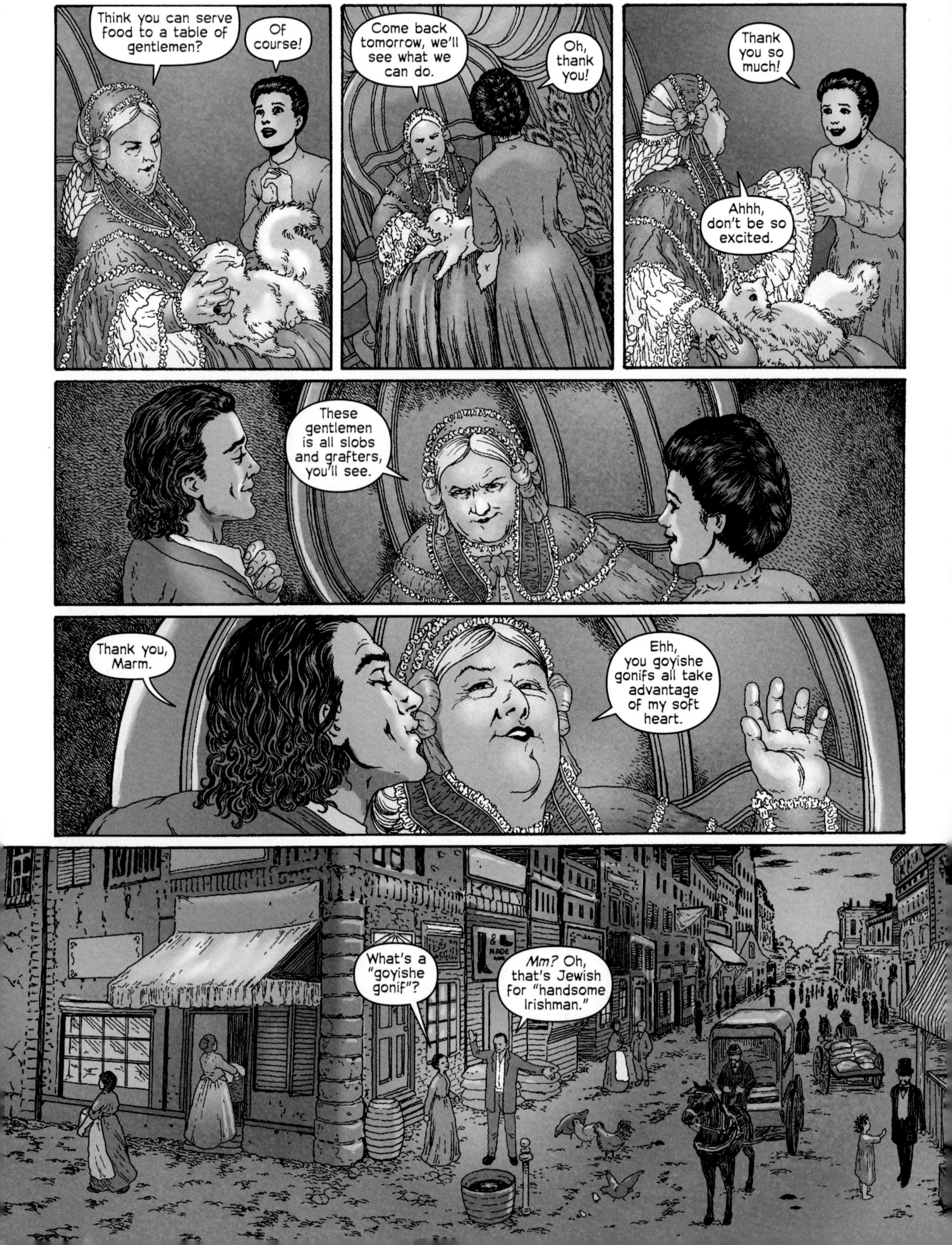
Think you can serve food to a table of gentlemen?
Of course!
Come back tomorrow, we'll see what we can do.
Oh, thank you!
Thank you so much!
Ahhh, don't be so excited.
These gentlemen is all slobs and grafters, you'll see.
Thank you, Marm.
Ehh, you goyishe gonifs all take advantage of my soft heart.
What's a "goyishe gonif"?
Mm? Oh, that's Jewish for "handsome Irishman."

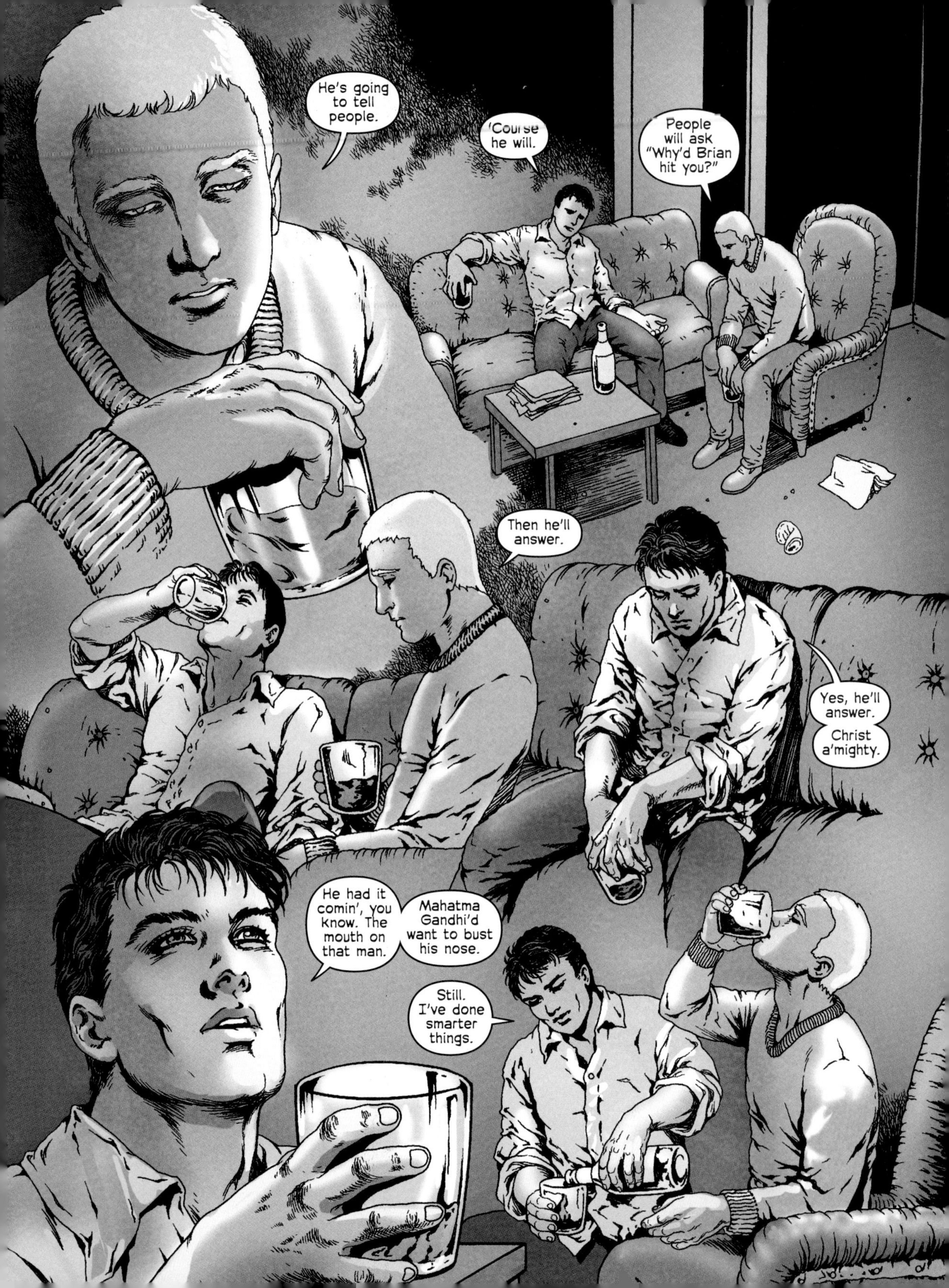

He's going to tell people.
'Course he will.
People will ask "Why'd Brian hit you?"
Then he'll answer.
Yes, he'll answer.
Christ a'mighty.
He had it comin', you know. The mouth on that man.
Mahatma Gandhi'd want to bust his nose.
Still. I've done smarter things.

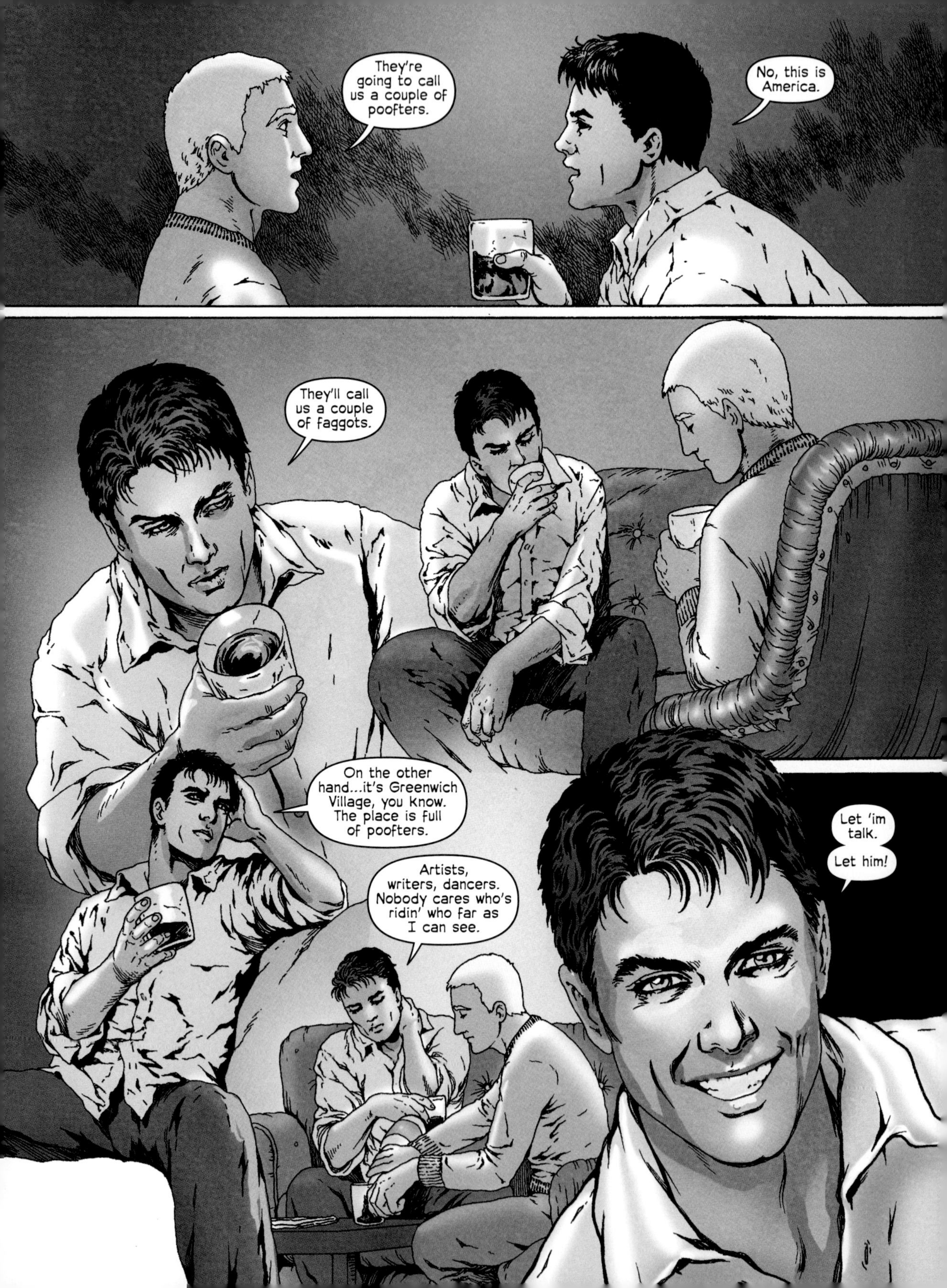
They're going to call us a couple of poofters.
No, this is America.
They'll call us a couple of faggots.
On the other hand...it's Greenwich Village, you know. The place is full of poofters.
Artists, writers, dancers. Nobody cares who's ridin' who far as I can see.
Let 'im talk.
Let him!

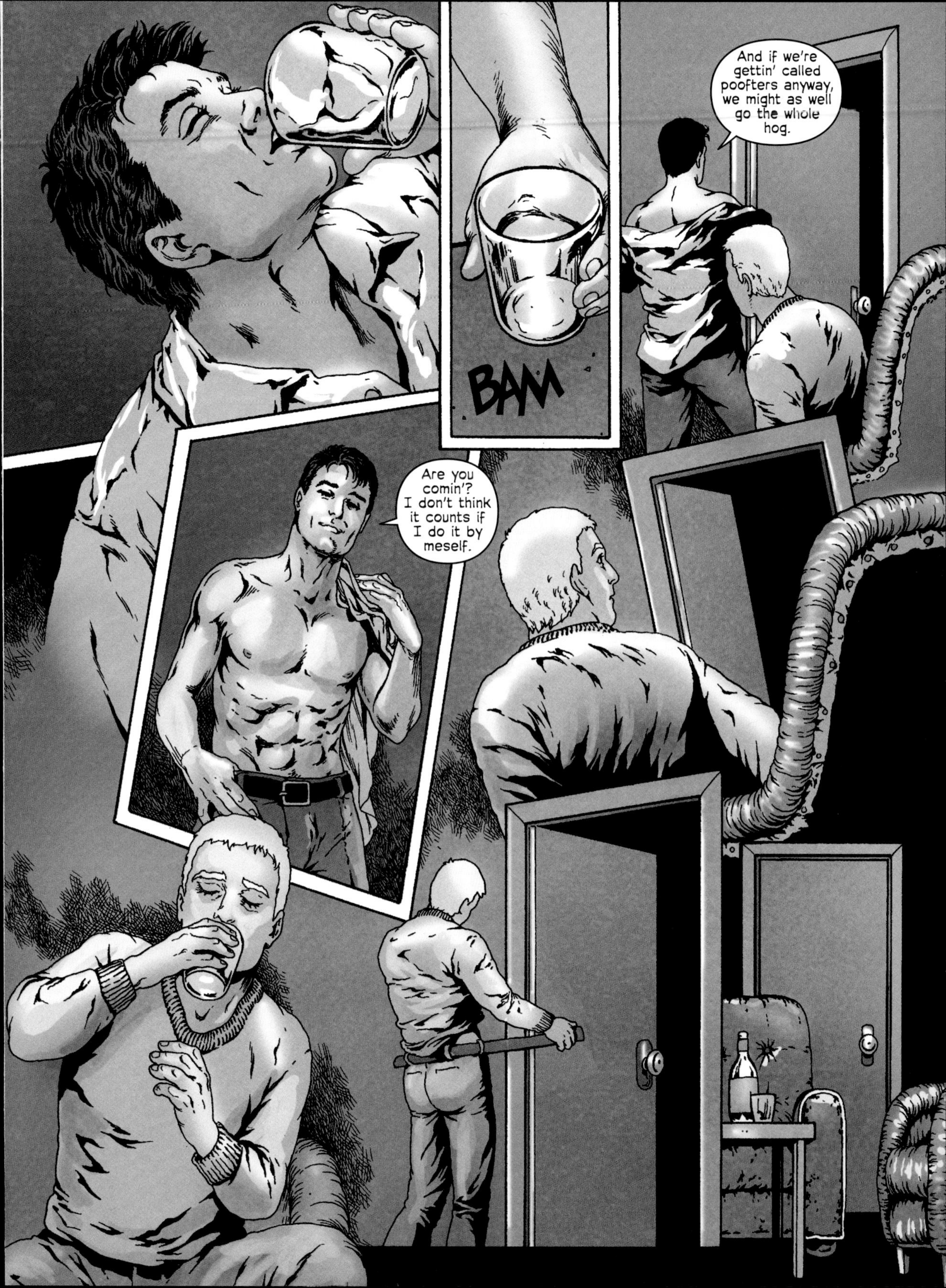
BAM
And if we're gettin' called poofters anyway, we might as well go the whole hog.
Are you comin'? I don't think it counts if I do it by meself.

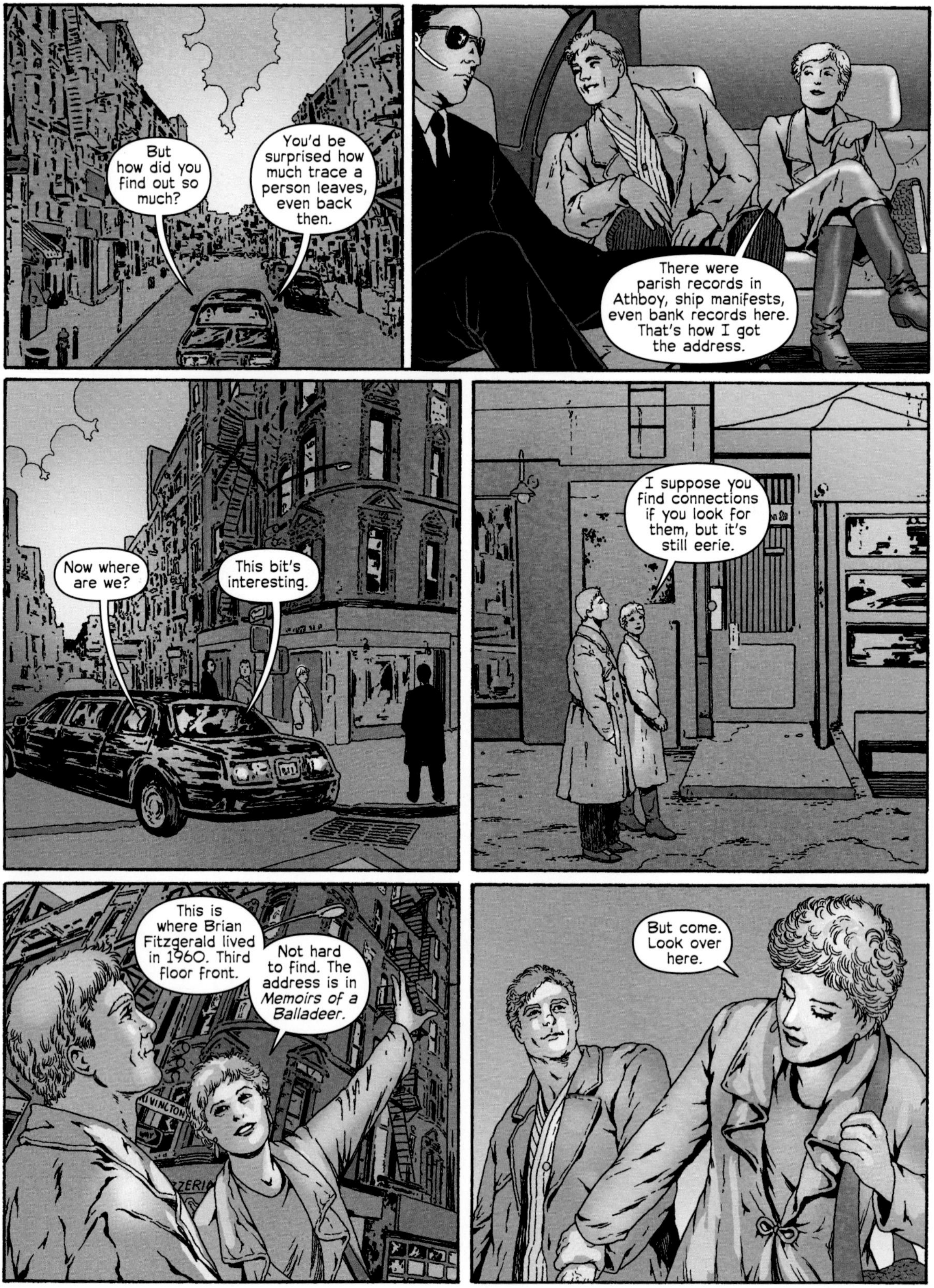
But how did you find out so much?
You'd be surprised how much trace a person leaves, even back then.
There were parish records in Athboy, ship manifests, even bank records here. That's how I got the address.
Now where are we?
This bit's interesting.
I suppose you find connections if you look for them, but it's still eerie.
This is where Brian Fitzgerald lived in 1960. Third floor front.
Not hard to find. The address is in *Memoirs of a Balladeer.*
But come. Look over here.

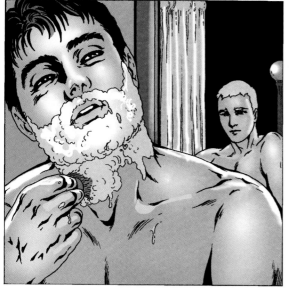

Are we
a couple of
poofters,
then?

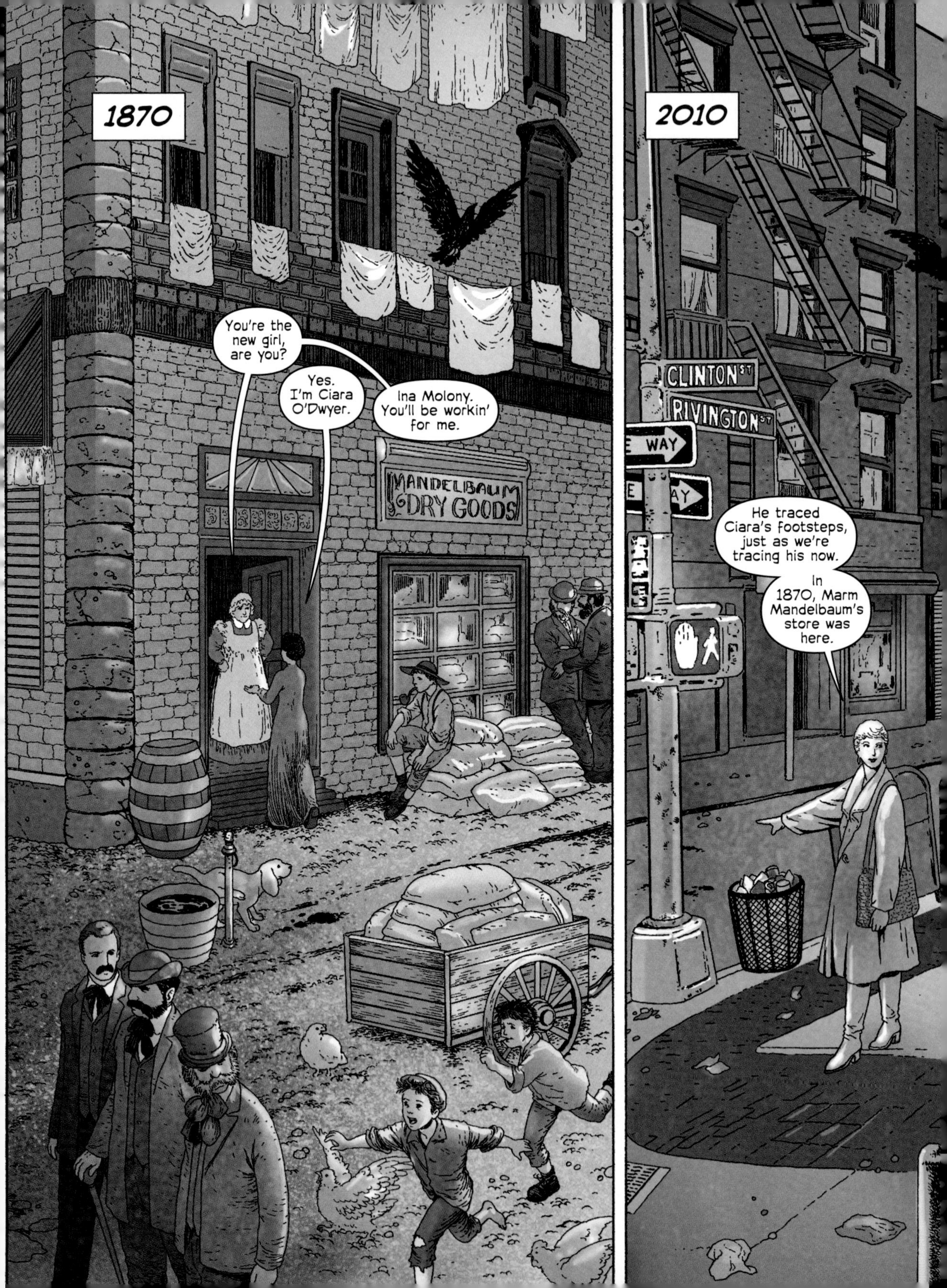
1870
You're the new girl, are you?
Yes. I'm Ciara O'Dwyer.
Ina Molony. You'll be workin' for me.
MANDELBAUM DRY GOODS
2010
CLINTON ST
RIVINGTON ST
He traced Ciara's footsteps, just as we're tracing his now.
In 1870, Marm Mandelbaum's store was here.

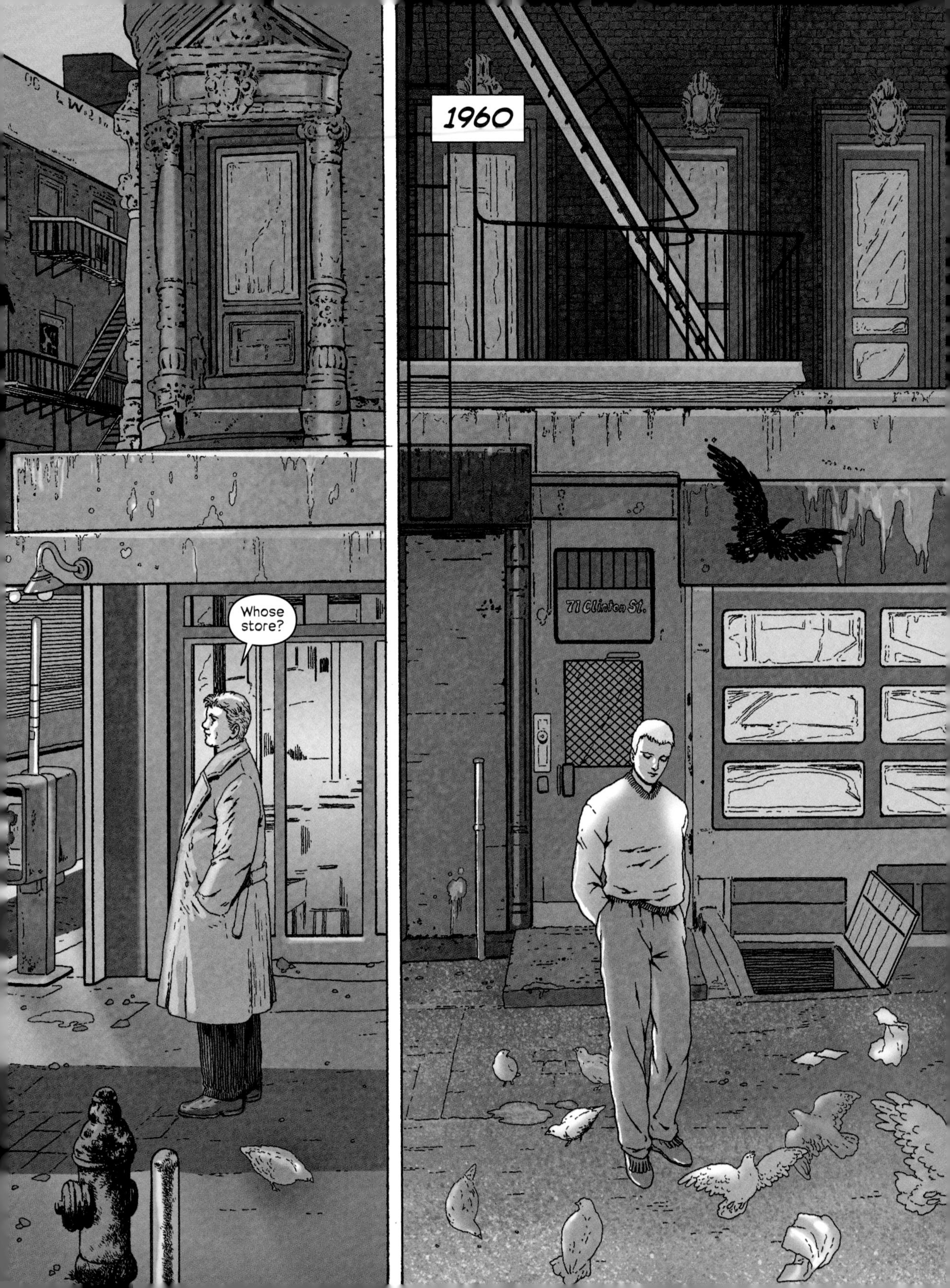
Whose store?
1960
71 Clinton St.

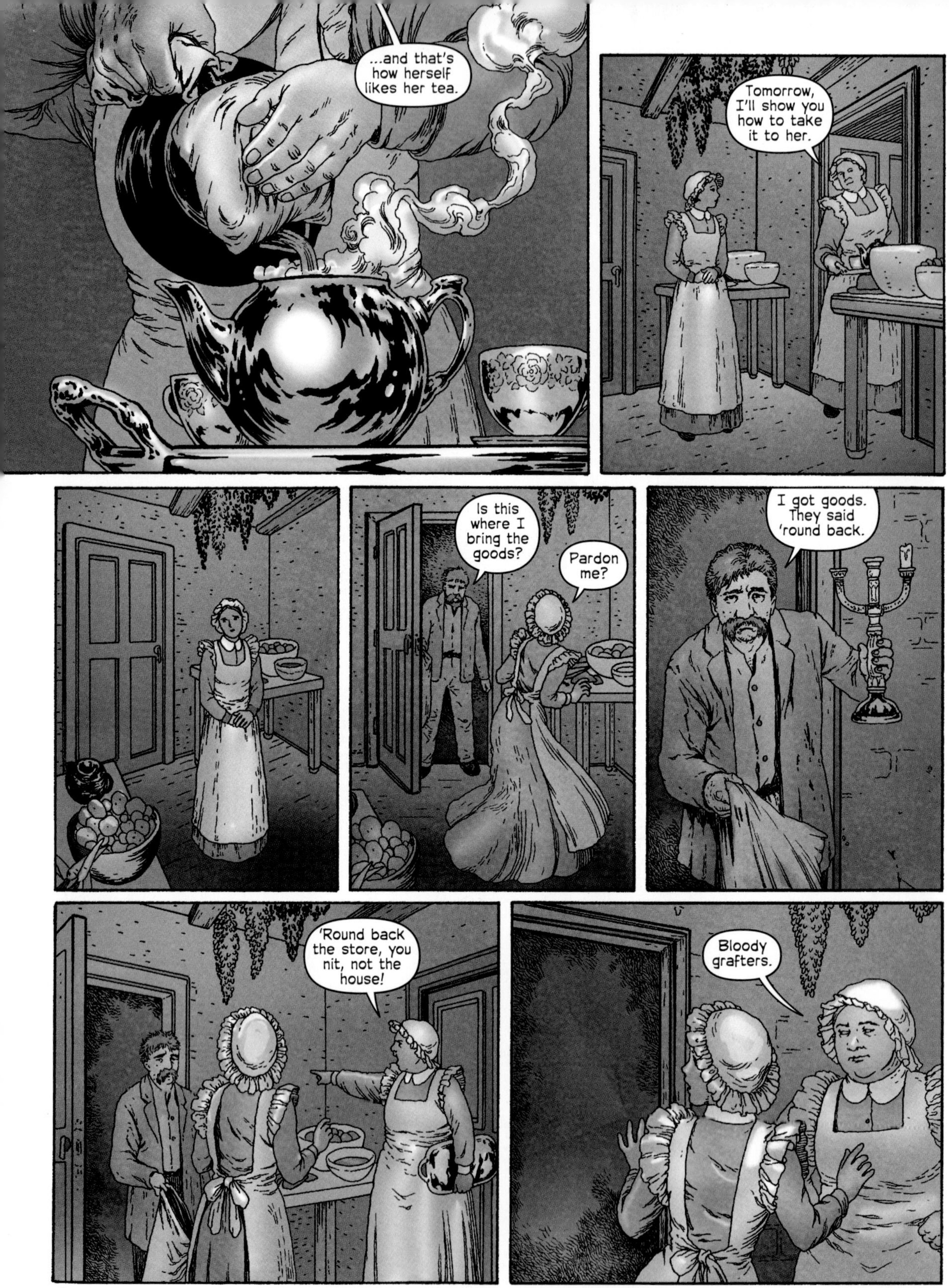
...and that's how herself likes her tea.
Tomorrow, I'll show you how to take it to her.
Is this where I bring the goods?
Pardon me?
I got goods. They said 'round back.
'Round back the store, you nit, not the house!
Bloody grafters.

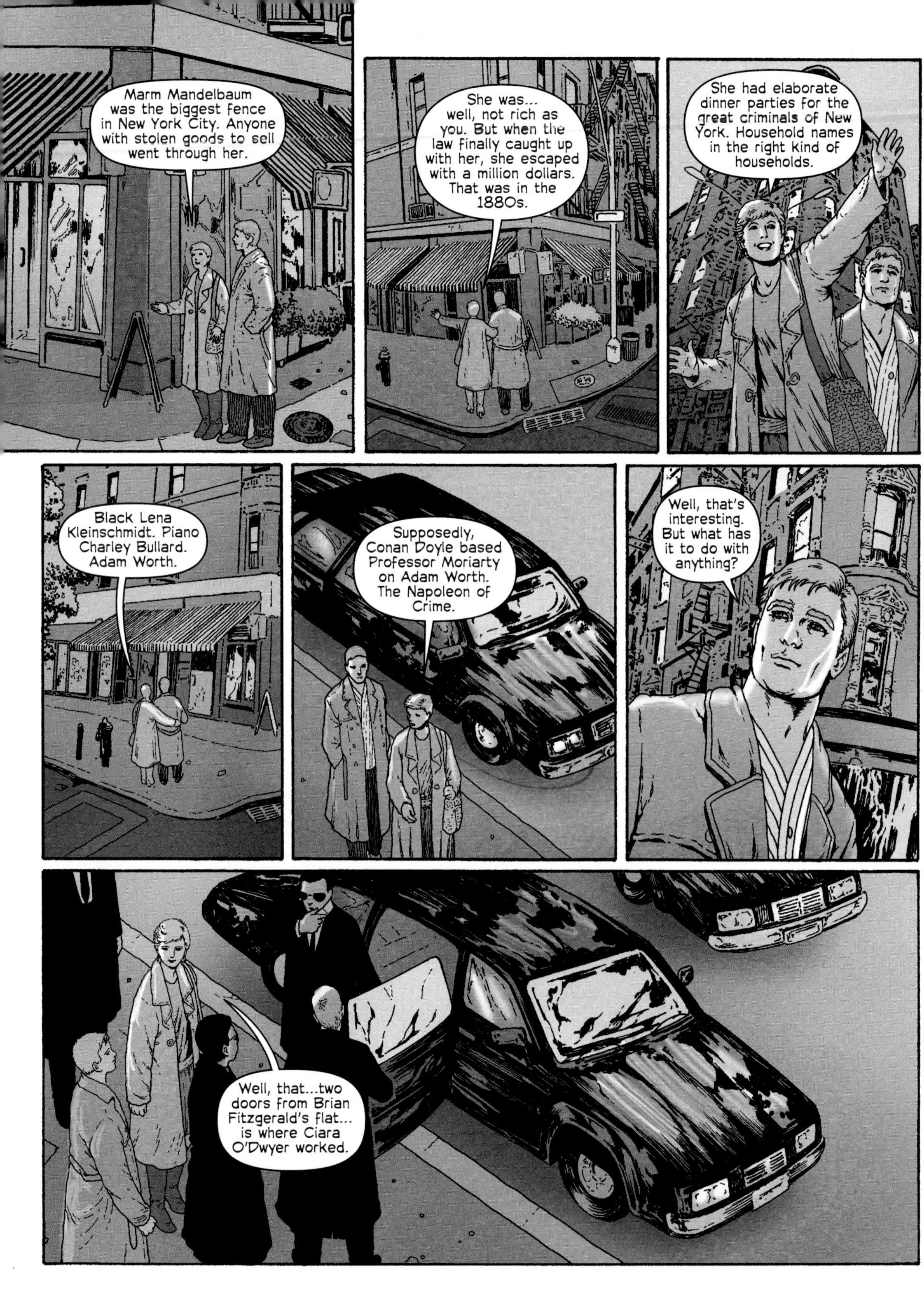
Marm Mandelbaum was the biggest fence in New York City. Anyone with stolen goods to sell went through her.
She was... well, not rich as you. But when the law finally caught up with her, she escaped with a million dollars. That was in the 1880s.
She had elaborate dinner parties for the great criminals of New York. Household names in the right kind of households.
Black Lena Kleinschmidt. Piano Charley Bullard. Adam Worth.
Supposedly, Conan Doyle based Professor Moriarty on Adam Worth. The Napoleon of Crime.
Well, that's interesting. But what has it to do with anything?
Well, that...two doors from Brian Fitzgerald's flat... is where Ciara O'Dwyer worked.

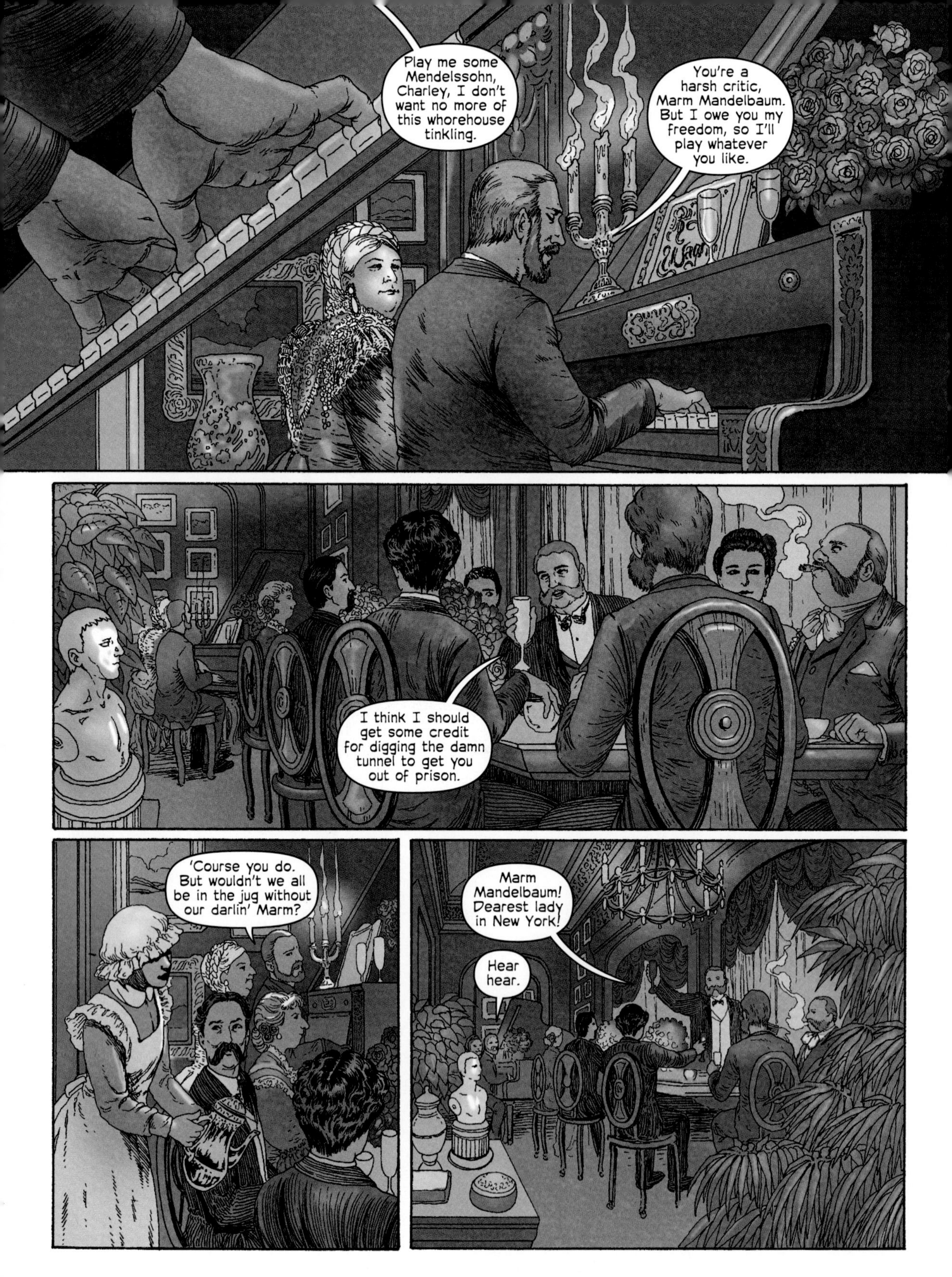
Play me some Mendelssohn, Charley, I don't want no more of this whorehouse tinkling.
You're a harsh critic, Marm Mandelbaum. But I owe you my freedom, so I'll play whatever you like.
I think I should get some credit for digging the damn tunnel to get you out of prison.
'Course you do. But wouldn't we all be in the jug without our darlin' Marm?
Marm Mandelbaum! Dearest lady in New York!
Hear hear.

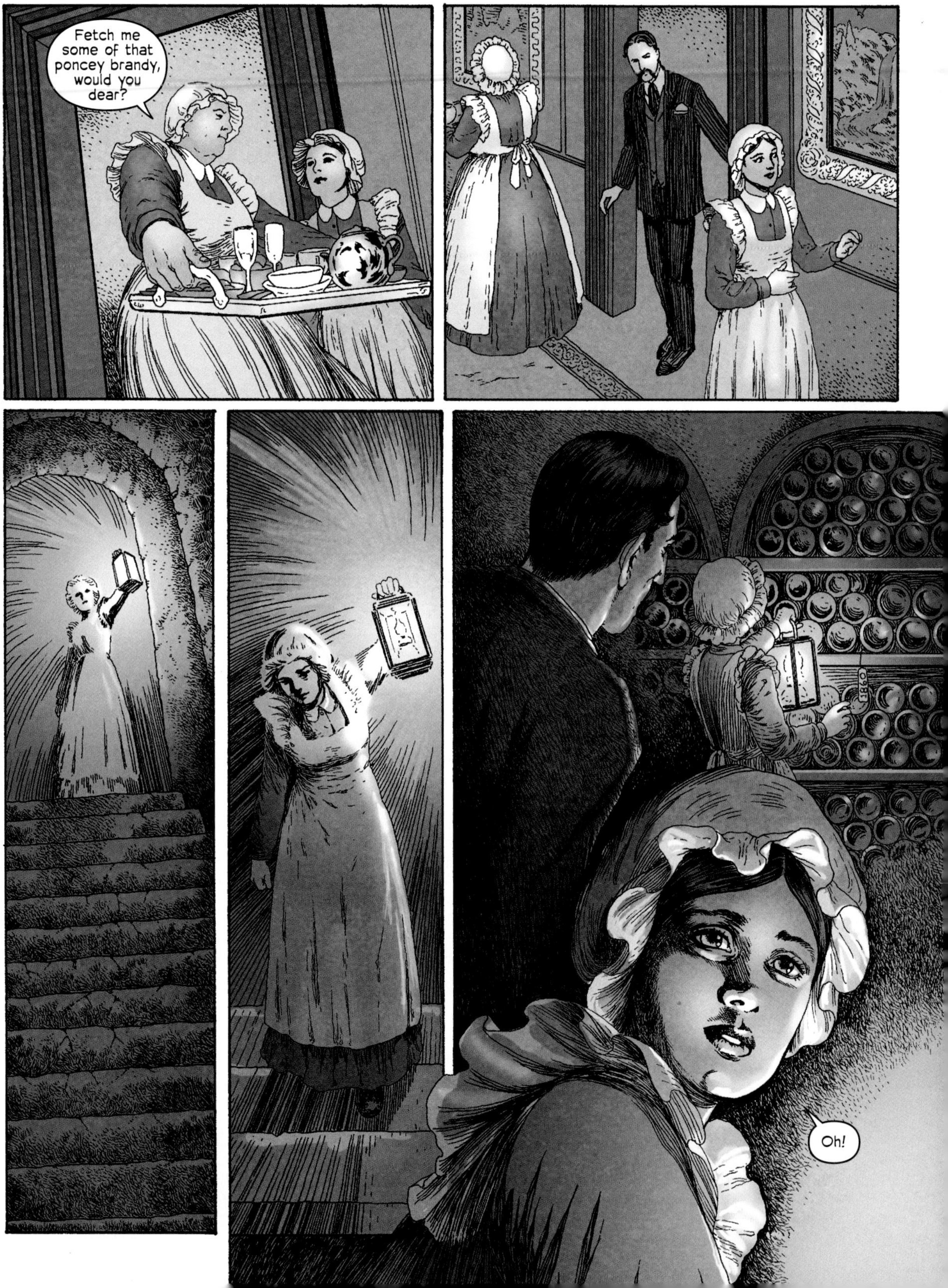
Fetch me some of that poncey brandy, would you dear?
1860
Oh!

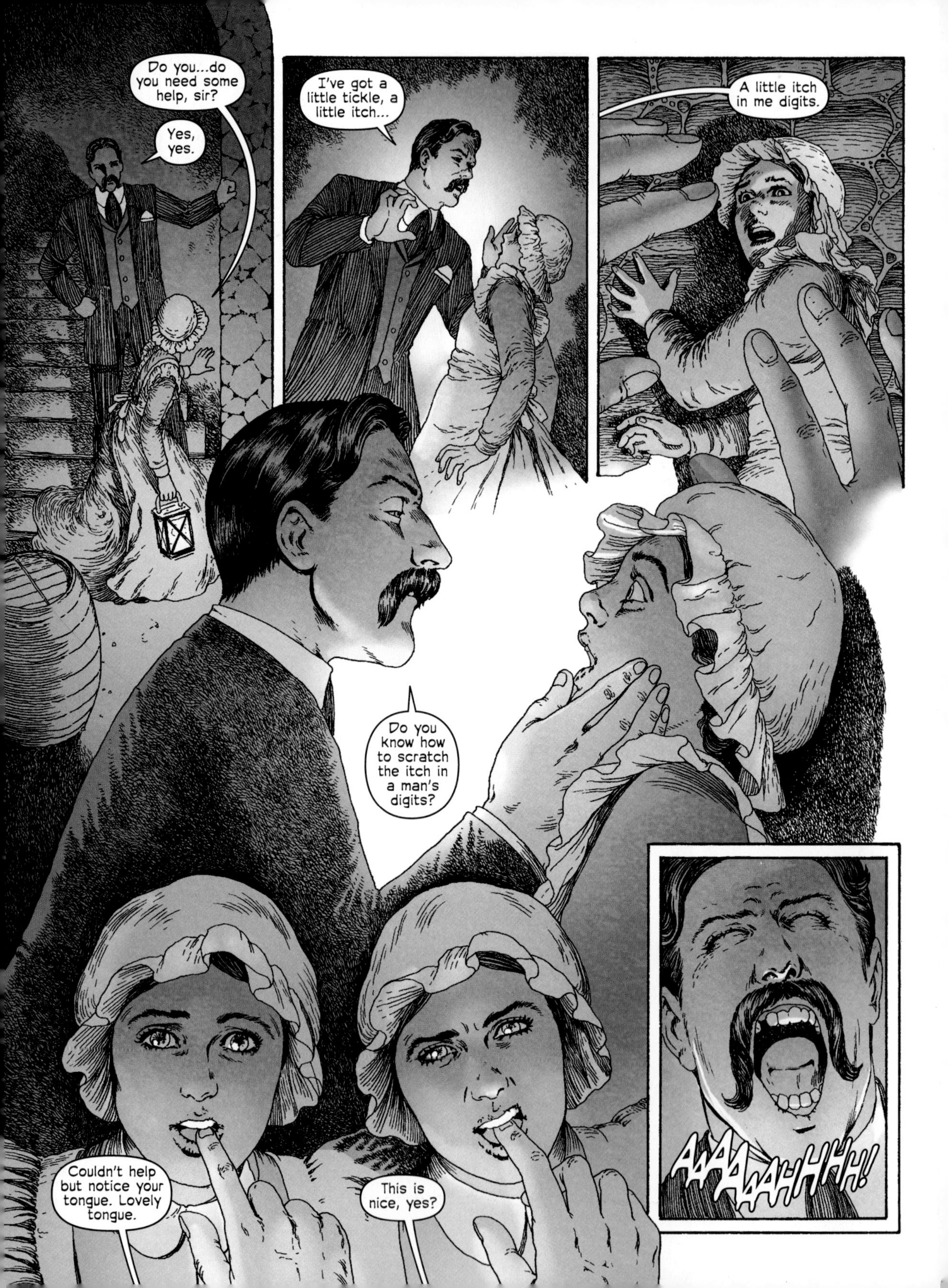
Do you...do you need some help, sir?
Yes, yes.
I've got a little tickle, a little itch...
A little itch in me digits.
Do you know how to scratch the itch in a man's digits?
Couldn't help but notice your tongue. Lovely tongue.
This is nice, yes?
AAAAAAHHHH!

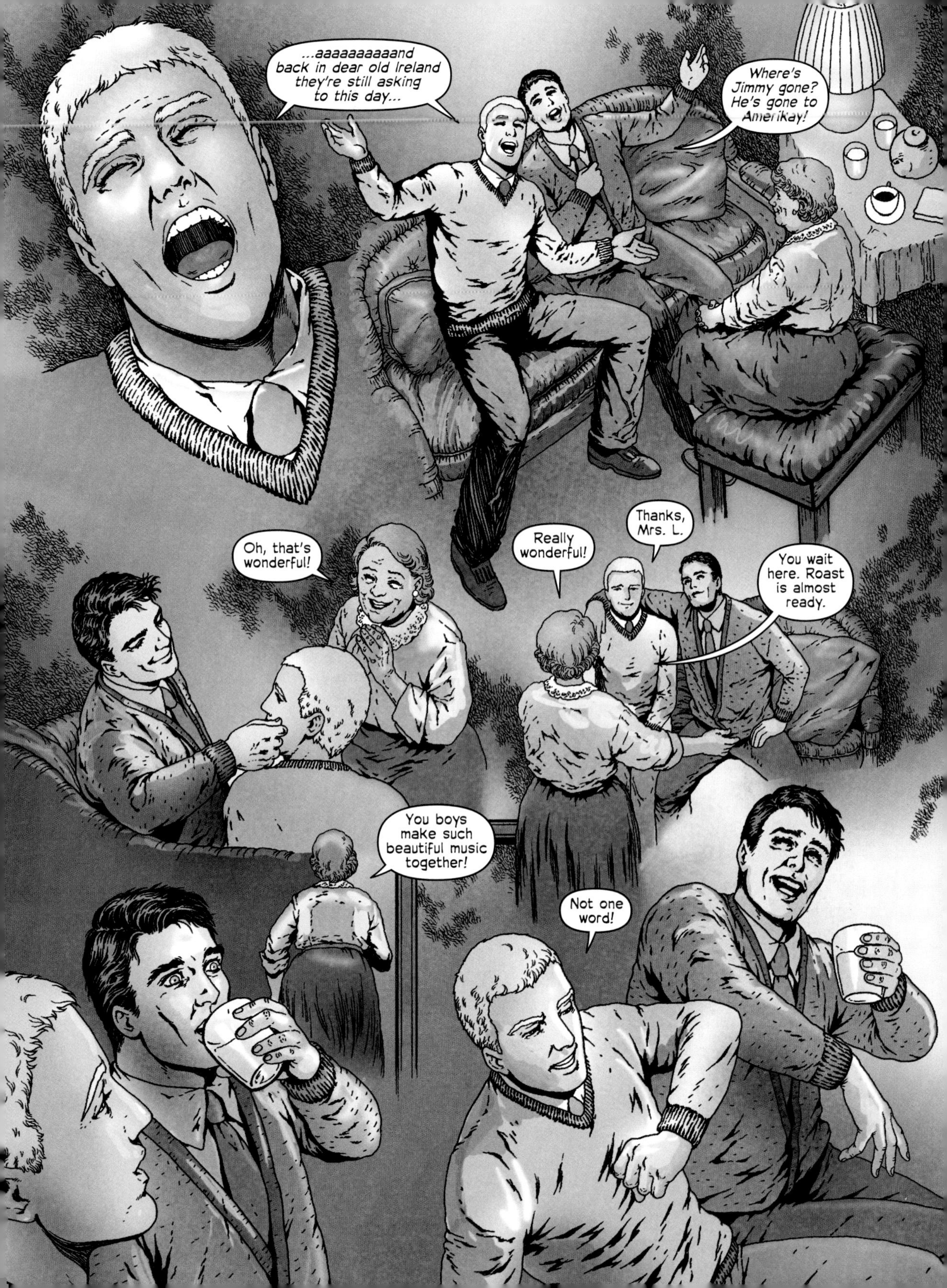
...aaaaaaaaaand back in dear old Ireland they're still asking to this day...
Where's Jimmy gone? He's gone to Amerikay!
Oh, that's wonderful!
Really wonderful!
Thanks, Mrs. L.
You wait here. Roast is almost ready.
You boys make such beautiful music together!
Not one word!

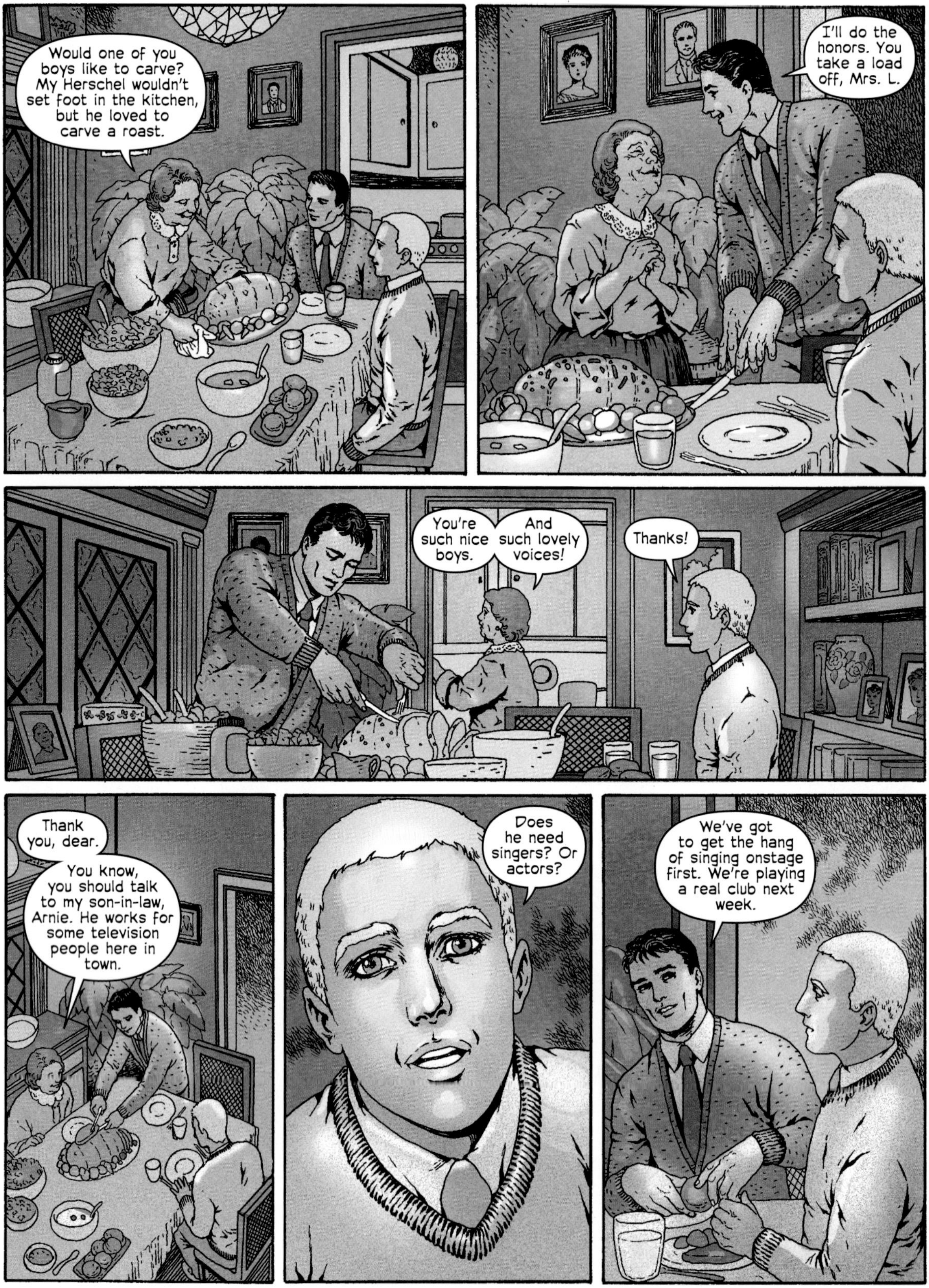
Would one of you boys like to carve? My Herschel wouldn't set foot in the kitchen, but he loved to carve a roast.
I'll do the honors. You take a load off, Mrs. L.
You're such nice boys.
And such lovely voices!
Thanks!
Thank you, dear.
You know, you should talk to my son-in-law, Arnie. He works for some television people here in town.
Does he need singers? Or actors?
We've got to get the hang of singing onstage first. We're playing a real club next week.

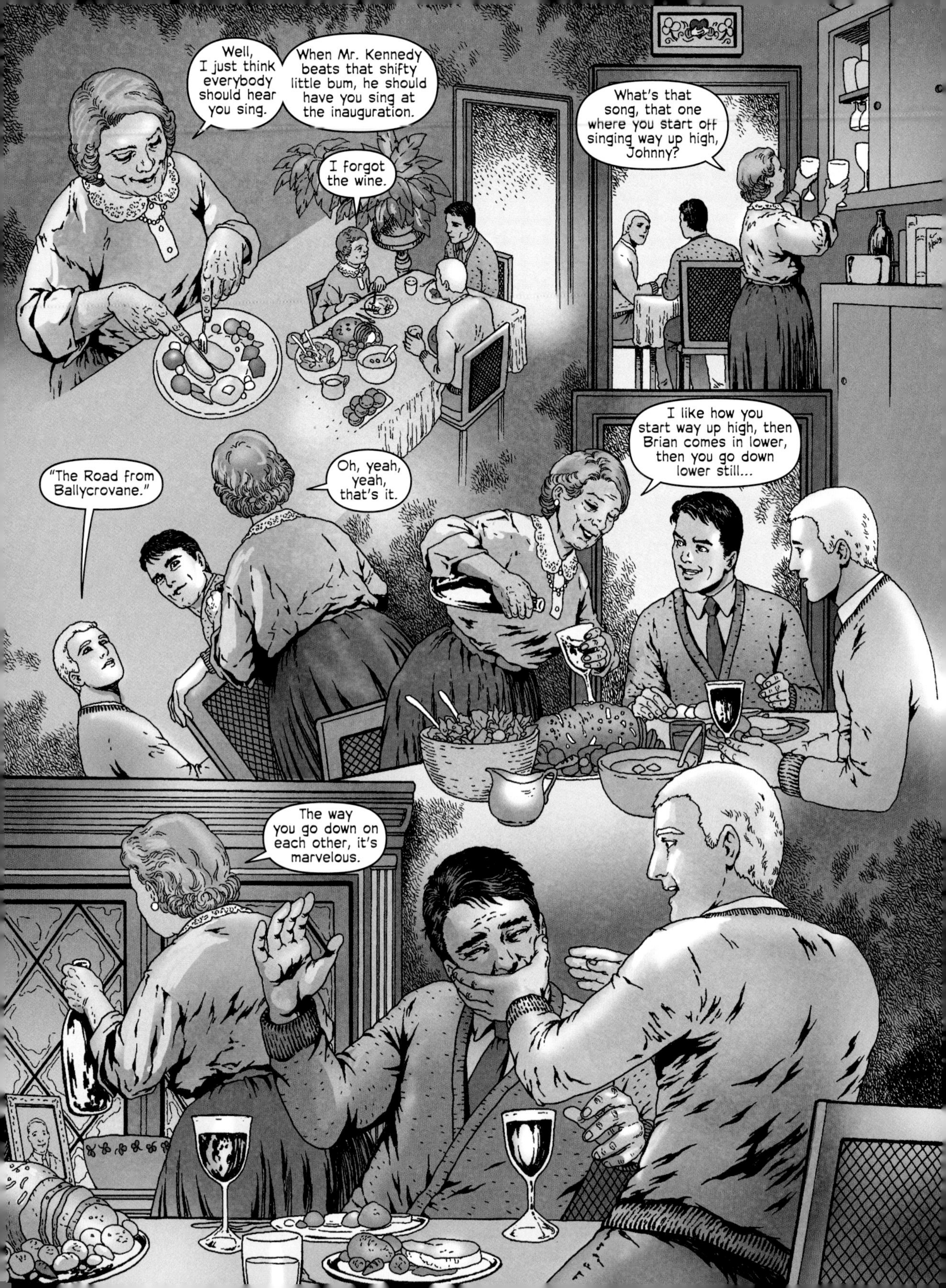
Well, I just think everybody should hear you sing.
When Mr. Kennedy beats that shifty little bum, he should have you sing at the inauguration.
I forgot the wine.
What's that song, that one where you start off singing way up high, Johnny?
"The Road from Ballycrovane."
Oh, yeah, yeah, that's it.
I like how you start way up high, then Brian comes in lower, then you go down lower still...
The way you go down on each other, it's marvelous.

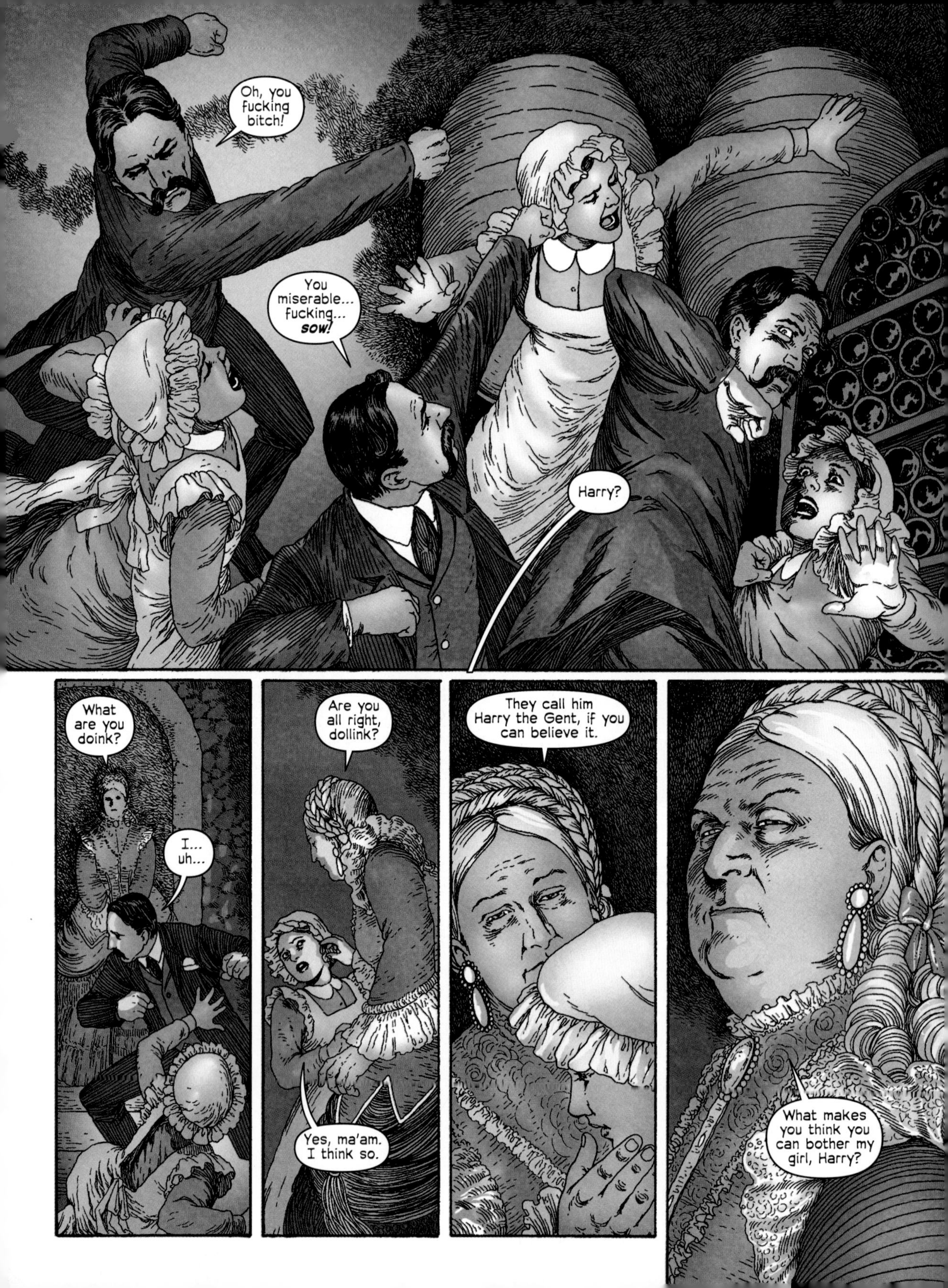
Oh, you fucking bitch!
You miserable... fucking... SOW!
Harry?
What are you doink?
I... uh...
Are you all right, dollink?
Yes, ma'am. I think so.
They call him Harry the Gent, if you can believe it.
What makes you think you can bother my girl, Harry?

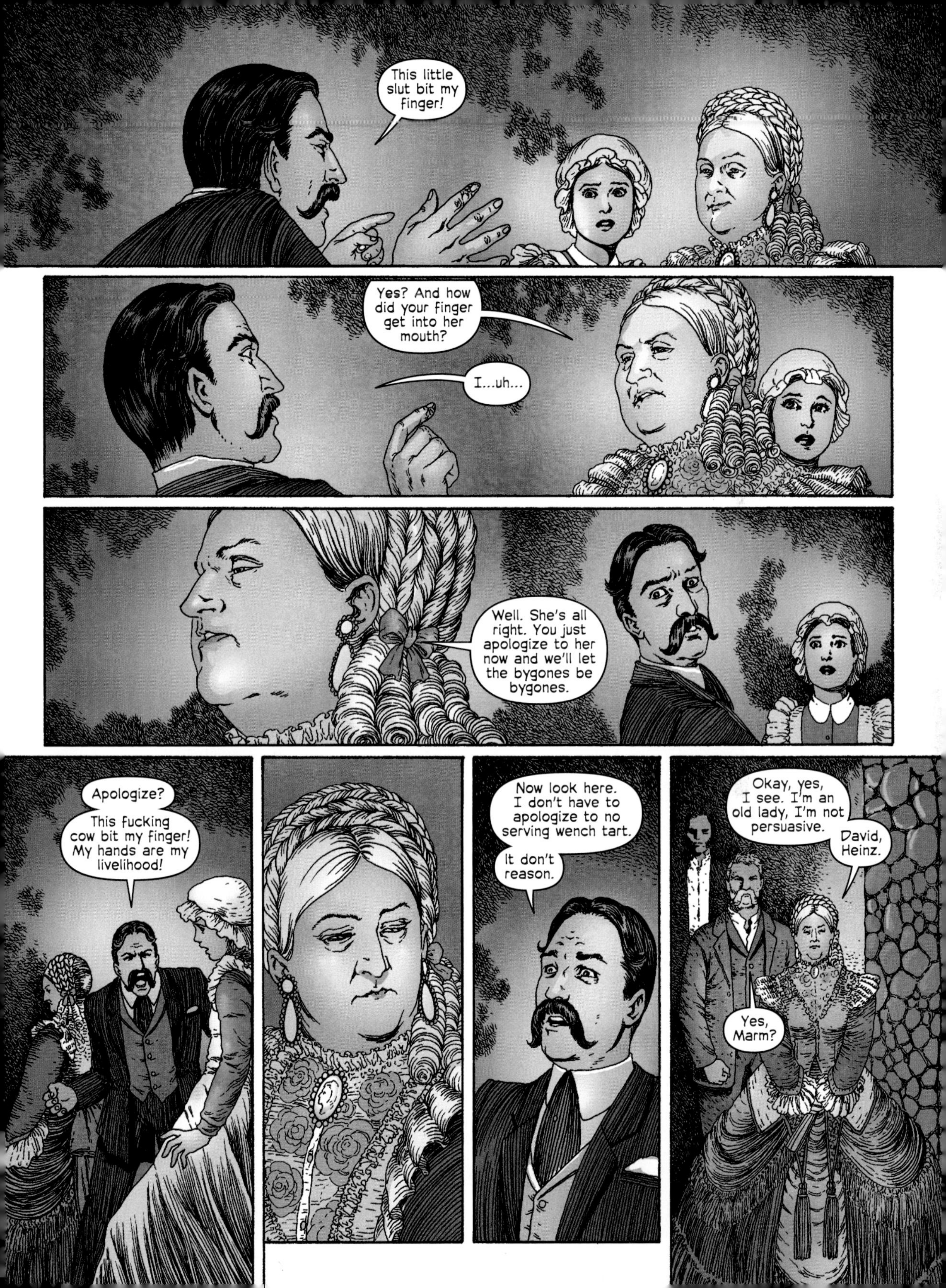
This little slut bit my finger!
Yes? And how did your finger get into her mouth?
I...uh...
Well. She's all right. You just apologize to her now and we'll let the bygones be bygones.
Apologize?
This fucking cow bit my finger! My hands are my livelihood!
Now look here. I don't have to apologize to no serving wench tart.
It don't reason.
Okay, yes, I see. I'm an old lady, I'm not persuasive.
David, Heinz.
Yes, Marm?

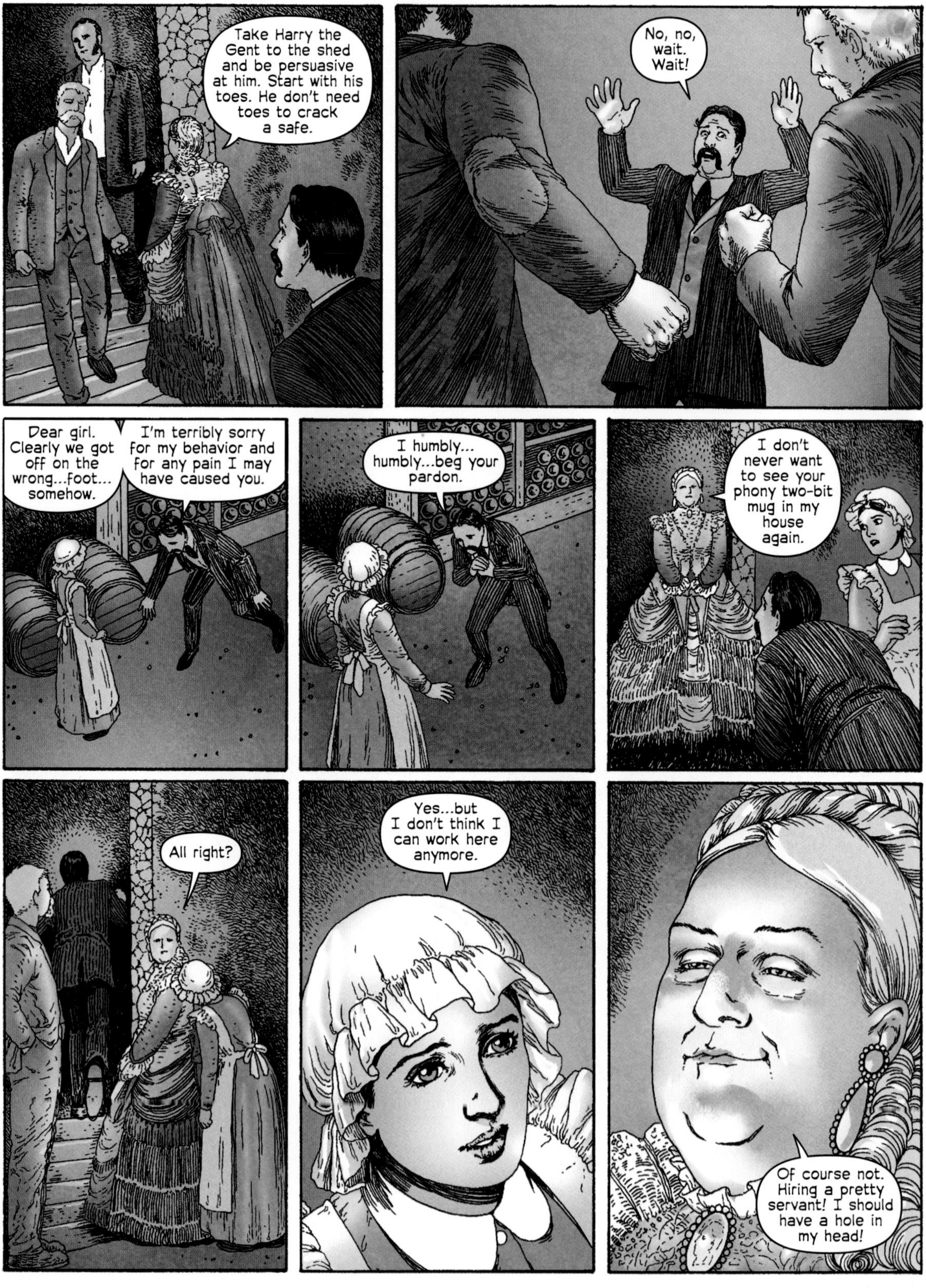
Take Harry the Gent to the shed and be persuasive at him. Start with his toes. He don't need toes to crack a safe.
No, no, wait. Wait!
Dear girl. Clearly we got off on the wrong...foot... somehow.
I'm terribly sorry for my behavior and for any pain I may have caused you.
I humbly... humbly...beg your pardon.
I don't never want to see your phony two-bit mug in my house again.
All right?
Yes...but I don't think I can work here anymore.
Of course not. Hiring a pretty servant! I should have a hole in my head!

Where's Jimmy gone? He's gone to Amerikay! ♪

Listen to them!

You done arrived, babies!

CLAP CLAP
WHOOOo! YEAH! YEAH!
CLAP CLAP

Couldn't have got here without you, darlin'.

Over to the corner there.

This is the man I want you to meet.

Aras Eismont.

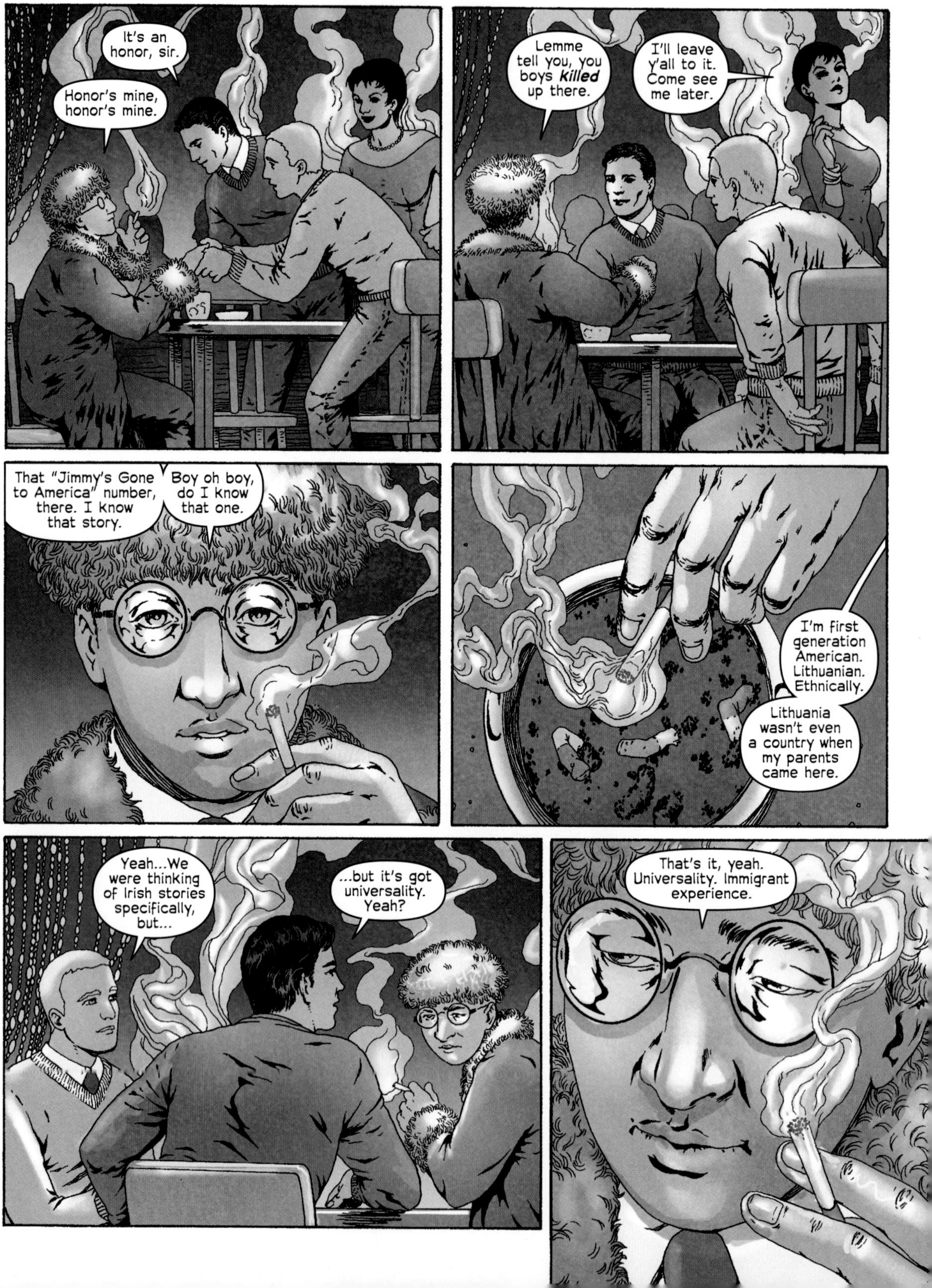

It's an honor, sir.
Honor's mine, honor's mine.
Lemme tell you, you boys *killed* up there.
I'll leave y'all to it. Come see me later.
That "Jimmy's Gone to America" number, there. I know that story.
Boy oh boy, do I know that one.
I'm first generation American. Lithuanian. Ethnically.
Lithuania wasn't even a country when my parents came here.
Yeah...We were thinking of Irish stories specifically, but...
...but it's got universality. Yeah?
That's it, yeah. Universality. Immigrant experience.

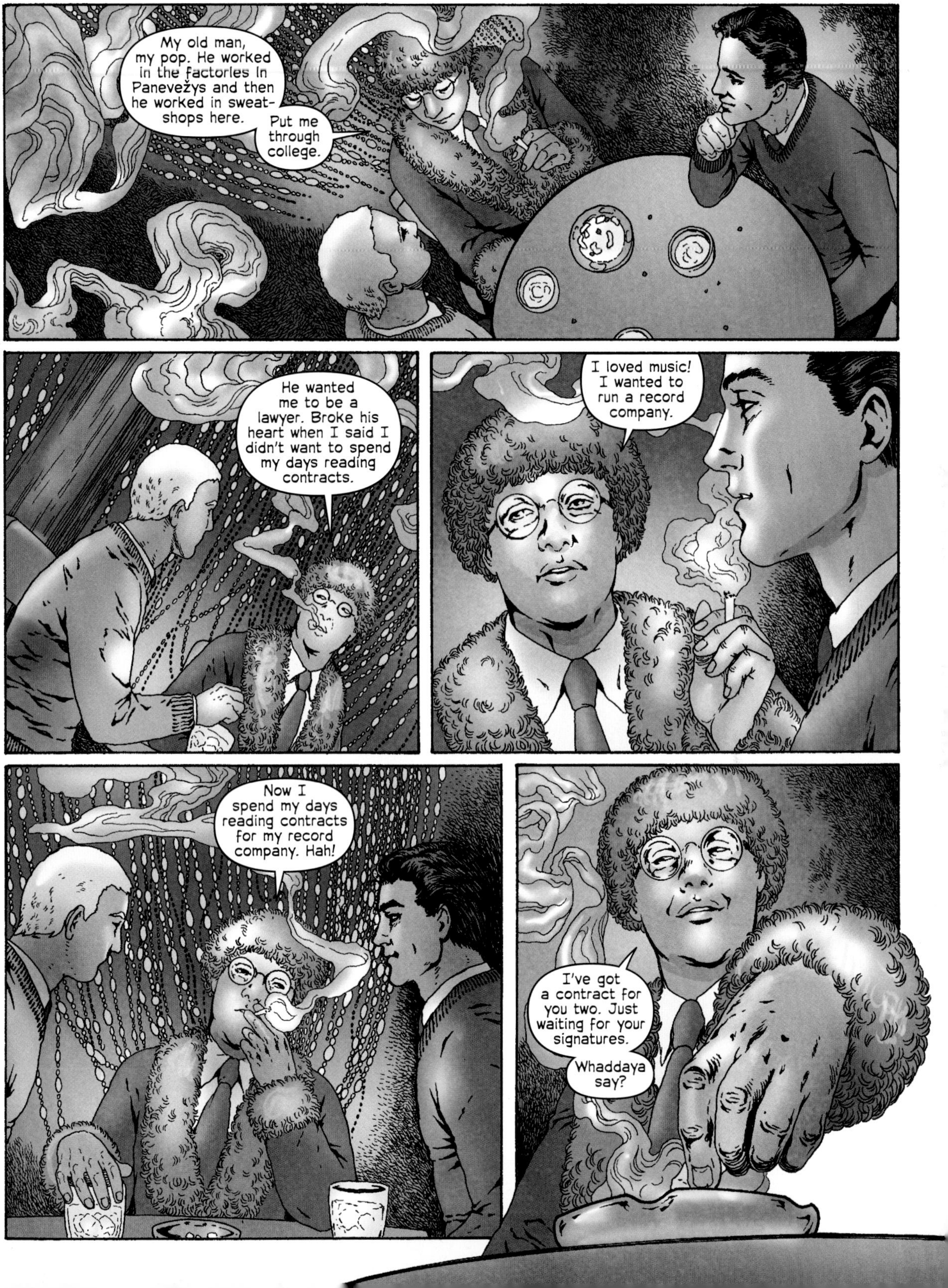
My old man, my pop. He worked in the factories in Panevežys and then he worked in sweat-shops here.
Put me through college.
He wanted me to be a lawyer. Broke his heart when I said I didn't want to spend my days reading contracts.
I loved music! I wanted to run a record company.
Now I spend my days reading contracts for my record company. Hah!
I've got a contract for you two. Just waiting for your signatures.
Whaddaya say?

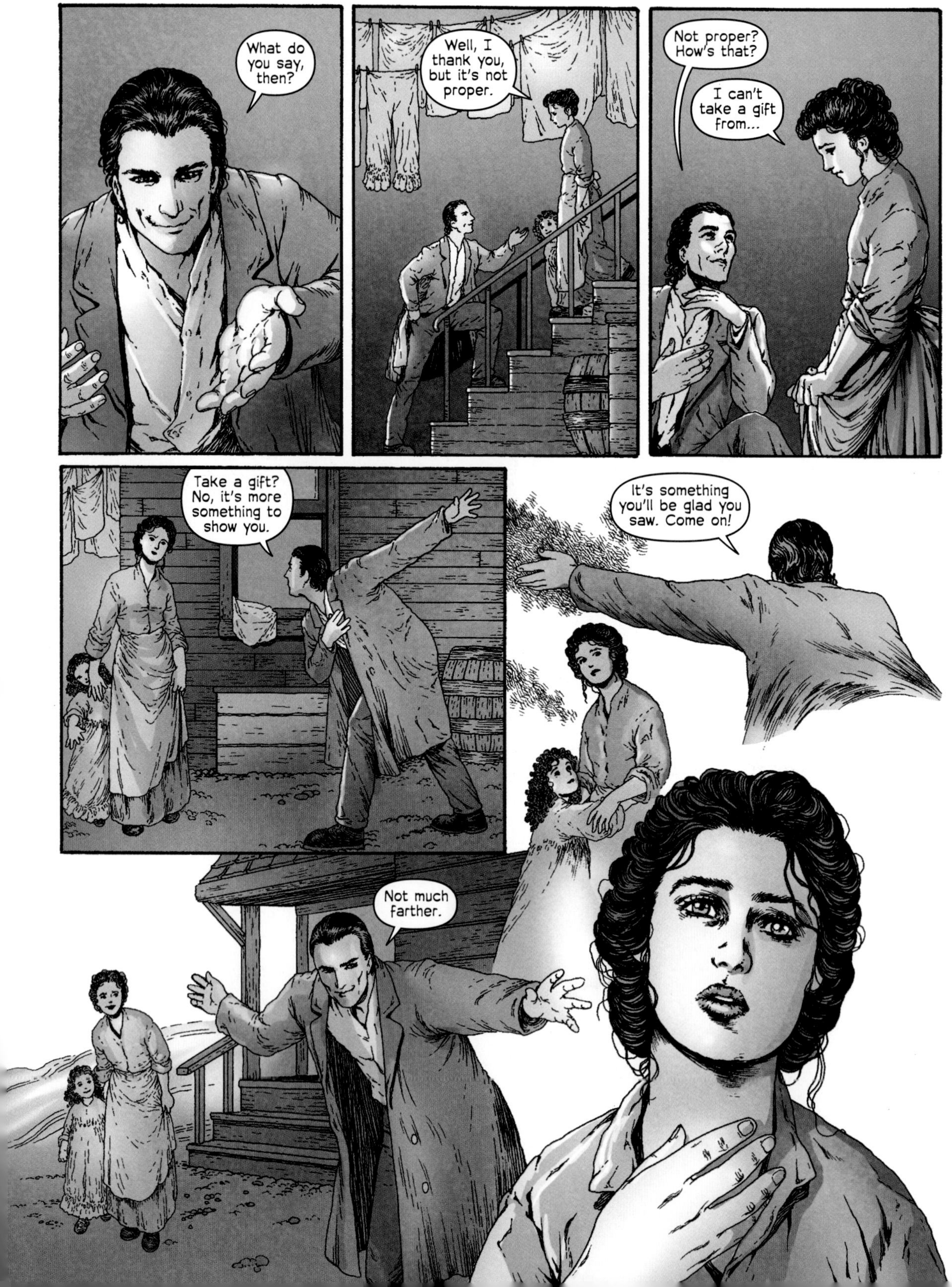
What do you say, then?
Well, I thank you, but it's not proper.
Not proper? How's that?
I can't take a gift from...
Take a gift? No, it's more something to show you.
It's something you'll be glad you saw. Come on!
Not much farther.

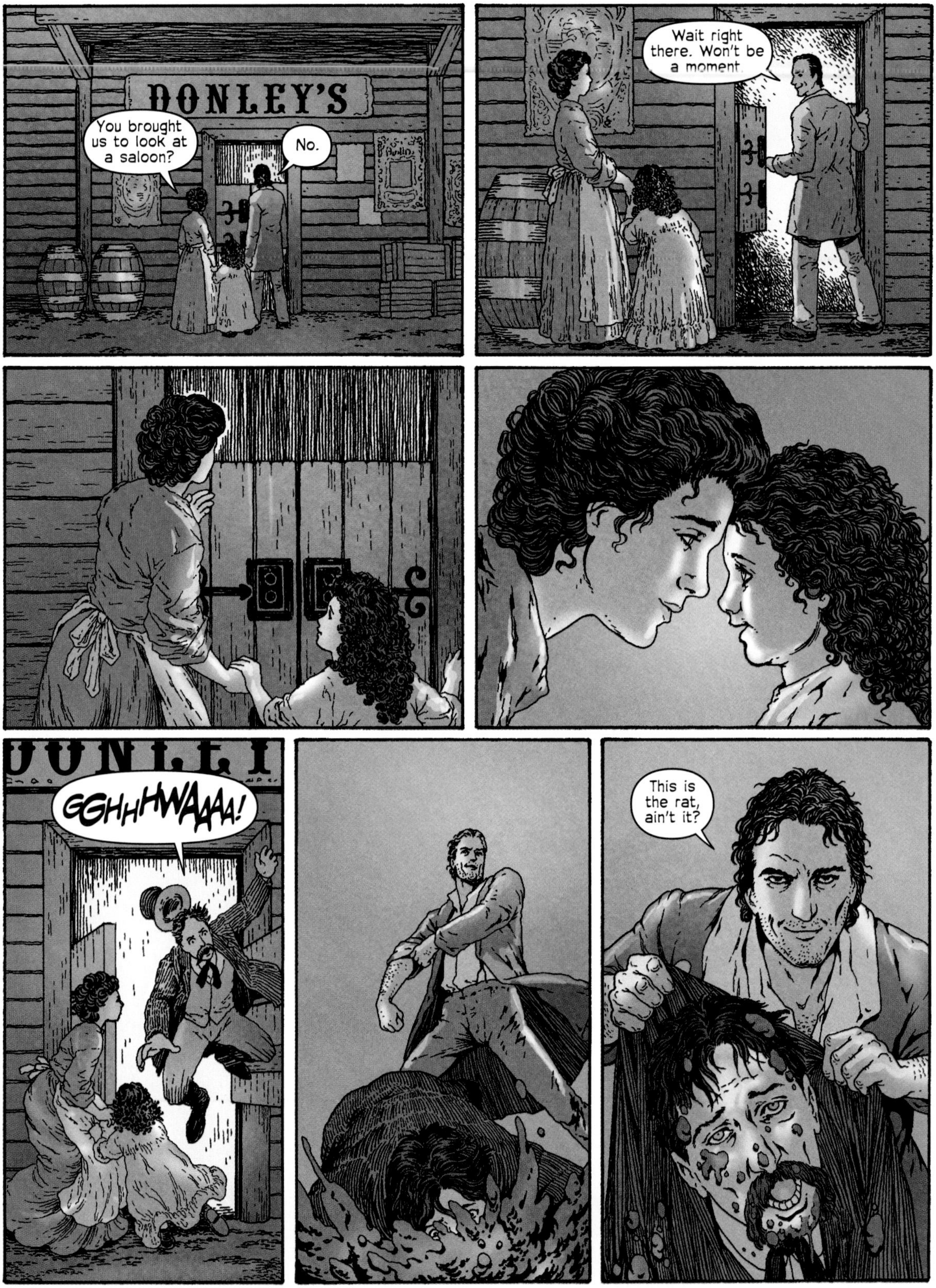
DONLEY'S
You brought us to look at a saloon?
No.
Wait right there. Won't be a moment.
GGHHHWAAAA!
This is the rat, ain't it?

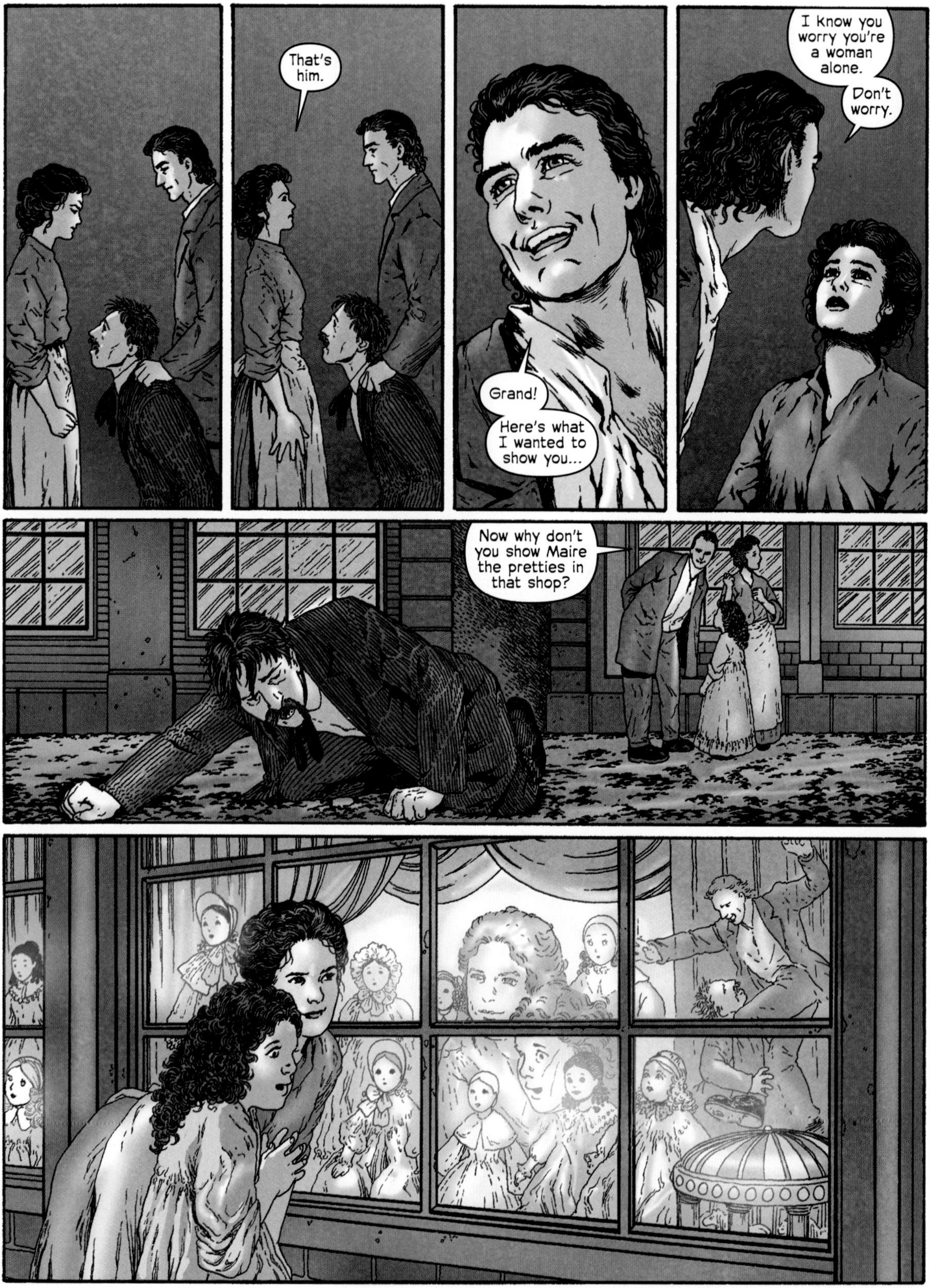
That's him.
Grand!
Here's what I wanted to show you...
I know you worry you're a woman alone.
Don't worry.
Now why don't you show Maire the pretties in that shop?

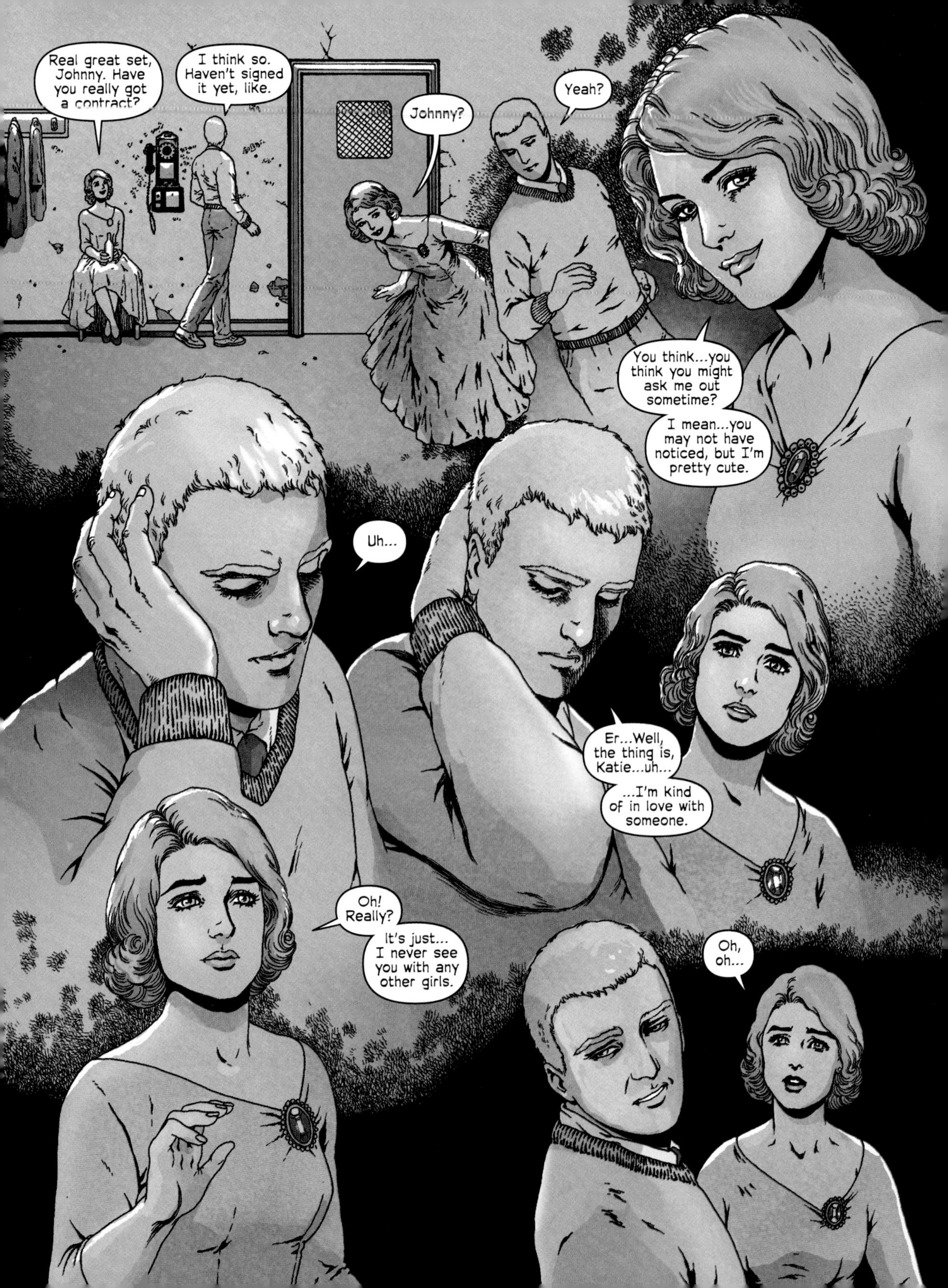
Real great set, Johnny. Have you really got a contract?
I think so. Haven't signed it yet, like.
Johnny?
Yeah?
You think...you think you might ask me out sometime?
I mean...you may not have noticed, but I'm pretty cute.
Uh...
Er...Well, the thing is, Katie...uh...
...I'm kind of in love with someone.
Oh! Really?
It's just... I never see you with any other girls.
Oh, oh...

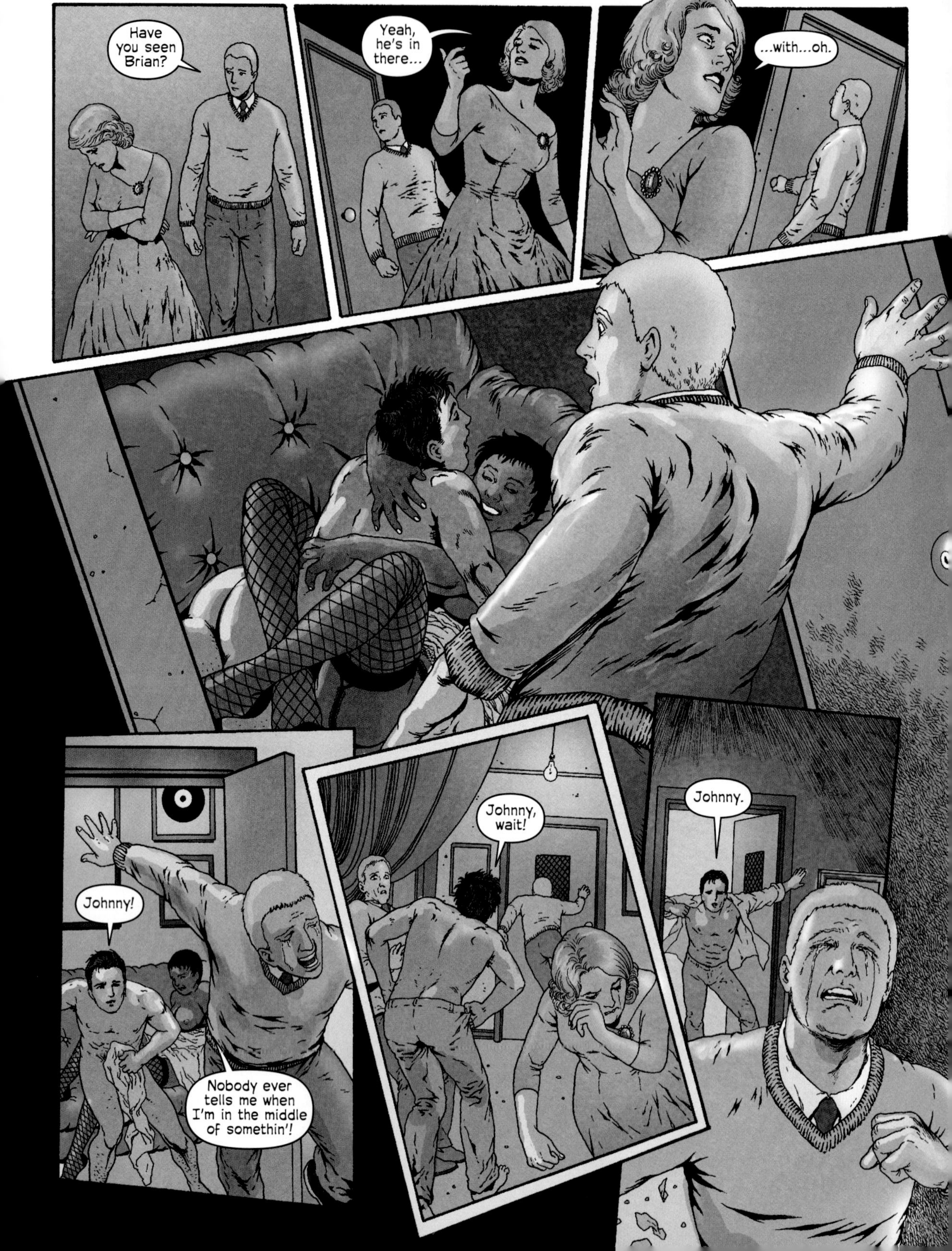
Have you seen Brian?
Yeah, he's in there...
...with...oh.
Johnny!
Nobody ever tells me when I'm in the middle of somethin'!
Johnny, wait!
Johnny.

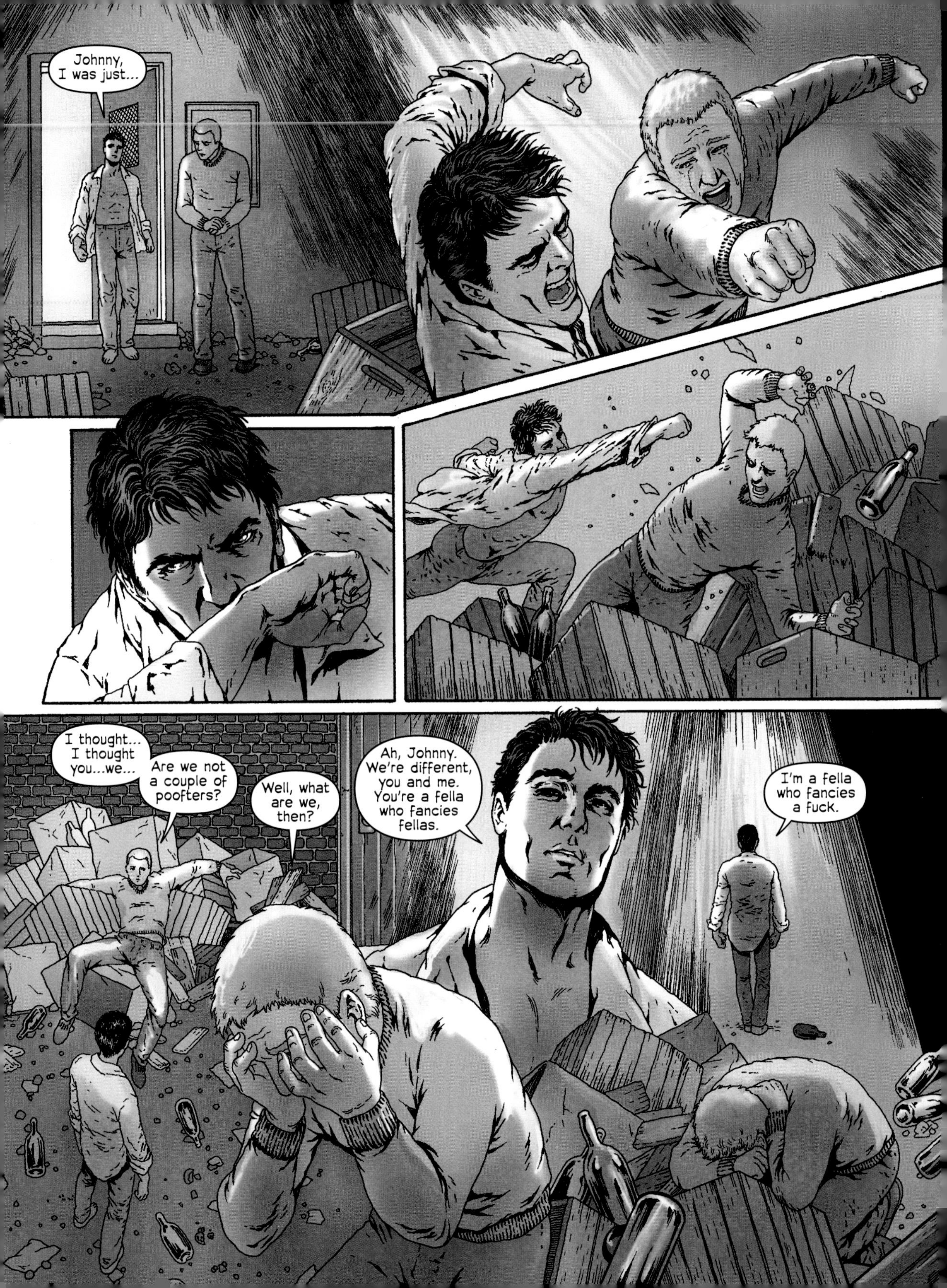
Johnny, I was just...
I thought... I thought you...we...
Are we not a couple of poofters?
Well, what are we, then?
Ah, Johnny. We're different, you and me. You're a fella who fancies fellas.
I'm a fella who fancies a fuck.

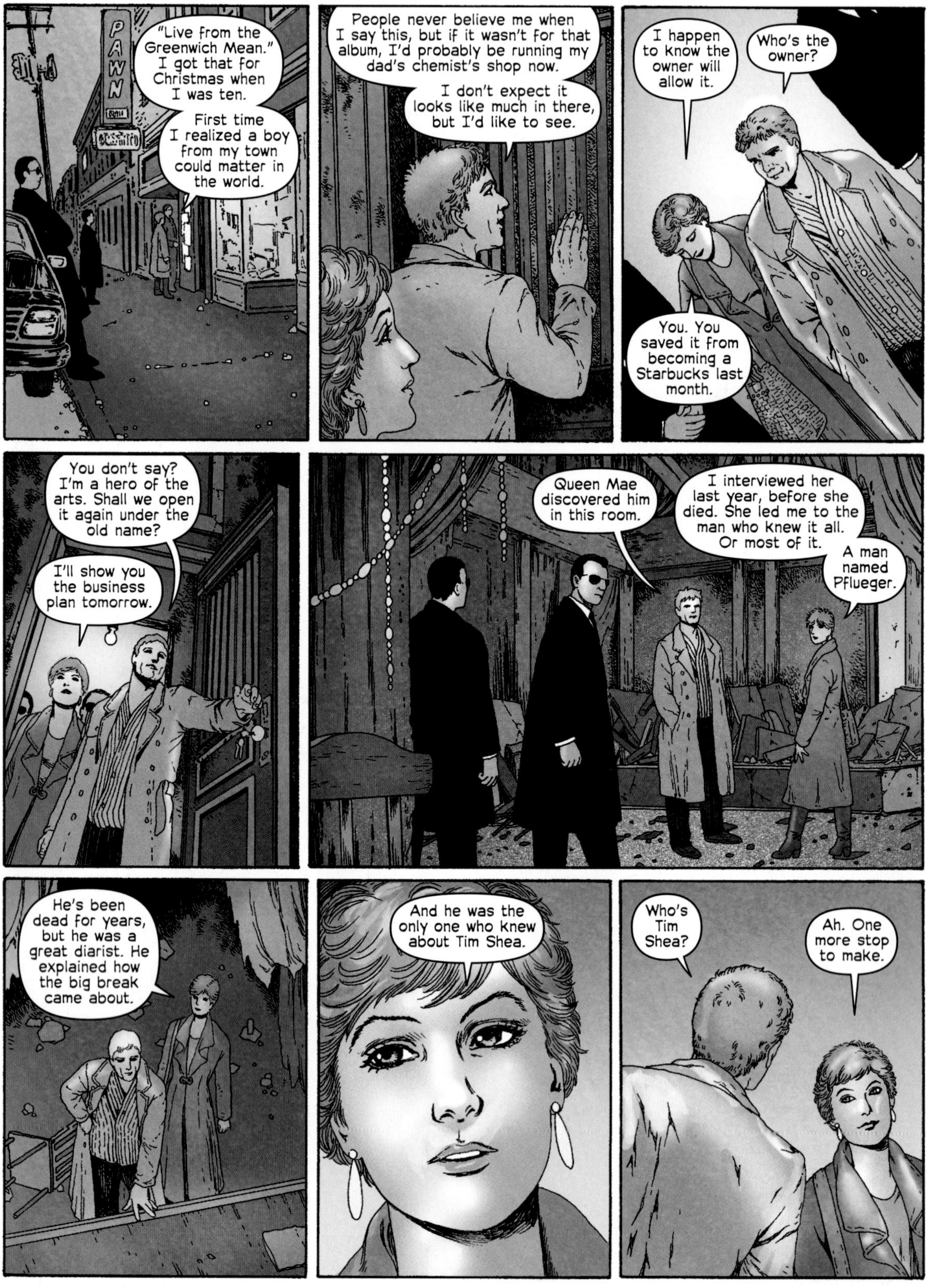
PAWN
"Live from the Greenwich Mean." I got that for Christmas when I was ten.
First time I realized a boy from my town could matter in the world.
People never believe me when I say this, but if it wasn't for that album, I'd probably be running my dad's chemist's shop now.
I don't expect it looks like much in there, but I'd like to see.
I happen to know the owner will allow it.
Who's the owner?
You. You saved it from becoming a Starbucks last month.
You don't say? I'm a hero of the arts. Shall we open it again under the old name?
I'll show you the business plan tomorrow.
Queen Mae discovered him in this room.
I interviewed her last year, before she died. She led me to the man who knew it all. Or most of it.
A man named Pflueger.
He's been dead for years, but he was a great diarist. He explained how the big break came about.
And he was the only one who knew about Tim Shea.
Who's Tim Shea?
Ah. One more stop to make.

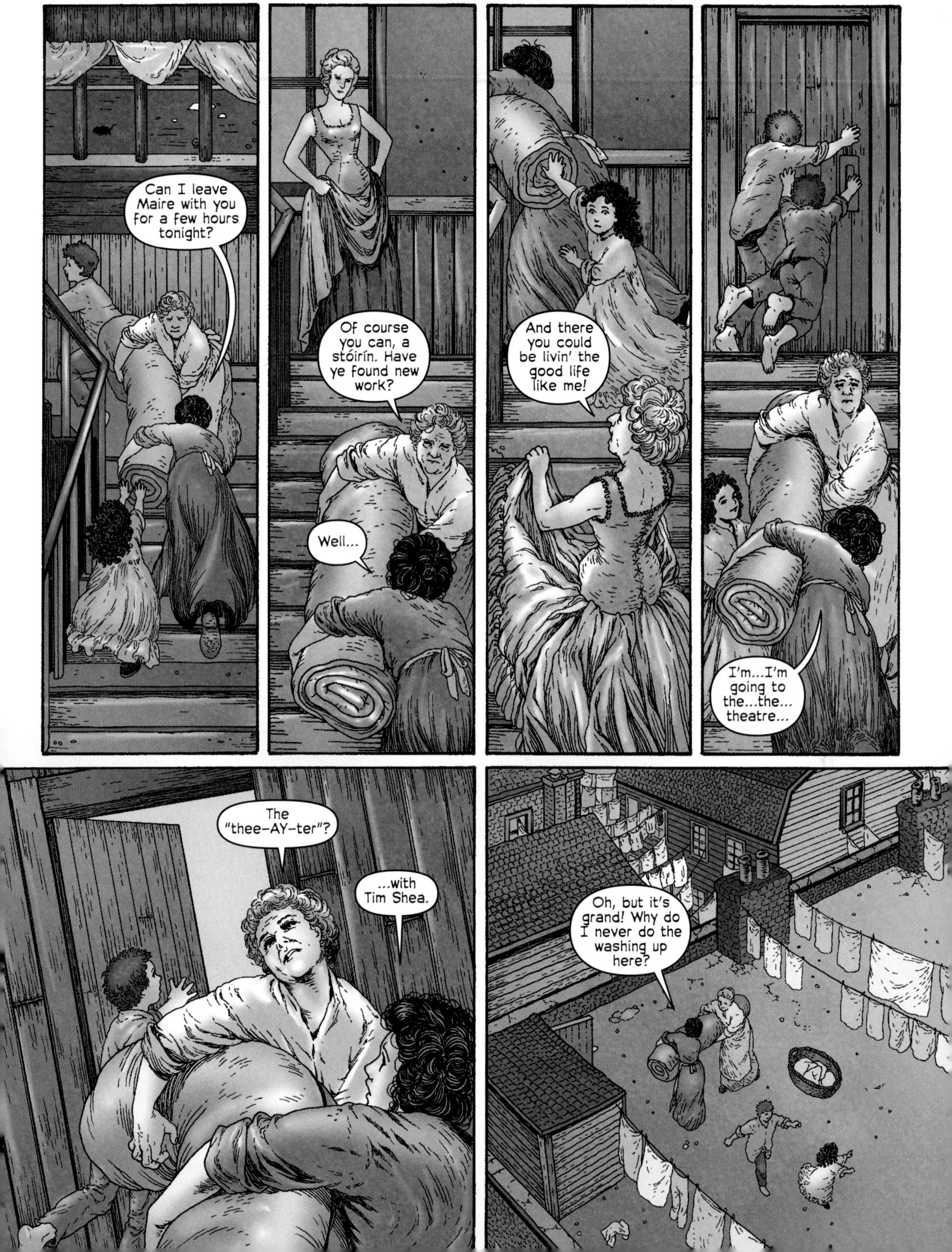
Can I leave Maire with you for a few hours tonight?
Of course you can, a stóirín. Have ye found new work?
Well...
And there you could be livin' the good life like me!
I'm...I'm going to the...the... theatre...
The "thee-AY-ter"?
...with Tim Shea.
Oh, but it's grand! Why do I never do the washing up here?

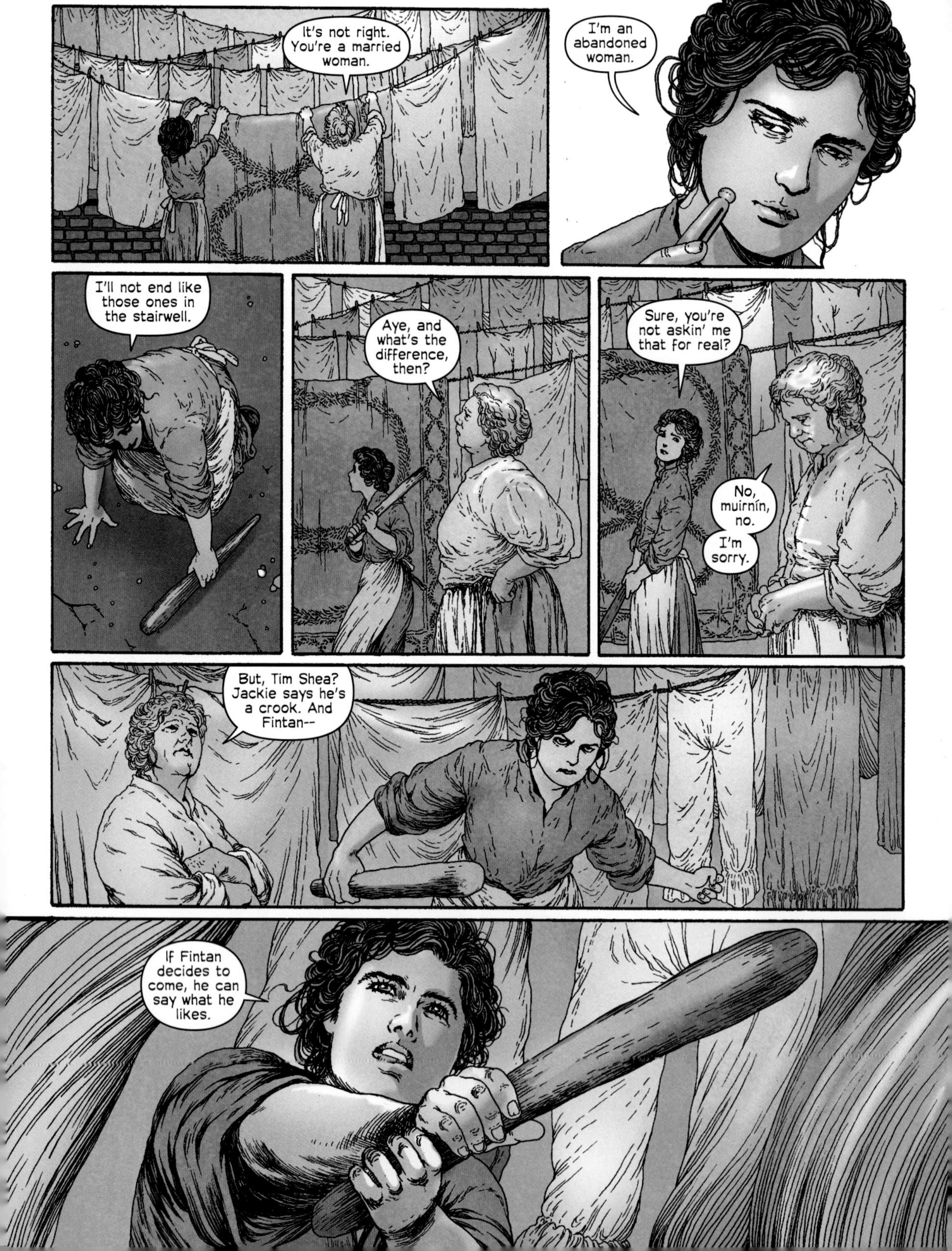
It's not right. You're a married woman.
I'm an abandoned woman.
I'll not end like those ones in the stairwell.
Aye, and what's the difference, then?
Sure, you're not askin' me that for real?
No, muirnín, no.
I'm sorry.
But, Tim Shea? Jackie says he's a crook. And Fintan--
If Fintan decides to come, he can say what he likes.

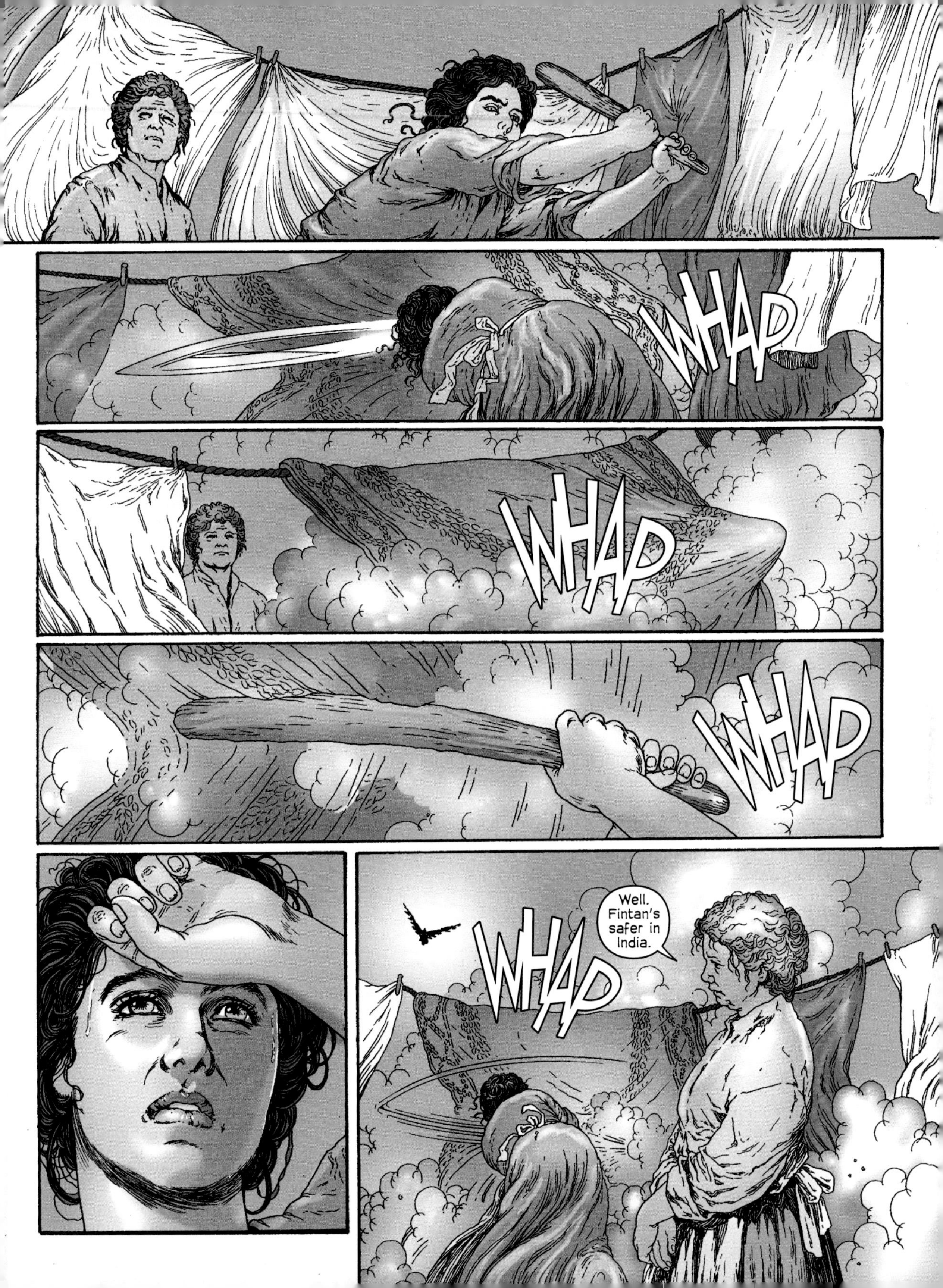
WHAP
WHAP
WHAP
WHAP
Well. Fintan's safer in India.

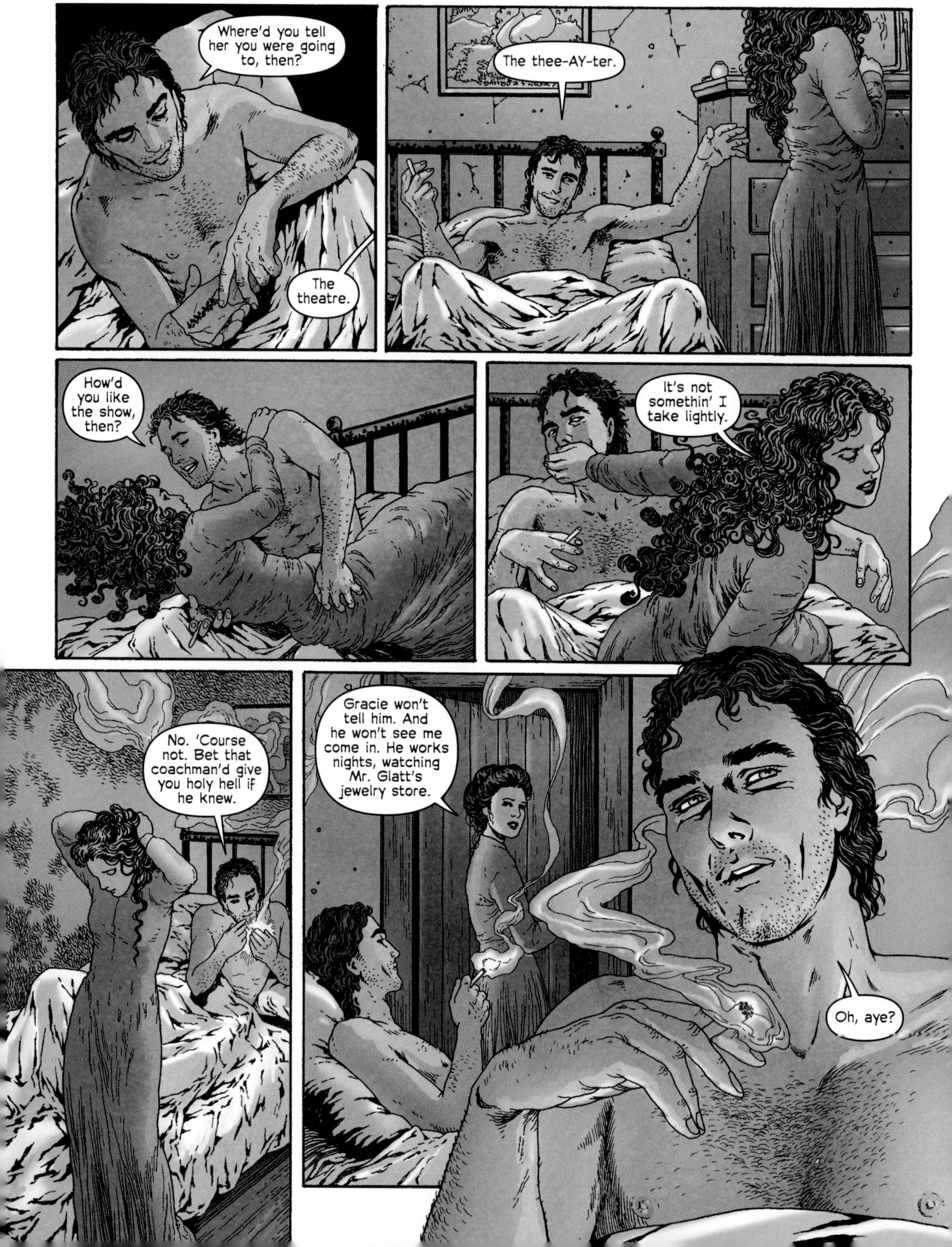
Where'd you tell her you were going to, then?
The theatre.
The thee-AY-ter.
How'd you like the show, then?
It's not somethin' I take lightly.
No. 'Course not. Bet that coachman'd give you holy hell if he knew.
Gracie won't tell him. And he won't see me come in. He works nights, watching Mr. Glatt's jewelry store.
Oh, aye?

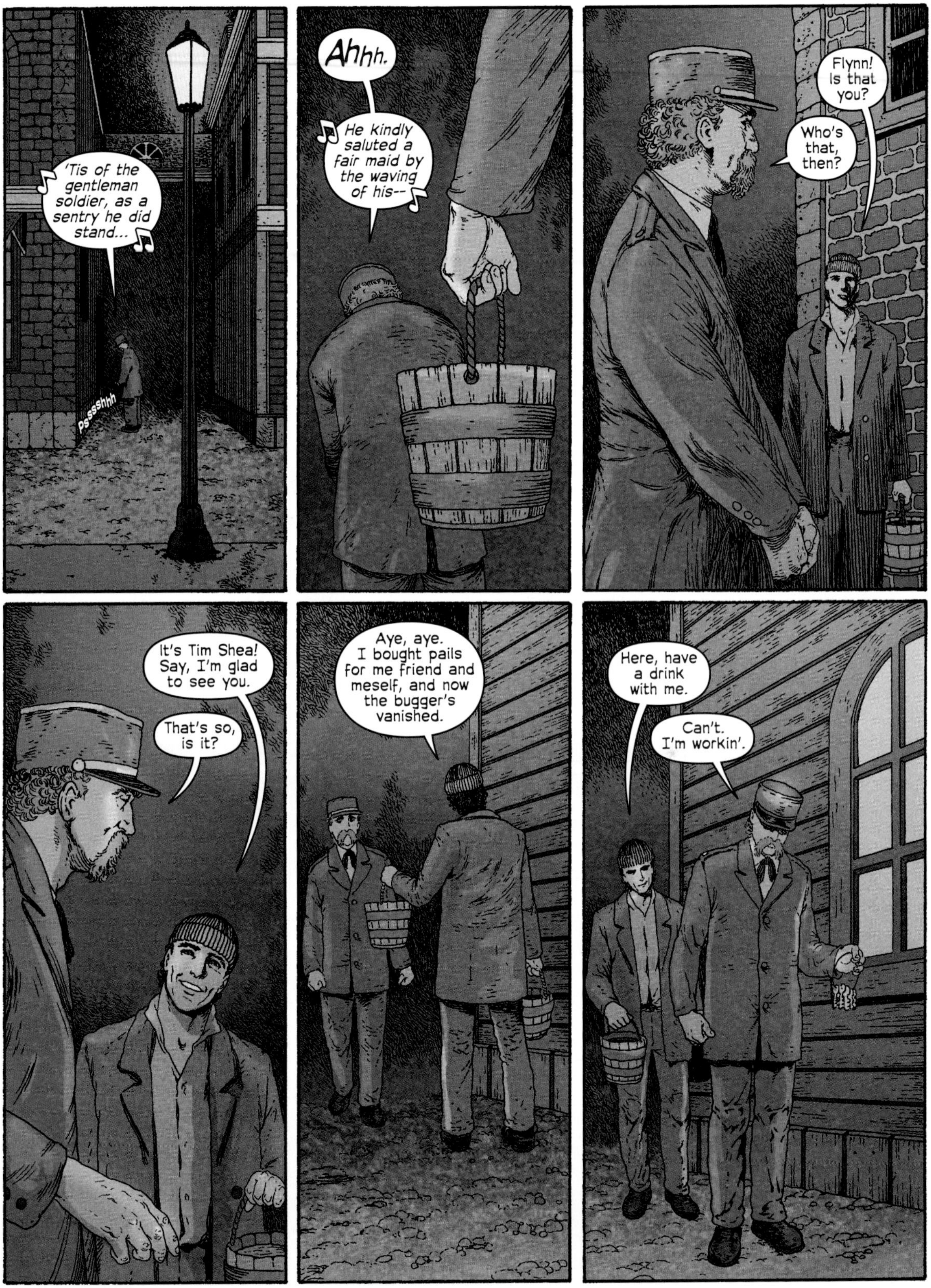
'Tis of the gentleman soldier, as a sentry he did stand...
Pssssshhh
Ahhh.
He kindly saluted a fair maid by the waving of his--
Flynn! Is that you?
Who's that, then?
It's Tim Shea! Say, I'm glad to see you.
That's so, is it?
Aye, aye. I bought pails for me friend and meself, and now the bugger's vanished.
Here, have a drink with me.
Can't. I'm workin'.

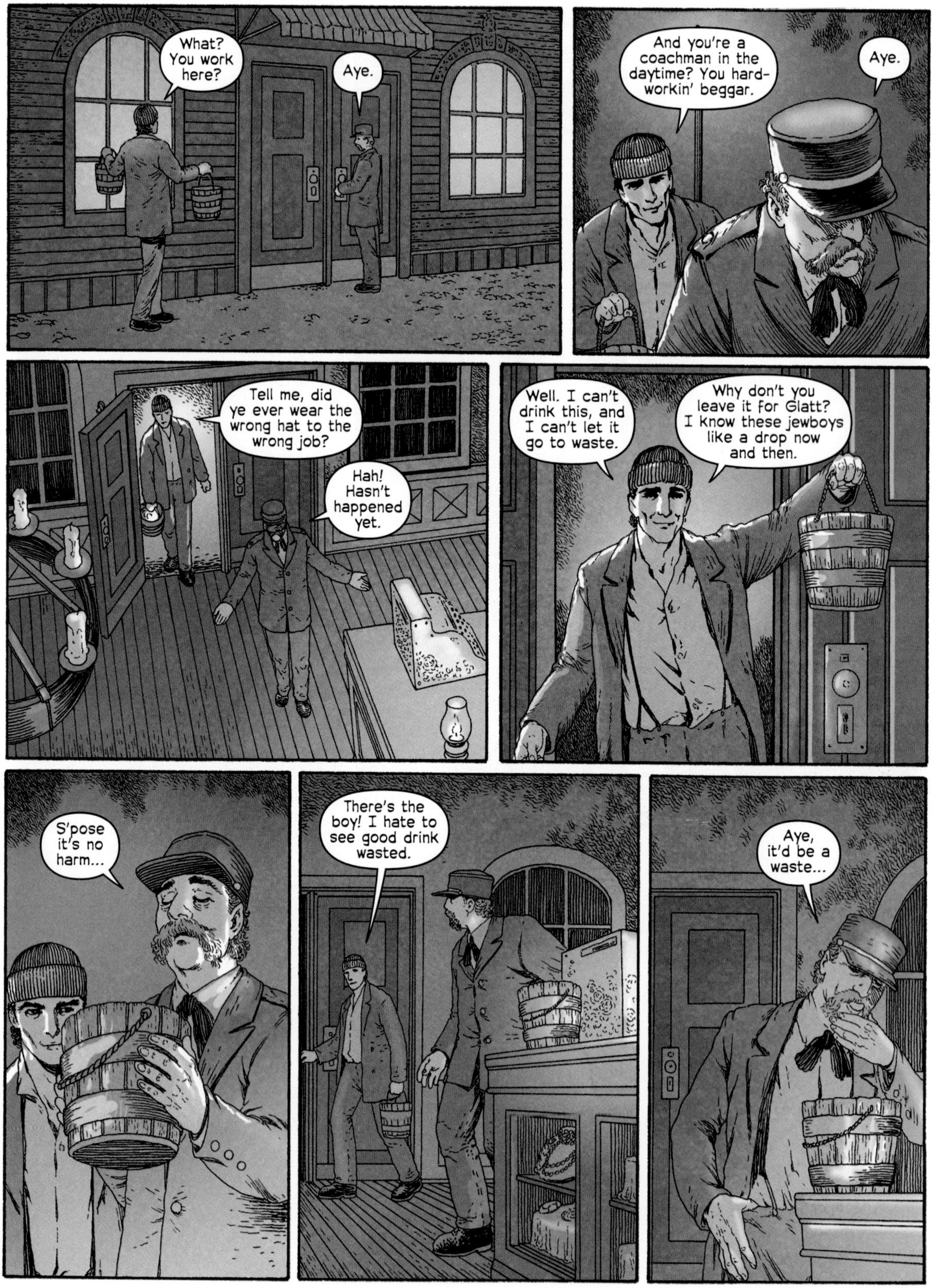
What? You work here?
Aye.
And you're a coachman in the daytime? You hard-workin' beggar.
Aye.
Tell me, did ye ever wear the wrong hat to the wrong job?
Hah! Hasn't happened yet.
Well. I can't drink this, and I can't let it go to waste.
Why don't you leave it for Glatt? I know these jewboys like a drop now and then.
S'pose it's no harm...
There's the boy! I hate to see good drink wasted.
Aye, it'd be a waste...

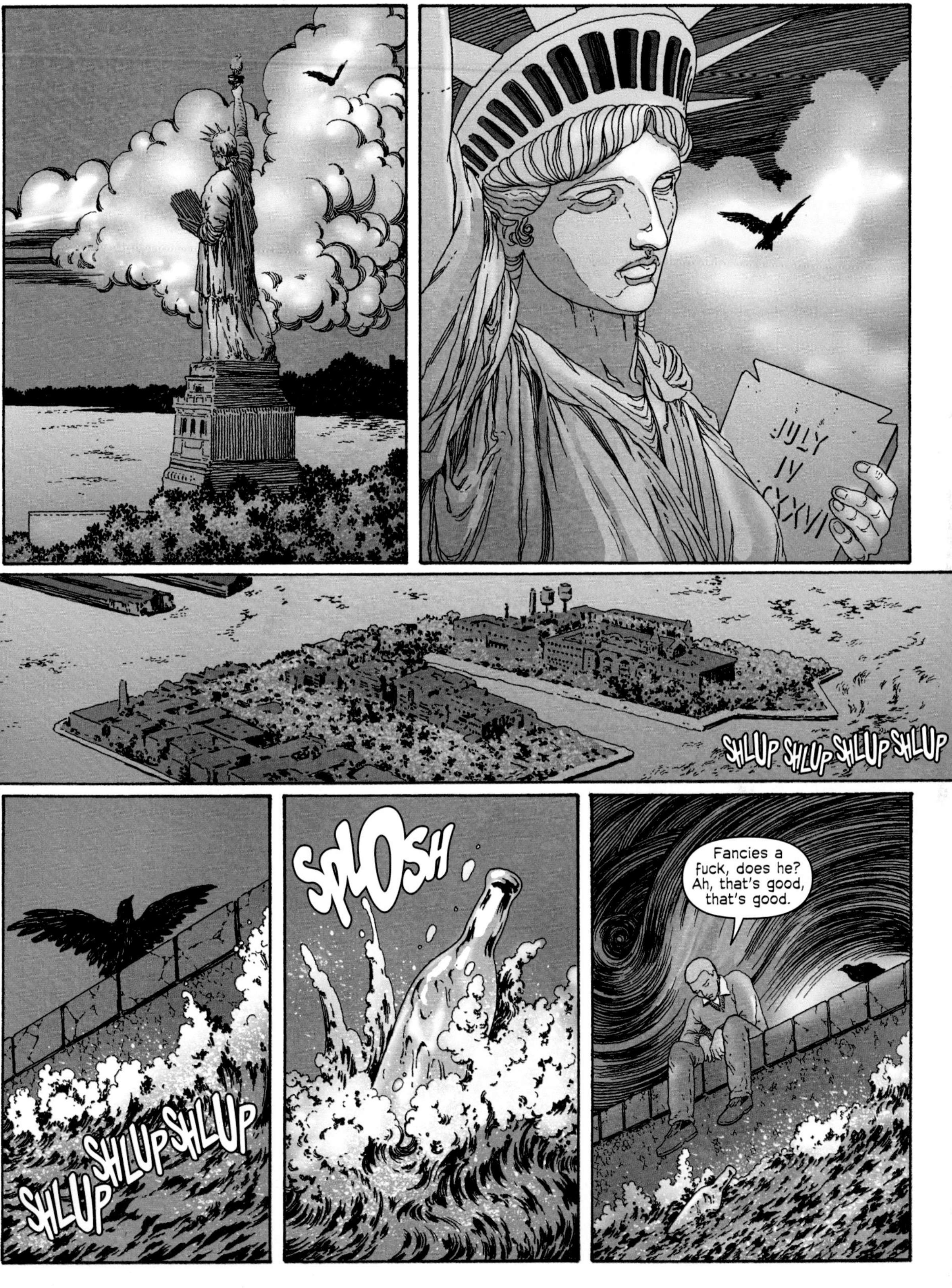
JULY
IV
MDCCLXXVI
SHLUP SHLUP SHLUP SHLUP
SHLUP SHLUP SHLUP
SPLOSH
Fancies a fuck, does he? Ah, that's good, that's good.

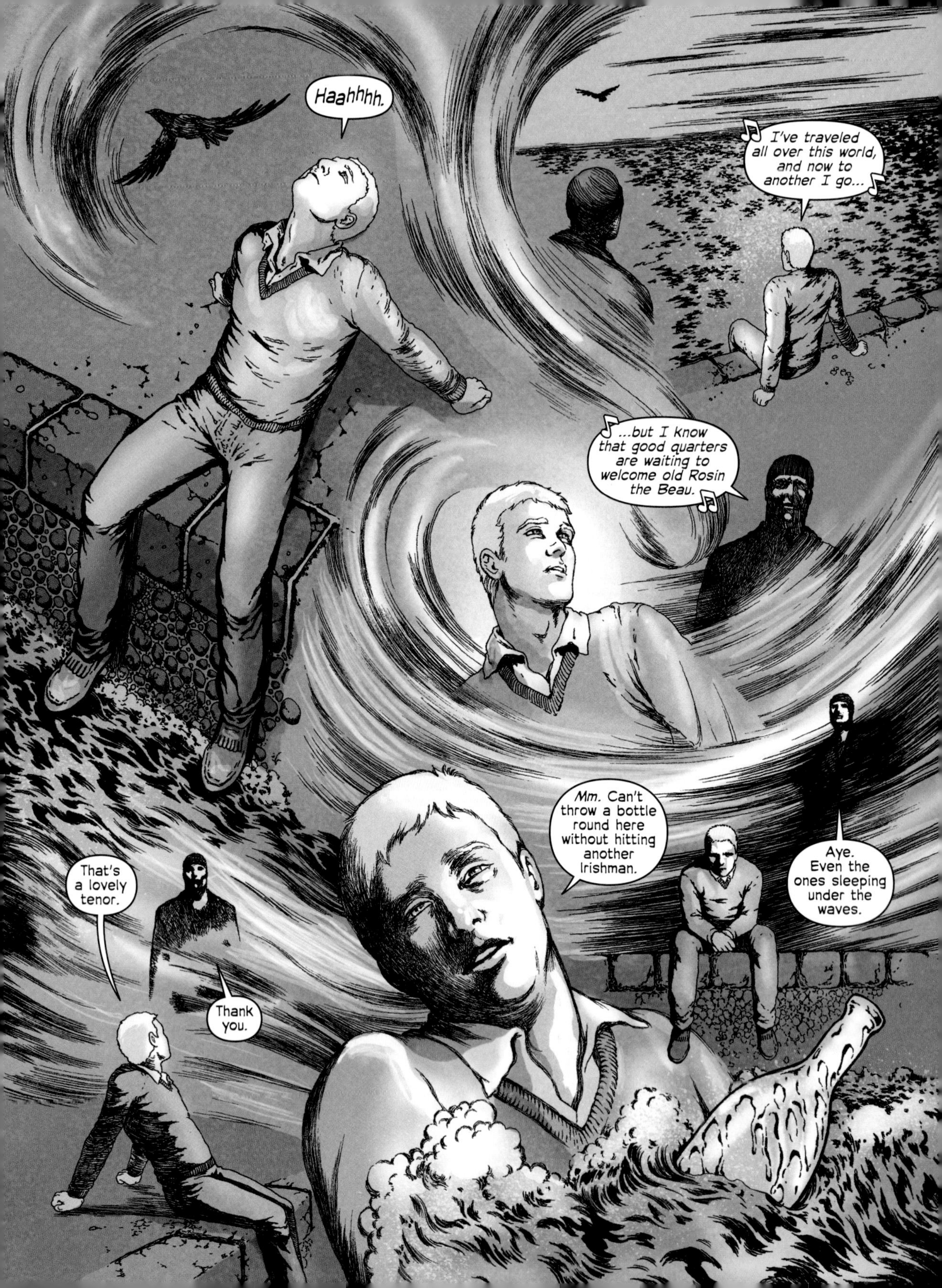
Haahhhh.
I've traveled all over this world, and now to another I go...
...but I know that good quarters are waiting to welcome old Rosin the Beau.
Mm. Can't throw a bottle round here without hitting another Irishman.
Aye. Even the ones sleeping under the waves.
That's a lovely tenor.
Thank you.

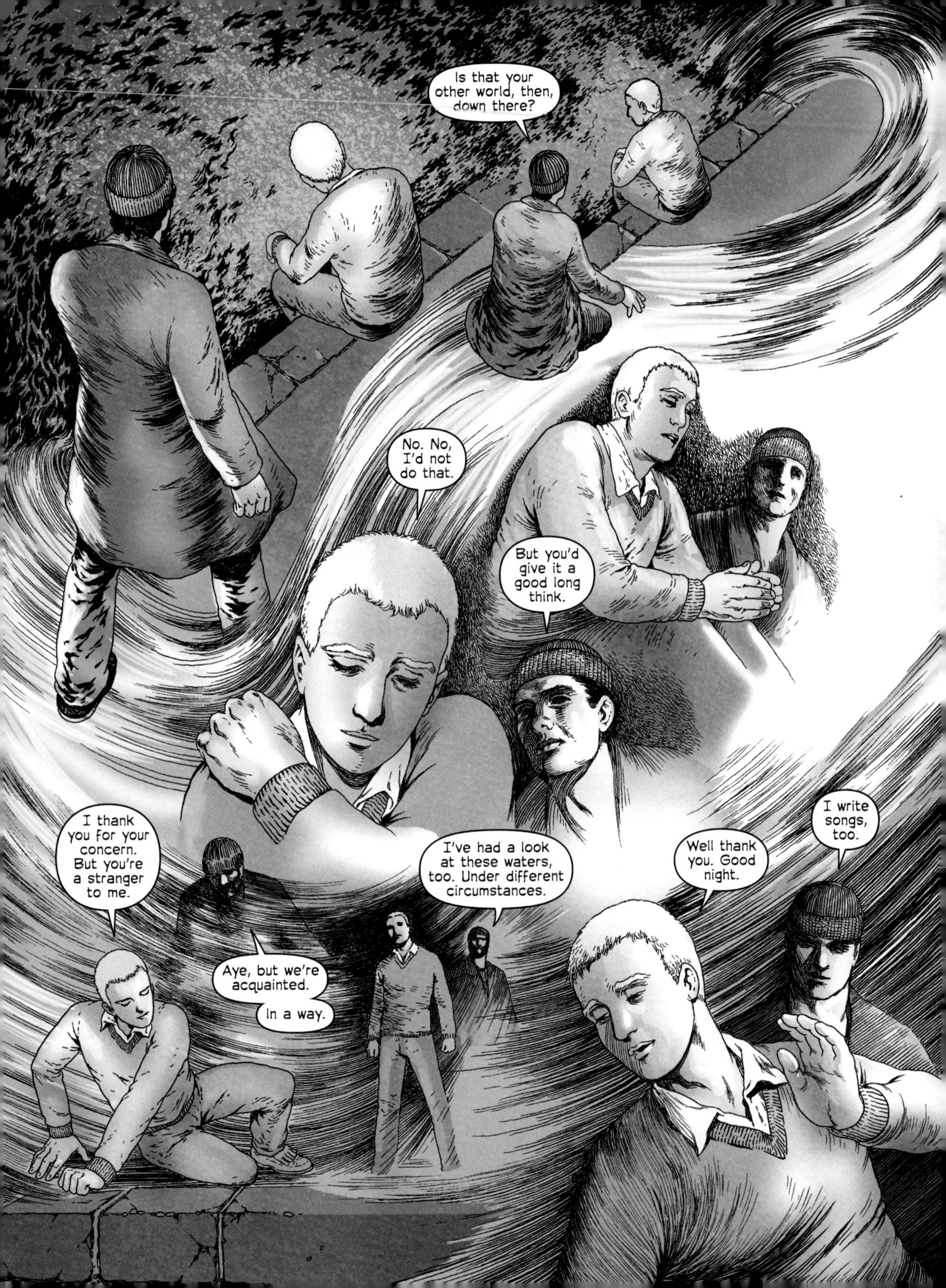
Is that your other world, then, down there?
No. No, I'd not do that.
But you'd give it a good long think.
I thank you for your concern. But you're a stranger to me.
Aye, but we're acquainted.
In a way.
I've had a look at these waters, too. Under different circumstances.
Well thank you. Good night.
I write songs, too.

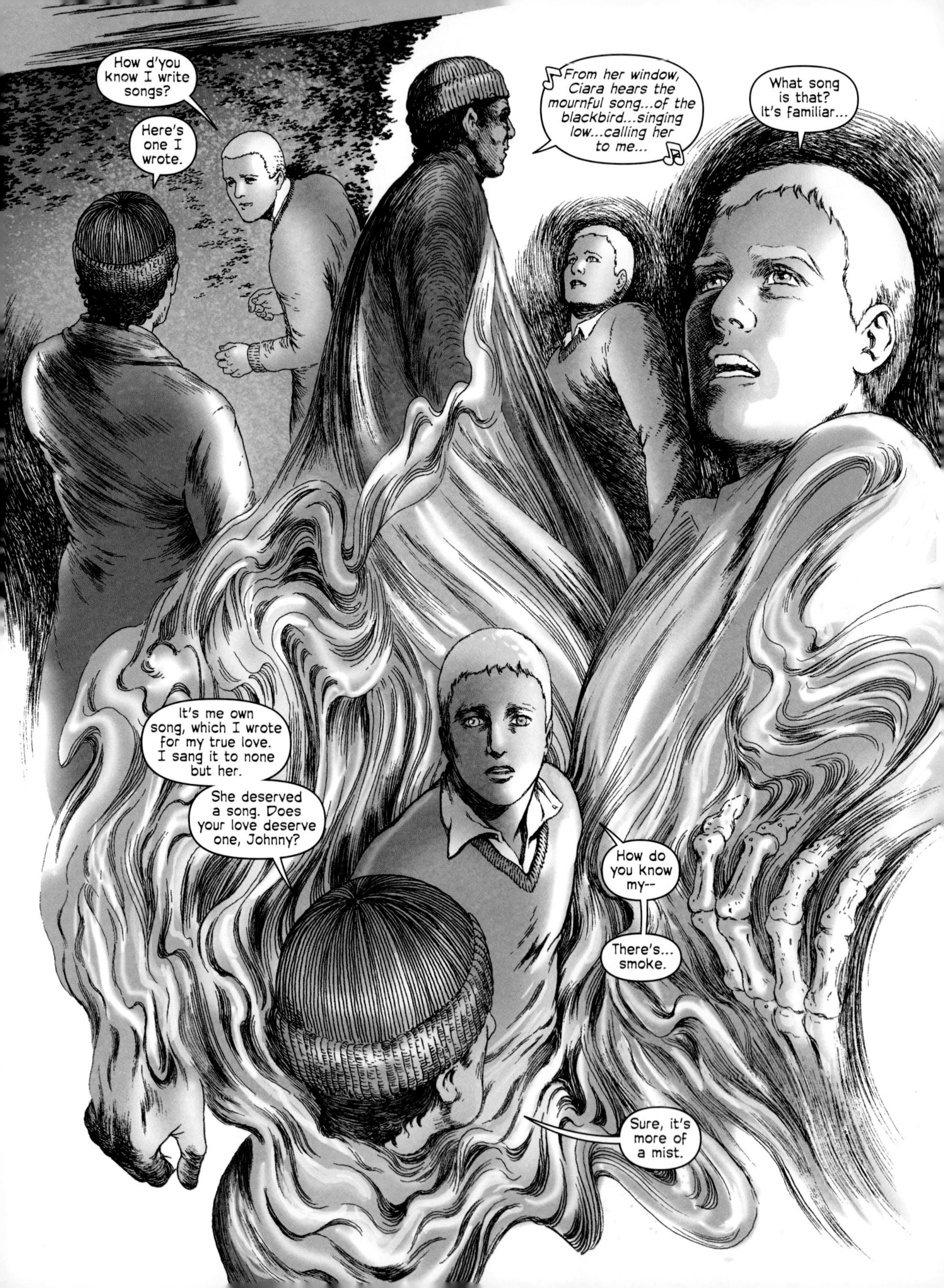

How d'you know I write songs?
Here's one I wrote.
From her window, Ciara hears the mournful song...of the blackbird...singing low...calling her to me...
What song is that? It's familiar...
It's me own song, which I wrote for my true love. I sang it to none but her.
She deserved a song. Does your love deserve one, Johnny?
How do you know my--
There's... smoke.
Sure, it's more of a mist.

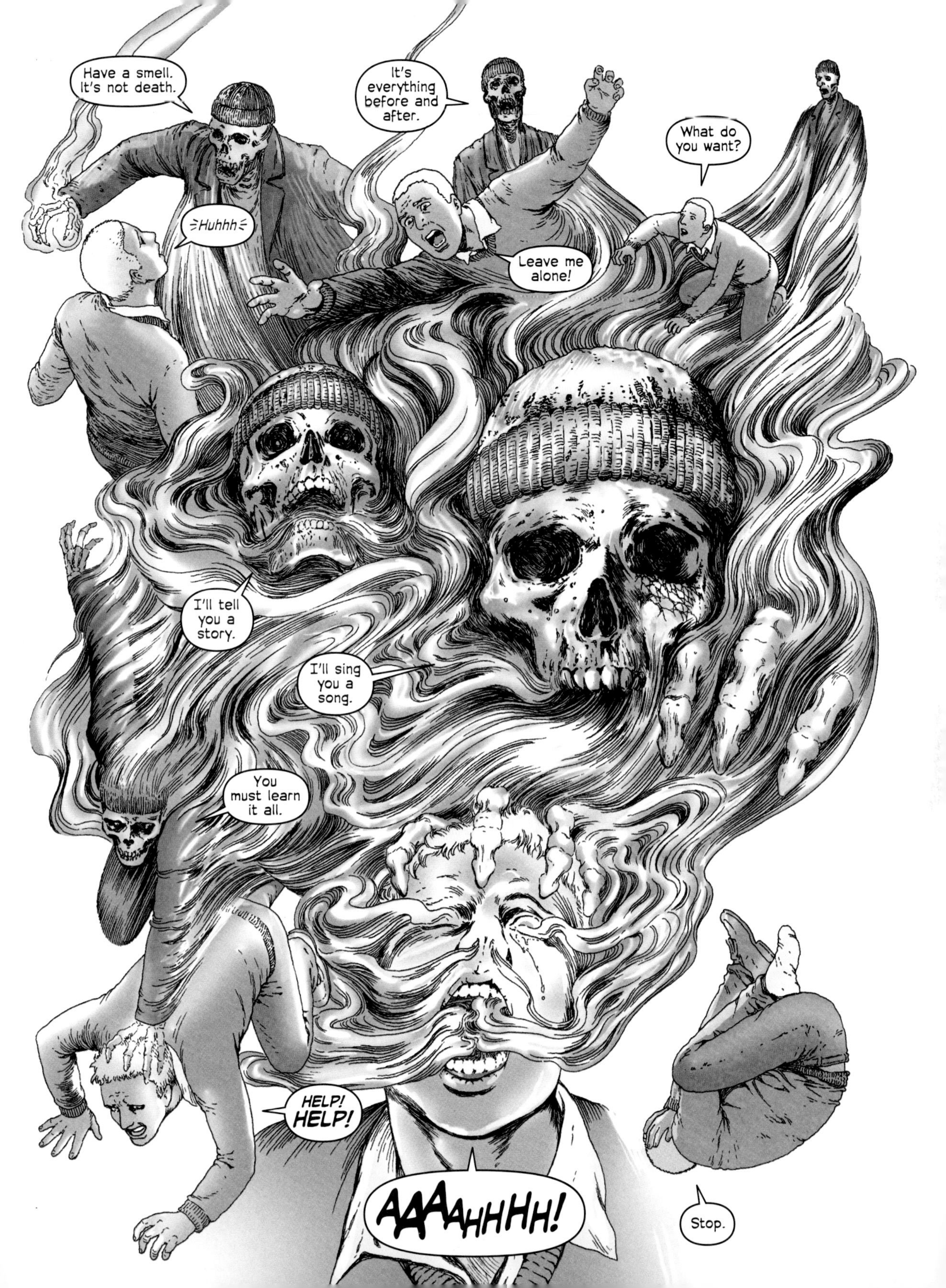
Have a smell. It's not death.
Huhhh
It's everything before and after.
Leave me alone!
What do you want?
I'll tell you a story.
I'll sing you a song.
You must learn it all.
HELP! HELP!
AAAAHHHH!
Stop.

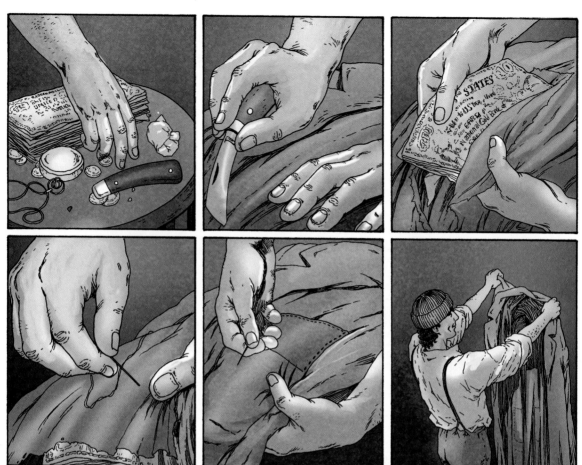

Ah, handsome Irishman.

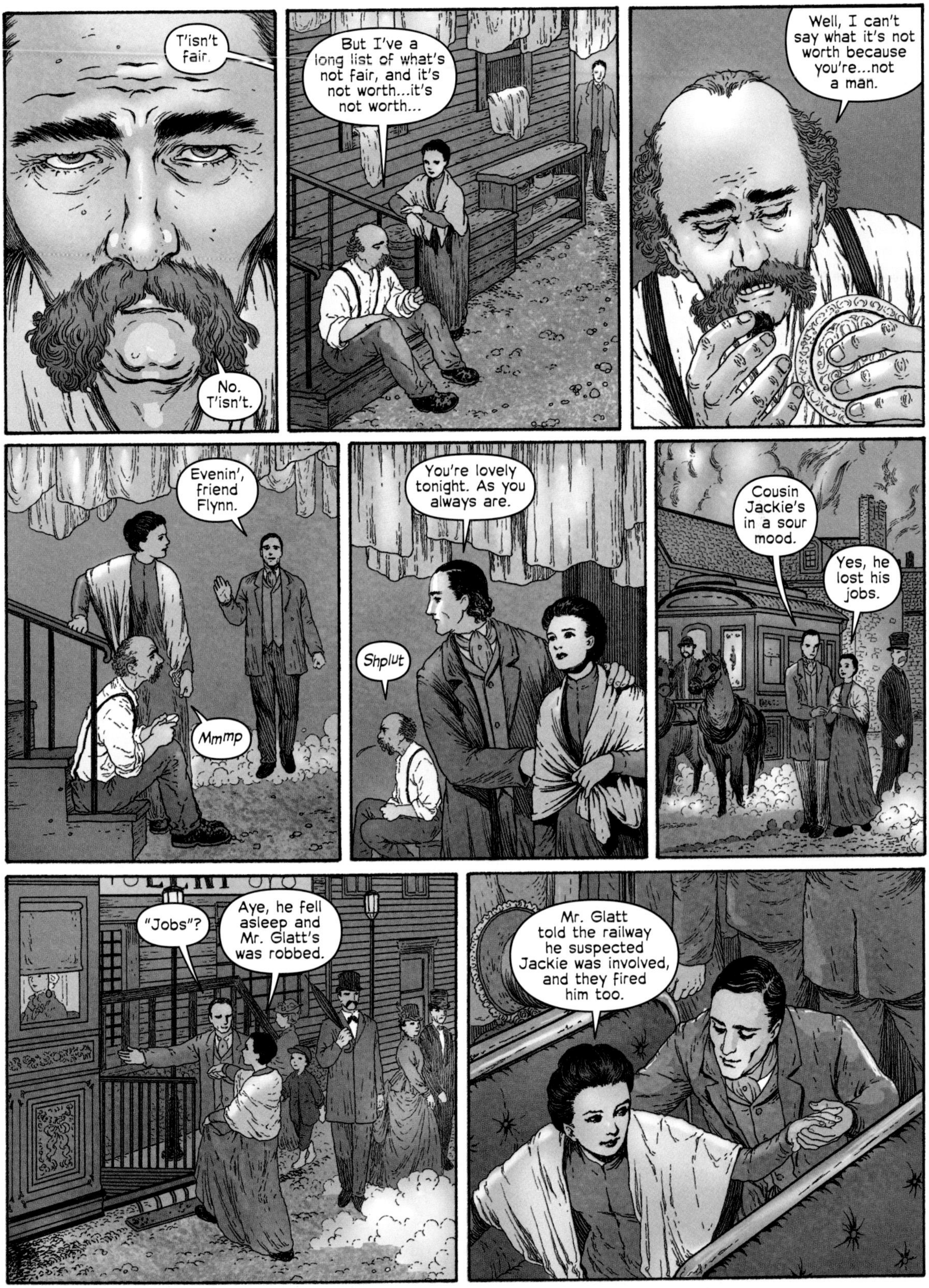
T'isn't fair.
No. T'isn't.
But I've a long list of what's not fair, and it's not worth...it's not worth...
Well, I can't say what it's not worth because you're...not a man.
Evenin', friend Flynn.
Mmmp
You're lovely tonight. As you always are.
Shplut
Cousin Jackie's in a sour mood.
Yes, he lost his jobs.
"Jobs"?
Aye, he fell asleep and Mr. Glatt's was robbed.
Mr. Glatt told the railway he suspected Jackie was involved, and they fired him too.

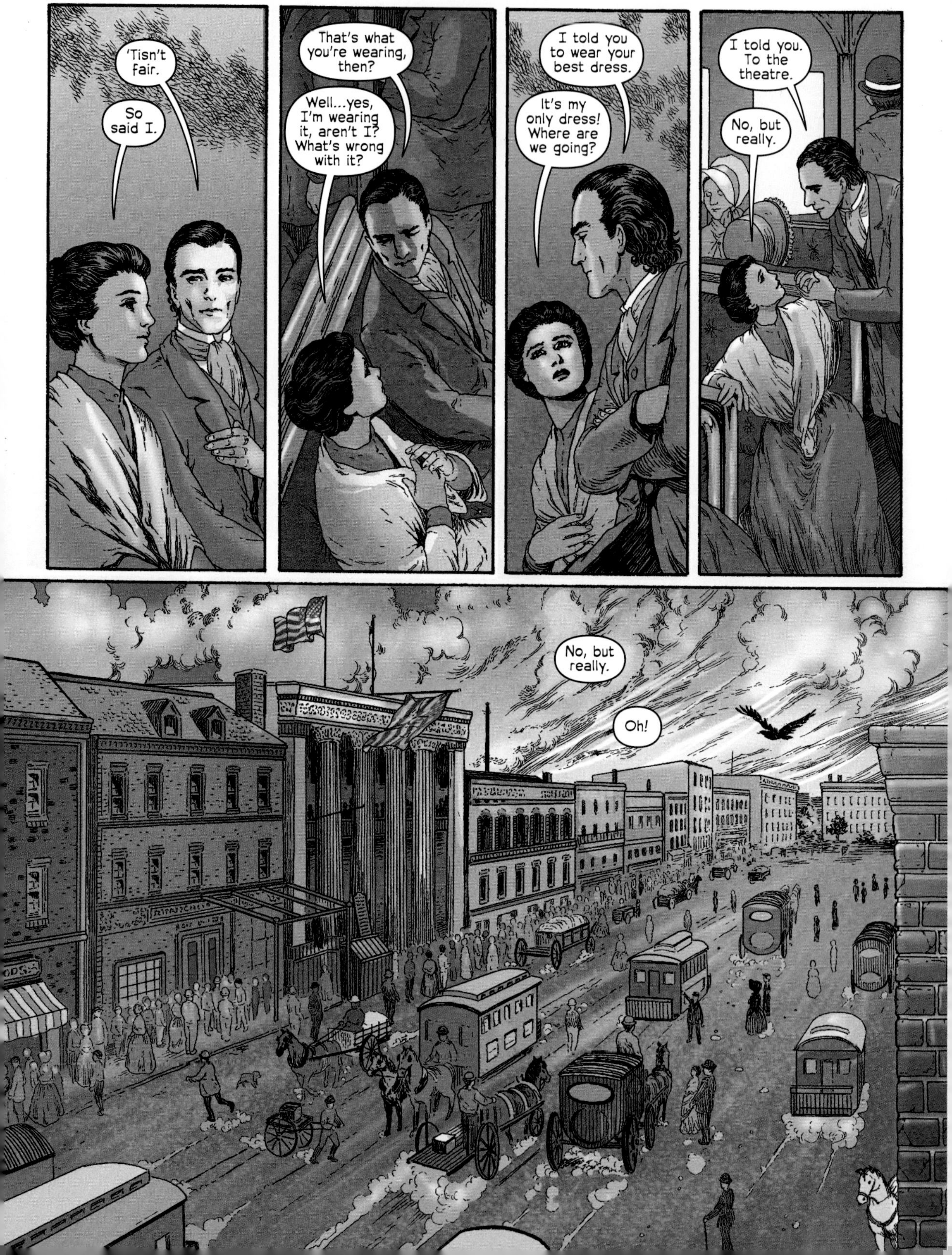
'Tisn't fair.
So said I.
That's what you're wearing, then?
Well...yes, I'm wearing it, aren't I? What's wrong with it?
I told you to wear your best dress.
It's my only dress! Where are we going?
I told you. To the theatre.
No, but really.
No, but really.
Oh!

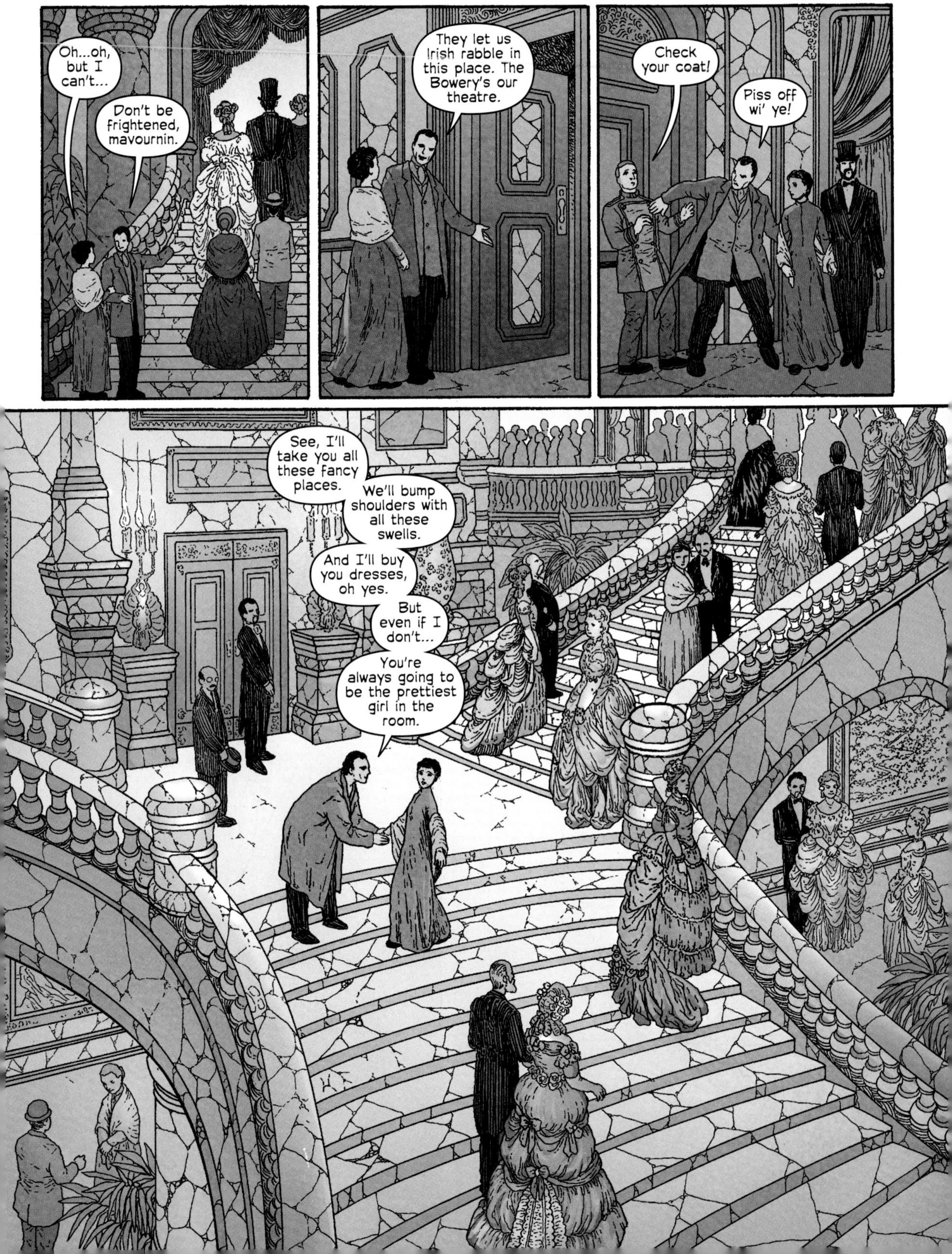
Oh...oh, but I can't...
Don't be frightened, mavournin.
They let us Irish rabble in this place. The Bowery's our theatre.
Check your coat!
Piss off wi' ye!
See, I'll take you all these fancy places.
We'll bump shoulders with all these swells.
And I'll buy you dresses, oh yes.
But even if I don't...
You're always going to be the prettiest girl in the room.

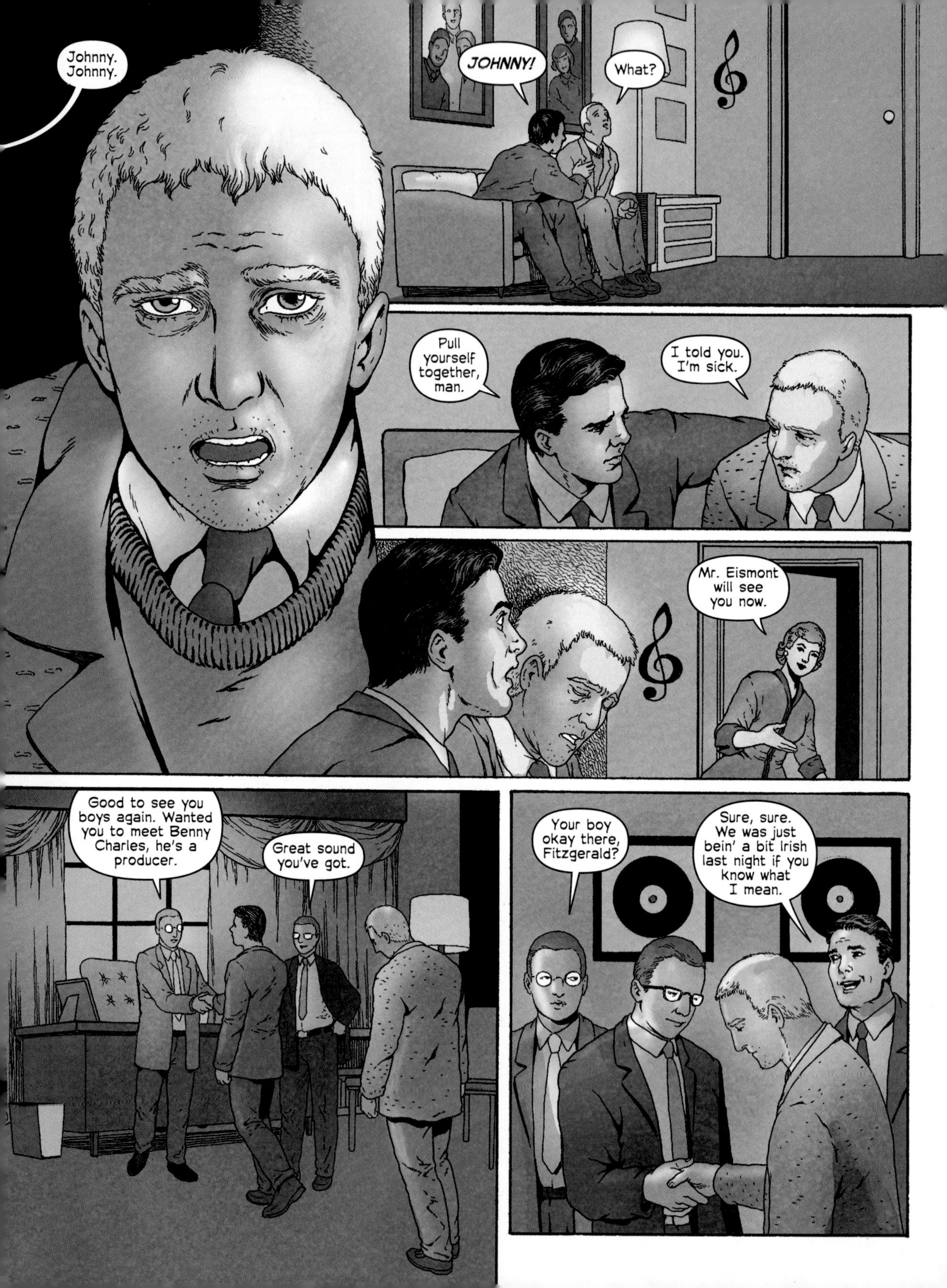
Johnny. Johnny.
JOHNNY!
What?
Pull yourself together, man.
I told you. I'm sick.
Mr. Eismont will see you now.
Good to see you boys again. Wanted you to meet Benny Charles, he's a producer.
Great sound you've got.
Your boy okay there, Fitzgerald?
Sure, sure. We was just bein' a bit Irish last night if you know what I mean.

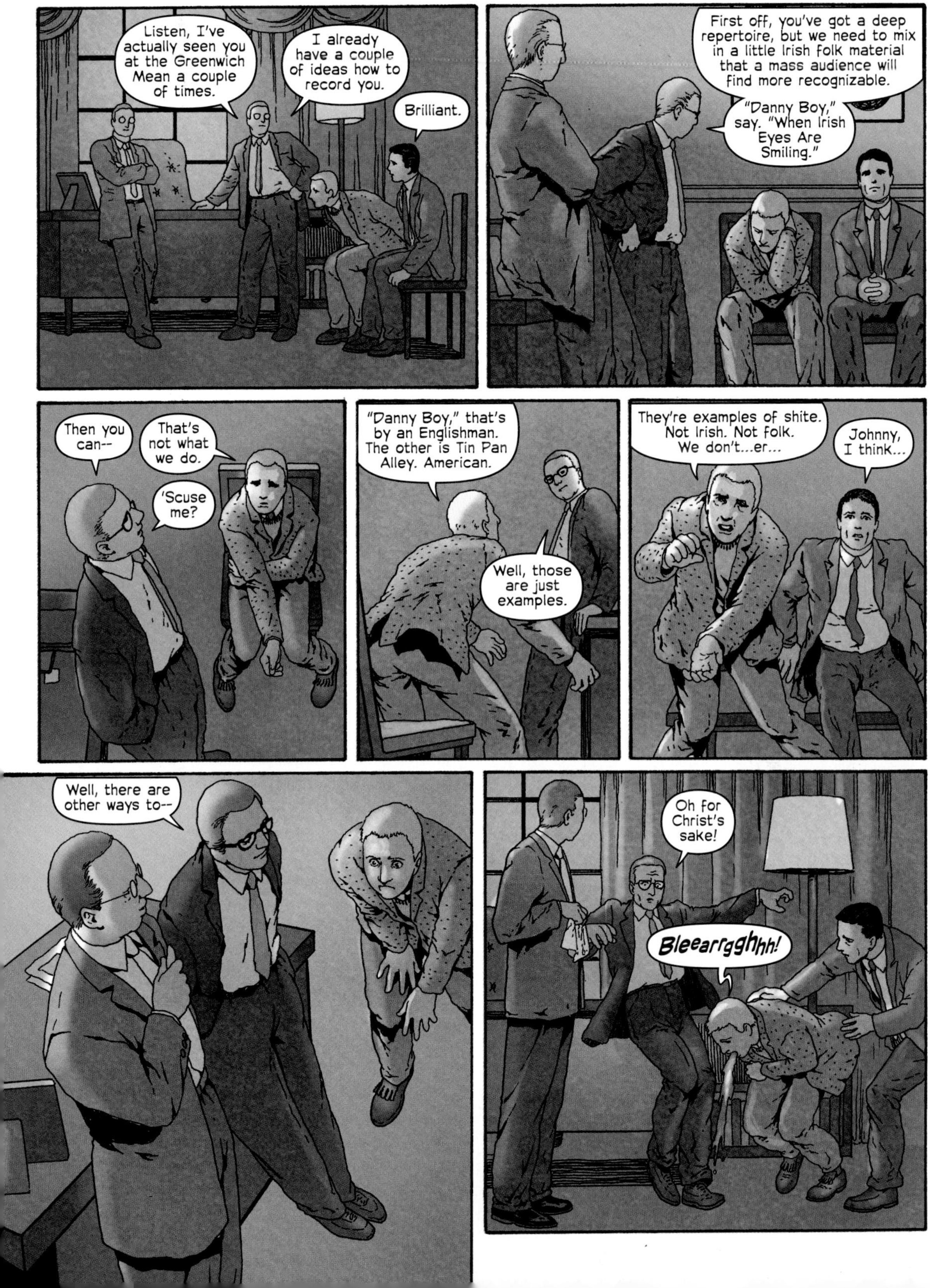
Listen, I've actually seen you at the Greenwich Mean a couple of times.
I already have a couple of ideas how to record you.
Brilliant.
First off, you've got a deep repertoire, but we need to mix in a little Irish folk material that a mass audience will find more recognizable.
"Danny Boy," say. "When Irish Eyes Are Smiling."
Then you can--
That's not what we do.
'Scuse me?
"Danny Boy," that's by an Englishman. The other is Tin Pan Alley. American.
Well, those are just examples.
They're examples of shite. Not Irish. Not folk. We don't...er...
Johnny, I think...
Well, there are other ways to--
Oh for Christ's sake!
Bleearrgghhh!

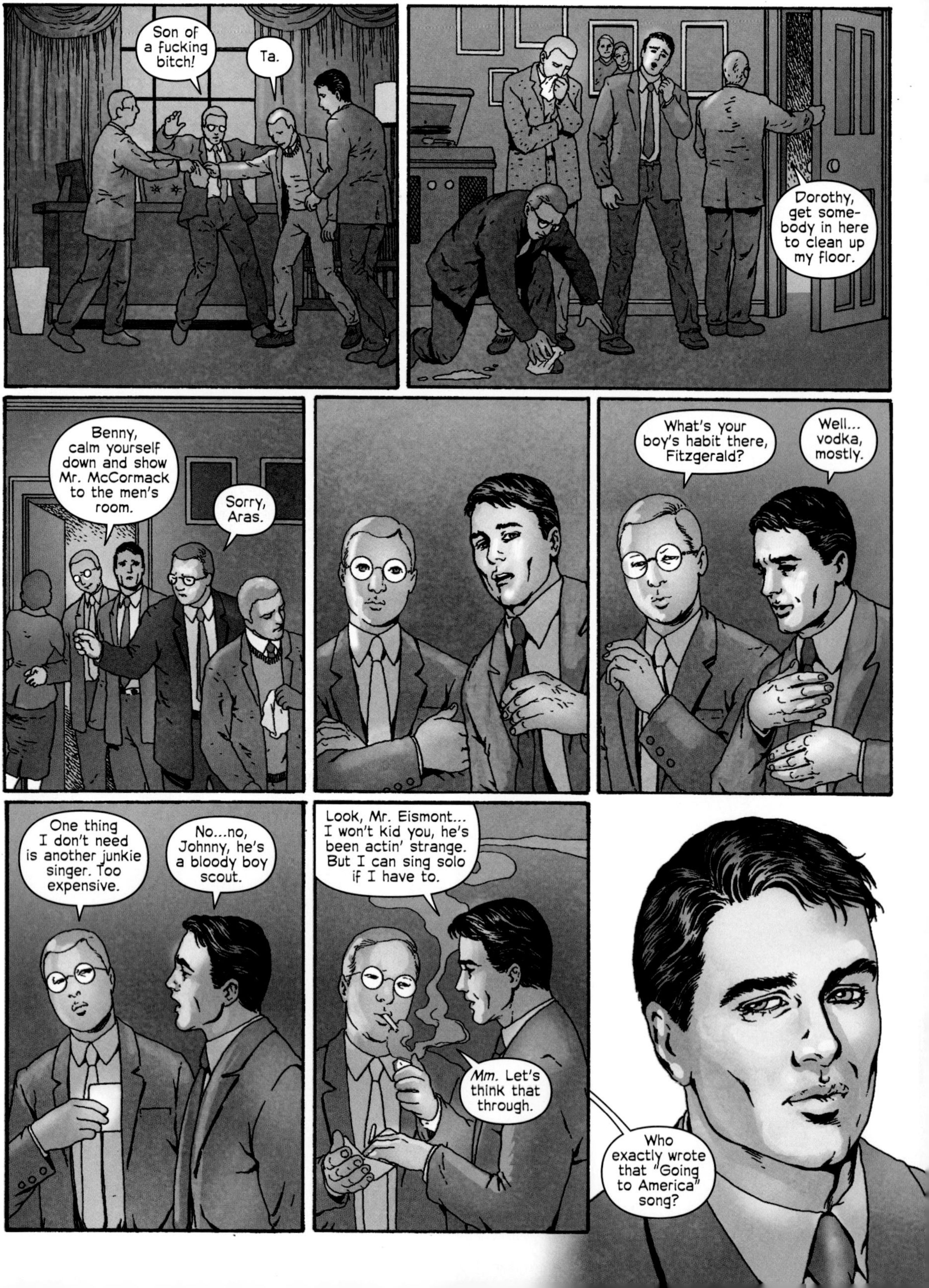
Son of a fucking bitch!
Ta.
Dorothy, get somebody in here to clean up my floor.
Benny, calm yourself down and show Mr. McCormack to the men's room.
Sorry, Aras.
What's your boy's habit there, Fitzgerald?
Well... vodka, mostly.
One thing I don't need is another junkie singer. Too expensive.
No...no, Johnny, he's a bloody boy scout.
Look, Mr. Eismont... I won't kid you, he's been actin' strange. But I can sing solo if I have to.
Mm. Let's think that through.
Who exactly wrote that "Going to America" song?

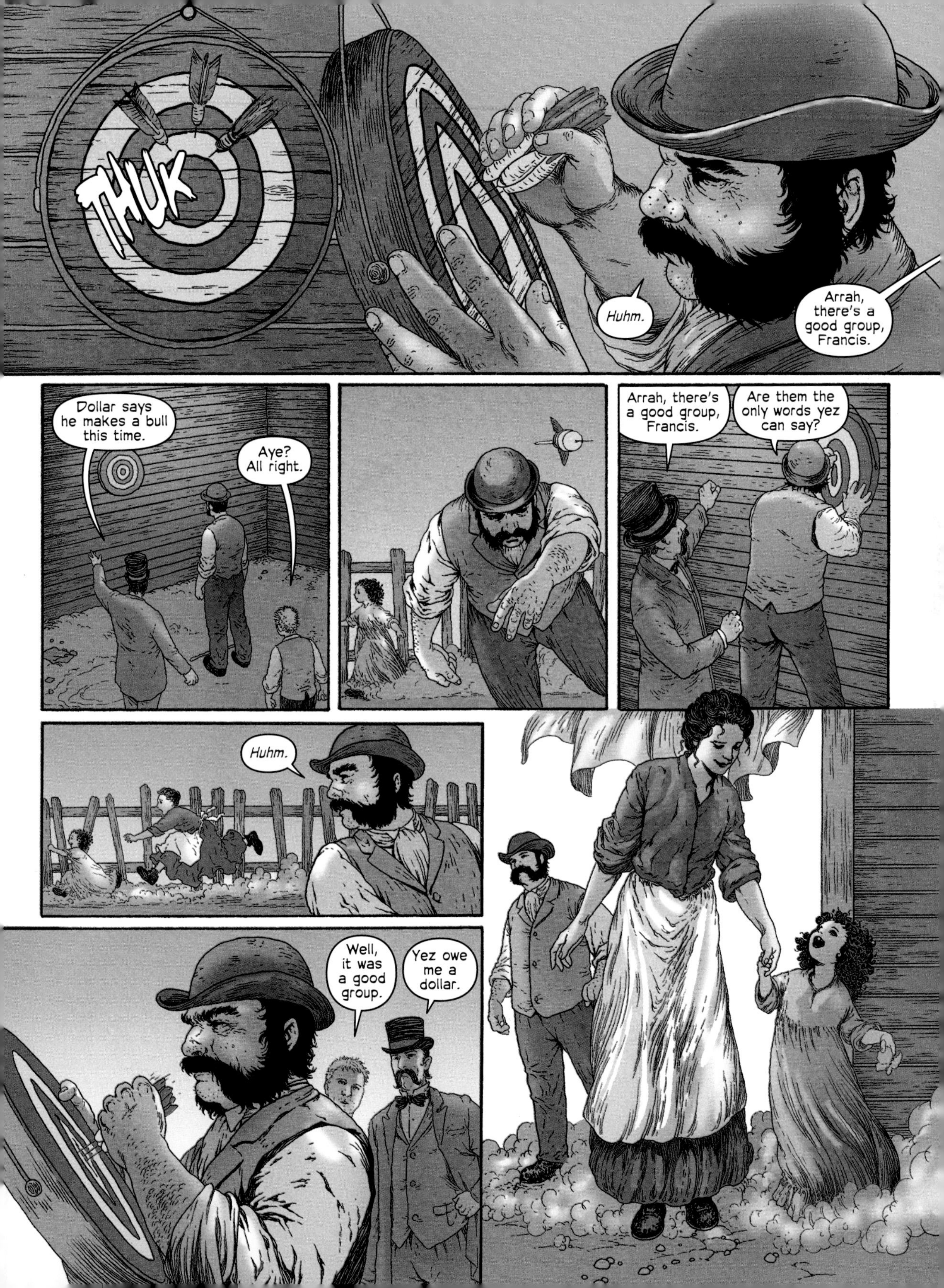
THUK
Huhm.
Arrah, there's a good group, Francis.
Dollar says he makes a bull this time.
Aye? All right.
Arrah, there's a good group, Francis.
Are them the only words yez can say?
Huhm.
Well, it was a good group.
Yez owe me a dollar.

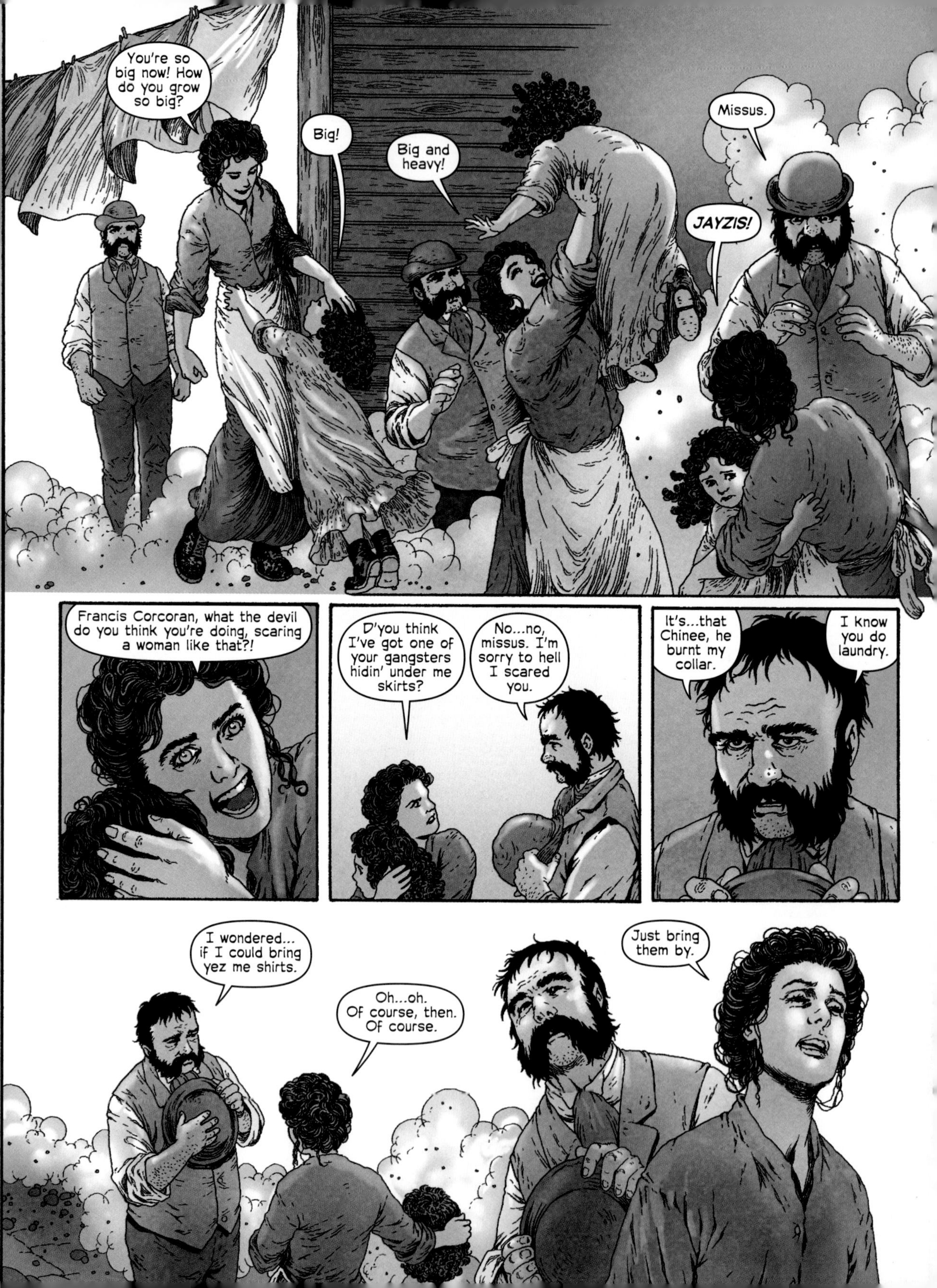
You're so big now! How do you grow so big?
Big!
Big and heavy!
Missus.
JAYZIS!
Francis Corcoran, what the devil do you think you're doing, scaring a woman like that?!
D'you think I've got one of your gangsters hidin' under me skirts?
No...no, missus. I'm sorry to hell I scared you.
It's...that Chinee, he burnt my collar.
I know you do laundry.
I wondered... if I could bring yez me shirts.
Oh...oh. Of course, then. Of course.
Just bring them by.

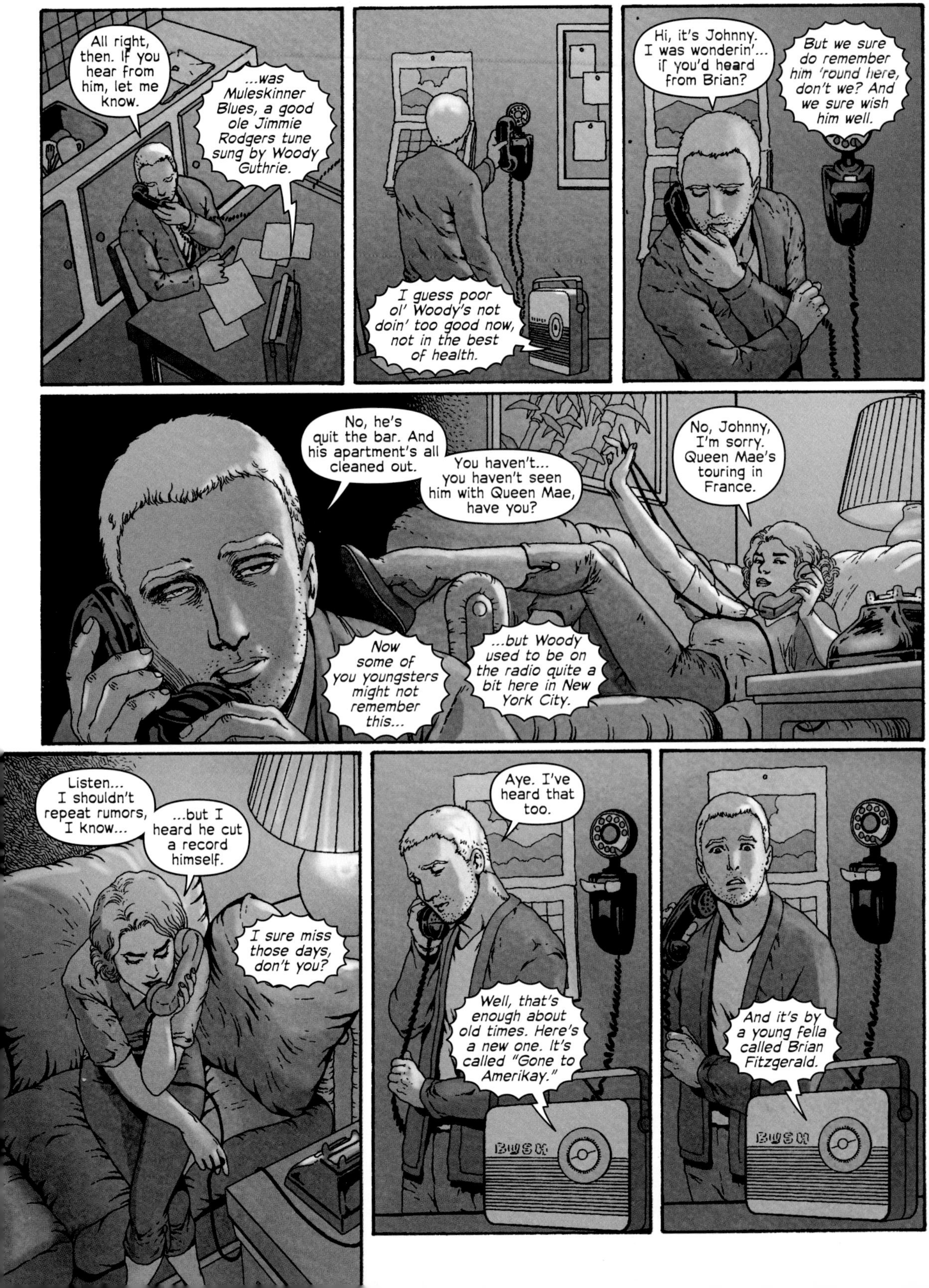
All right, then. If you hear from him, let me know.
...was Muleskinner Blues, a good ole Jimmie Rodgers tune sung by Woody Guthrie.
I guess poor ol' Woody's not doin' too good now, not in the best of health.
Hi, it's Johnny. I was wonderin'... if you'd heard from Brian?
But we sure do remember him 'round here, don't we? And we sure wish him well.
No, he's quit the bar. And his apartment's all cleaned out.
You haven't... you haven't seen him with Queen Mae, have you?
No, Johnny, I'm sorry. Queen Mae's touring in France.
Now some of you youngsters might not remember this...
...but Woody used to be on the radio quite a bit here in New York City.
Listen... I shouldn't repeat rumors, I know...
...but I heard he cut a record himself.
I sure miss those days, don't you?
Aye. I've heard that too.
Well, that's enough about old times. Here's a new one. It's called "Gone to Amerikay."
And it's by a young fella called Brian Fitzgerald.

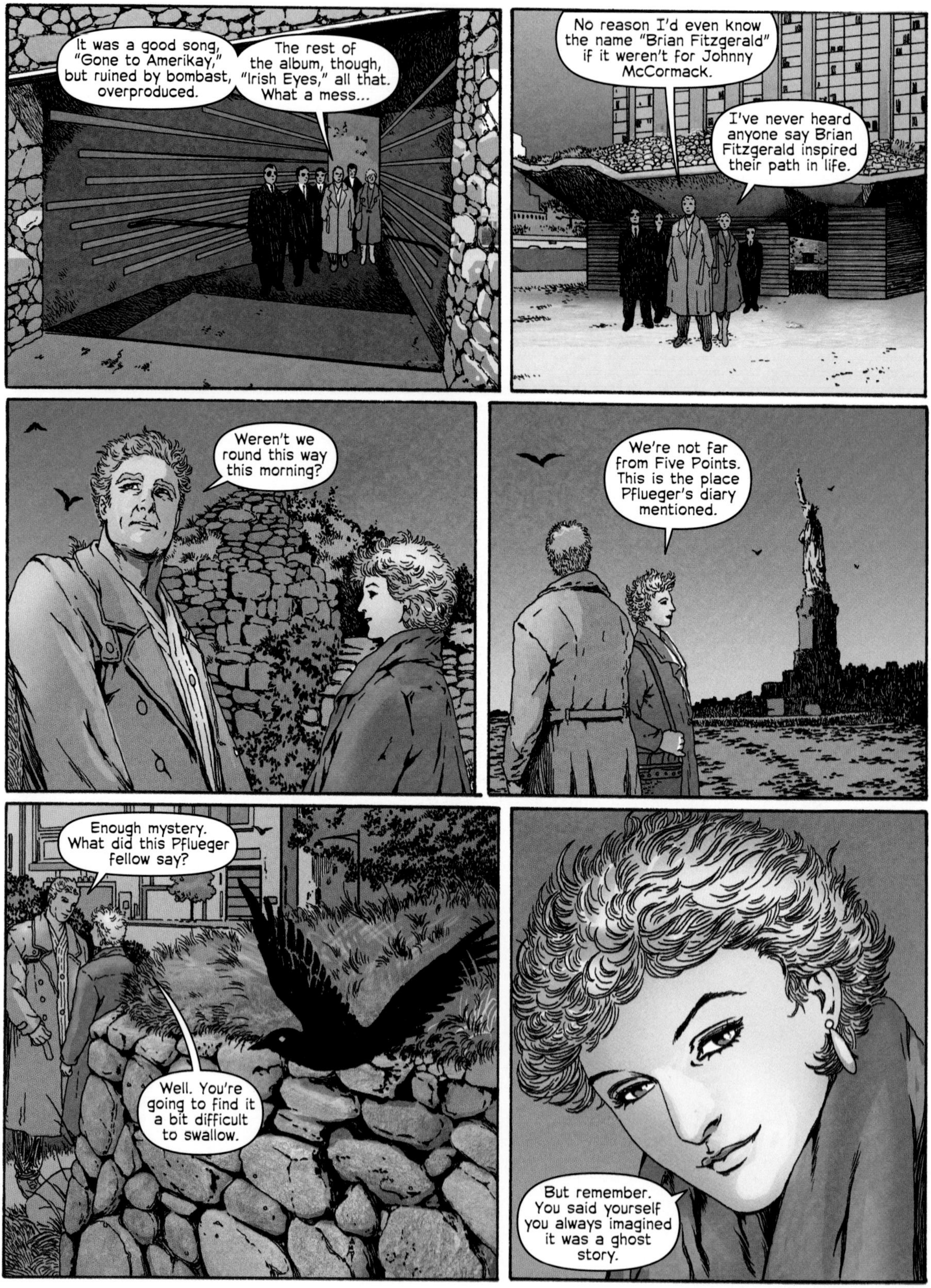
It was a good song, "Gone to AmeriKay," but ruined by bombast, overproduced.
The rest of the album, though, "Irish Eyes," all that. What a mess...
No reason I'd even know the name "Brian Fitzgerald" if it weren't for Johnny McCormack.
I've never heard anyone say Brian Fitzgerald inspired their path in life.
Weren't we round this way this morning?
We're not far from Five Points. This is the place Pflueger's diary mentioned.
Enough mystery. What did this Pflueger fellow say?
Well. You're going to find it a bit difficult to swallow.
But remember. You said yourself you always imagined it was a ghost story.

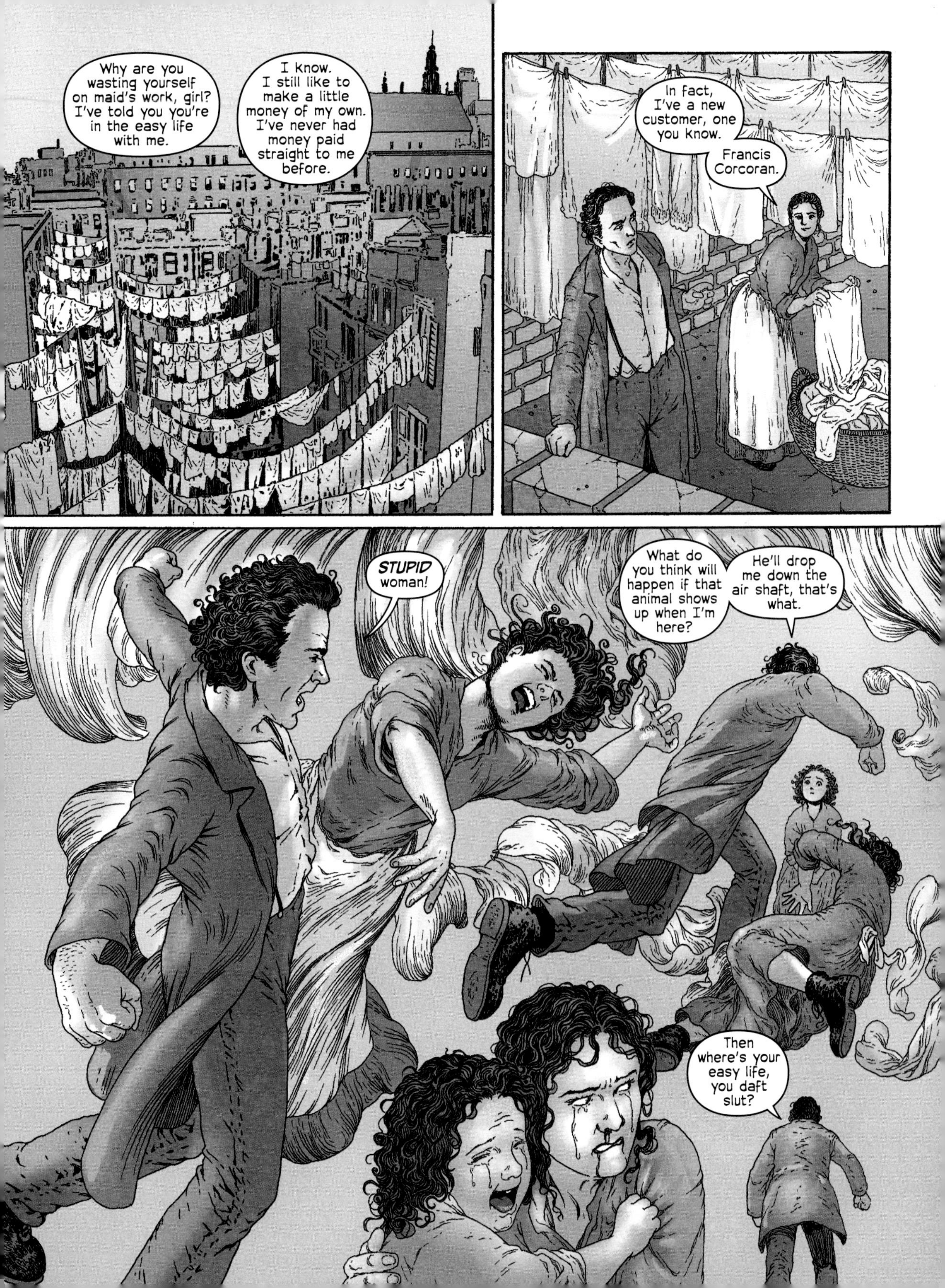
Why are you wasting yourself on maid's work, girl? I've told you you're in the easy life with me.
I know. I still like to make a little money of my own. I've never had money paid straight to me before.
In fact, I've a new customer, one you know.
Francis Corcoran.
STUPID woman!
What do you think will happen if that animal shows up when I'm here?
He'll drop me down the air shaft, that's what.
Then where's your easy life, you daft slut?

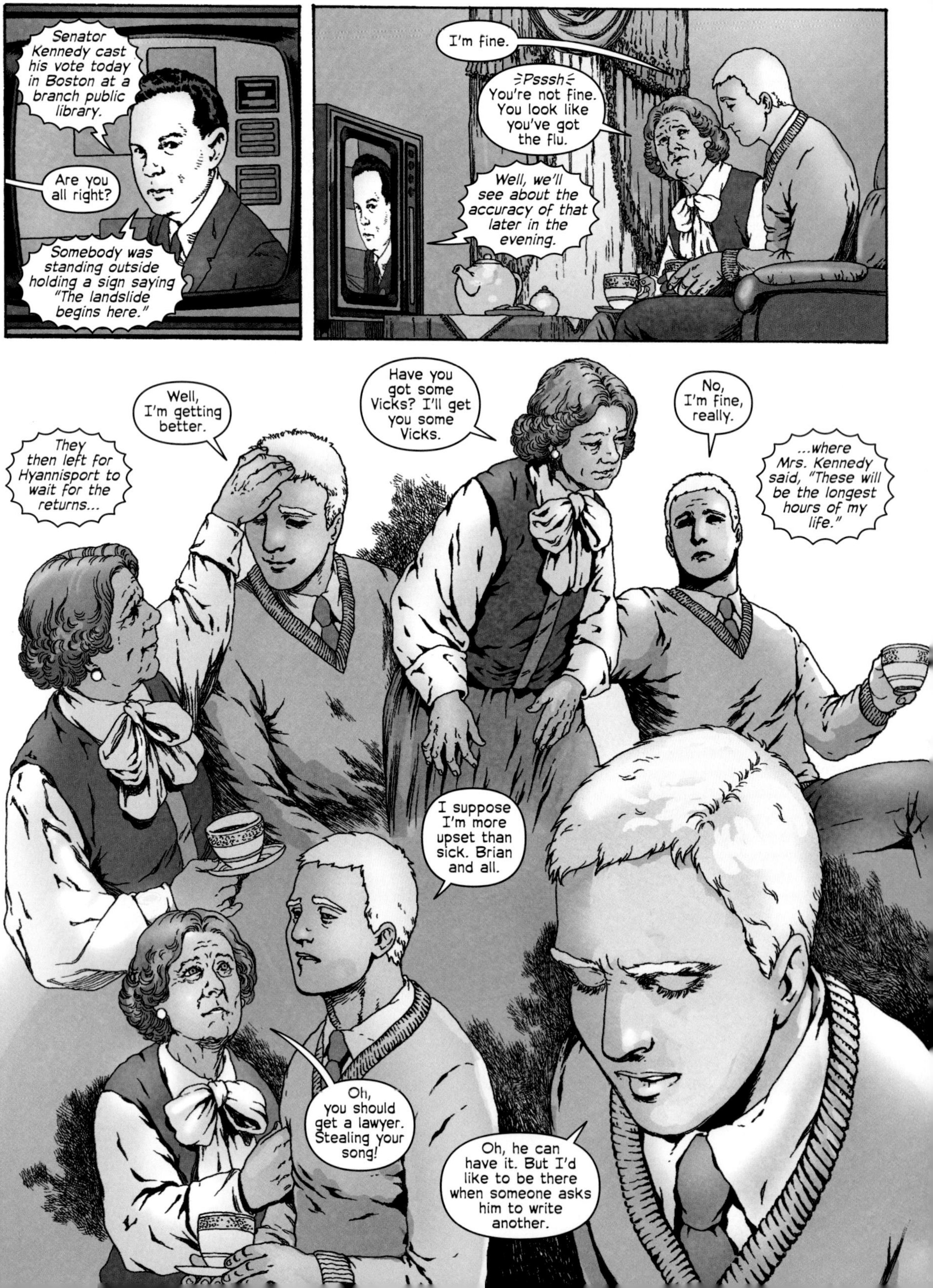

Senator Kennedy cast his vote today in Boston at a branch public library.
Are you all right?
Somebody was standing outside holding a sign saying "The landslide begins here."
I'm fine.
Psssh You're not fine. You look like you've got the flu.
Well, we'll see about the accuracy of that later in the evening.
They then left for Hyannisport to wait for the returns...
Well, I'm getting better.
Have you got some Vicks? I'll get you some Vicks.
No, I'm fine, really.
...where Mrs. Kennedy said, "These will be the longest hours of my life."
I suppose I'm more upset than sick. Brian and all.
Oh, you should get a lawyer. Stealing your song!
Oh, he can have it. But I'd like to be there when someone asks him to write another.

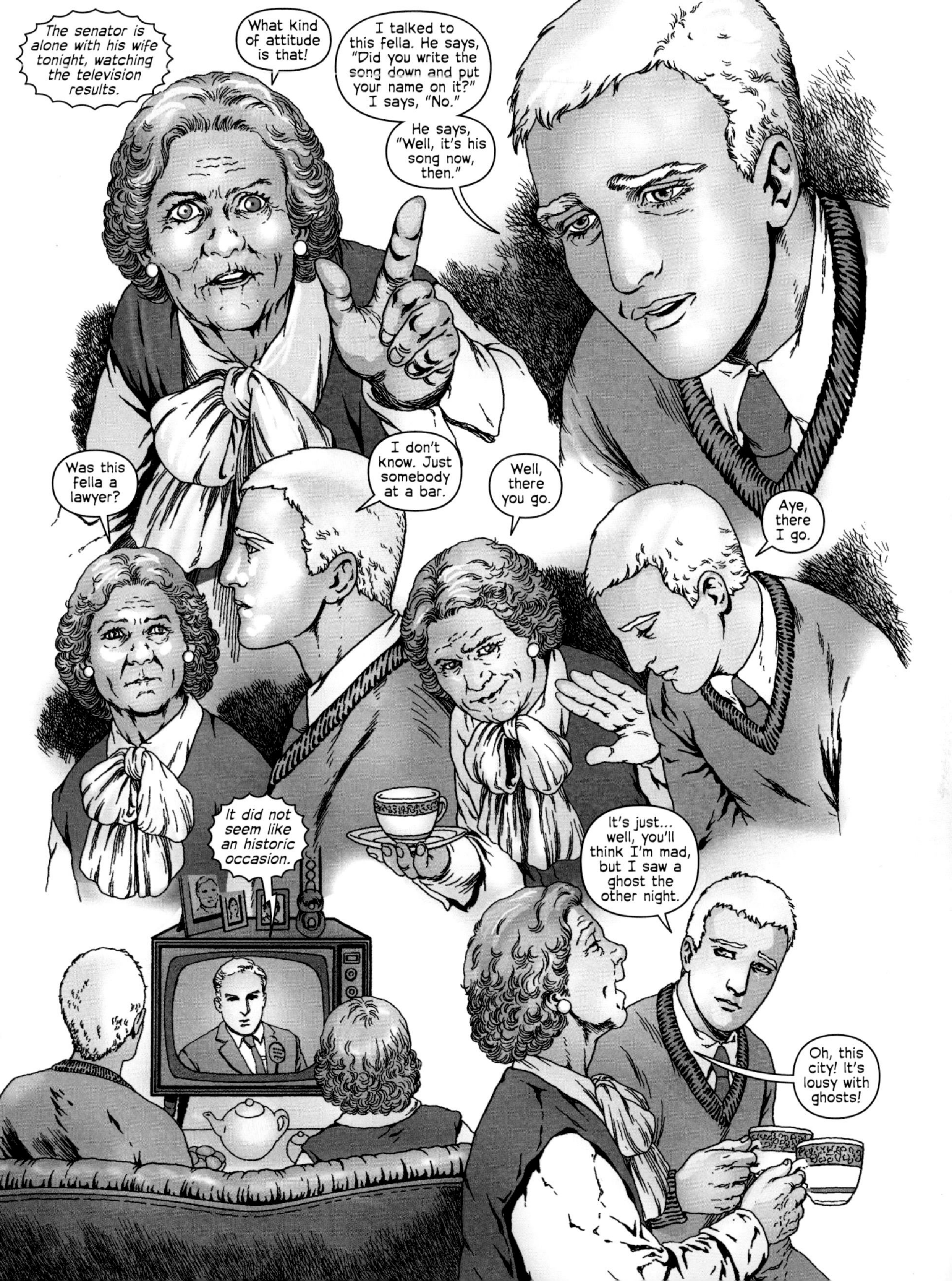
The senator is alone with his wife tonight, watching the television results.
What kind of attitude is that!
I talked to this fella. He says, "Did you write the song down and put your name on it?" I says, "No."
He says, "Well, it's his song now, then."
Was this fella a lawyer?
I don't know. Just somebody at a bar.
Well, there you go.
Aye, there I go.
It did not seem like an historic occasion.
It's just... well, you'll think I'm mad, but I saw a ghost the other night.
Oh, this city! It's lousy with ghosts!

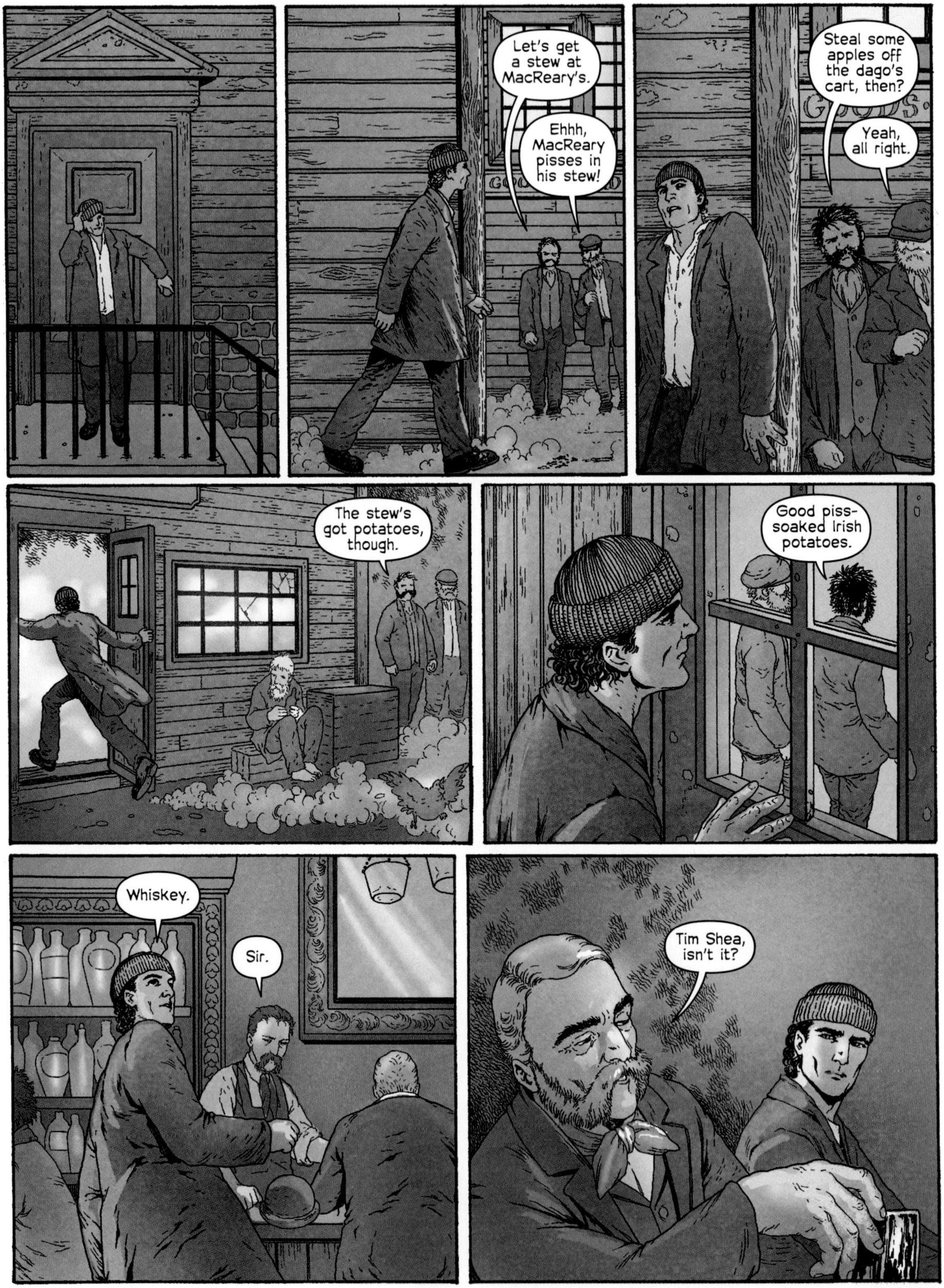
Let's get a stew at MacReary's.
Ehhh, MacReary pisses in his stew!
Steal some apples off the dago's cart, then?
Yeah, all right.
The stew's got potatoes, though.
Good piss-soaked Irish potatoes.
Whiskey.
Sir.
Tim Shea, isn't it?

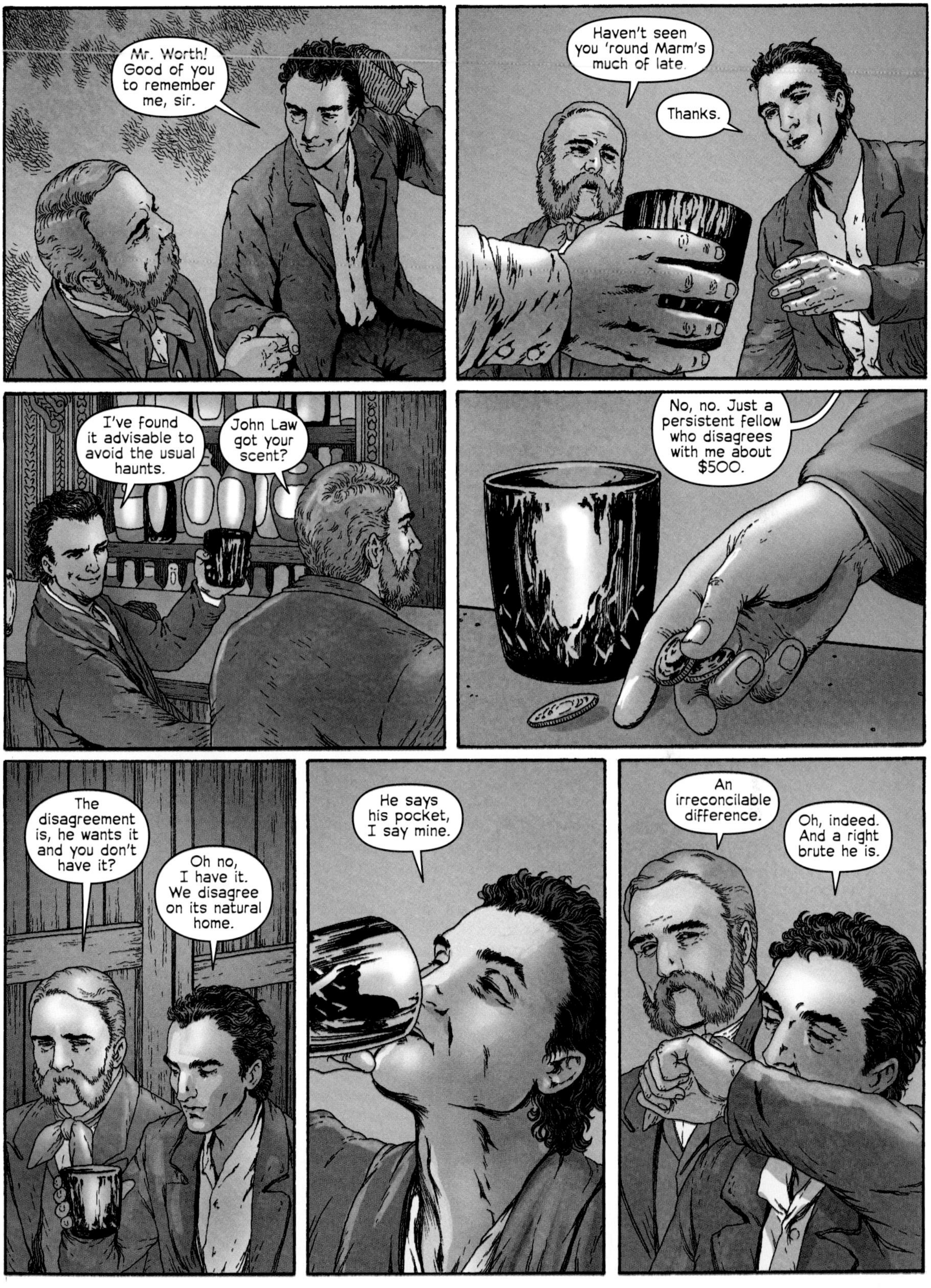
Mr. Worth! Good of you to remember me, sir.
Haven't seen you 'round Marm's much of late.
Thanks.
I've found it advisable to avoid the usual haunts.
John Law got your scent?
No, no. Just a persistent fellow who disagrees with me about $500.
The disagreement is, he wants it and you don't have it?
Oh no, I have it. We disagree on its natural home.
He says his pocket, I say mine.
An irreconcilable difference.
Oh, indeed. And a right brute he is.

My experience, that sort of fellow you have to either pay him or kill him.

Well, I obviously don't take to the first option.

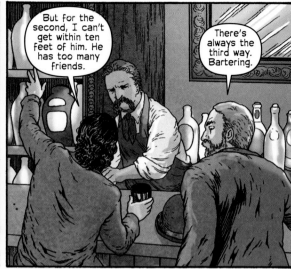

But for the second, I can't get within ten feet of him. He has too many friends.

There's always the third way. Bartering.

Aye?

I've had such problems. One fellow was pacified with an inside tip on the ponies. Another I cut in on a score.

And there you have a whole other problem. Such a fellow expects to be a formalized partner thereafter.

My conclusion was that a little unpleasantness in the short term is the best investment in the long term.

But still. If you know something he wants. Other than your money.

Aye.

Aye, there's food for thought.

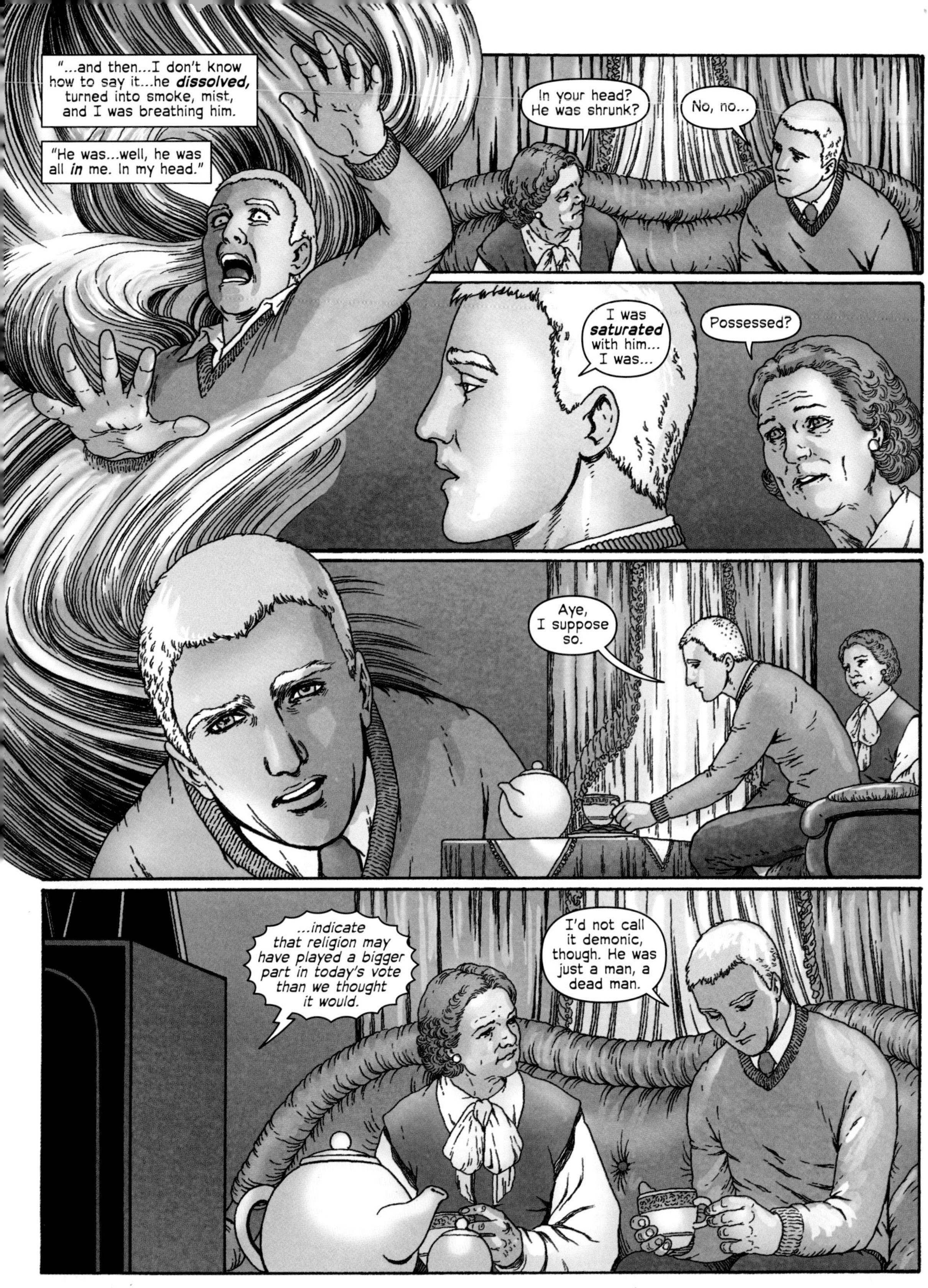
"...and then...I don't know how to say it...he *dissolved,* turned into smoke, mist, and I was breathing him.
"He was...well, he was all *in* me. In my head."
In your head? He was shrunk?
No, no...
I was *saturated* with him... I was...
Possessed?
Aye, I suppose so.
...indicate that religion may have played a bigger part in today's vote than we thought it would.
I'd not call it demonic, though. He was just a man, a dead man.

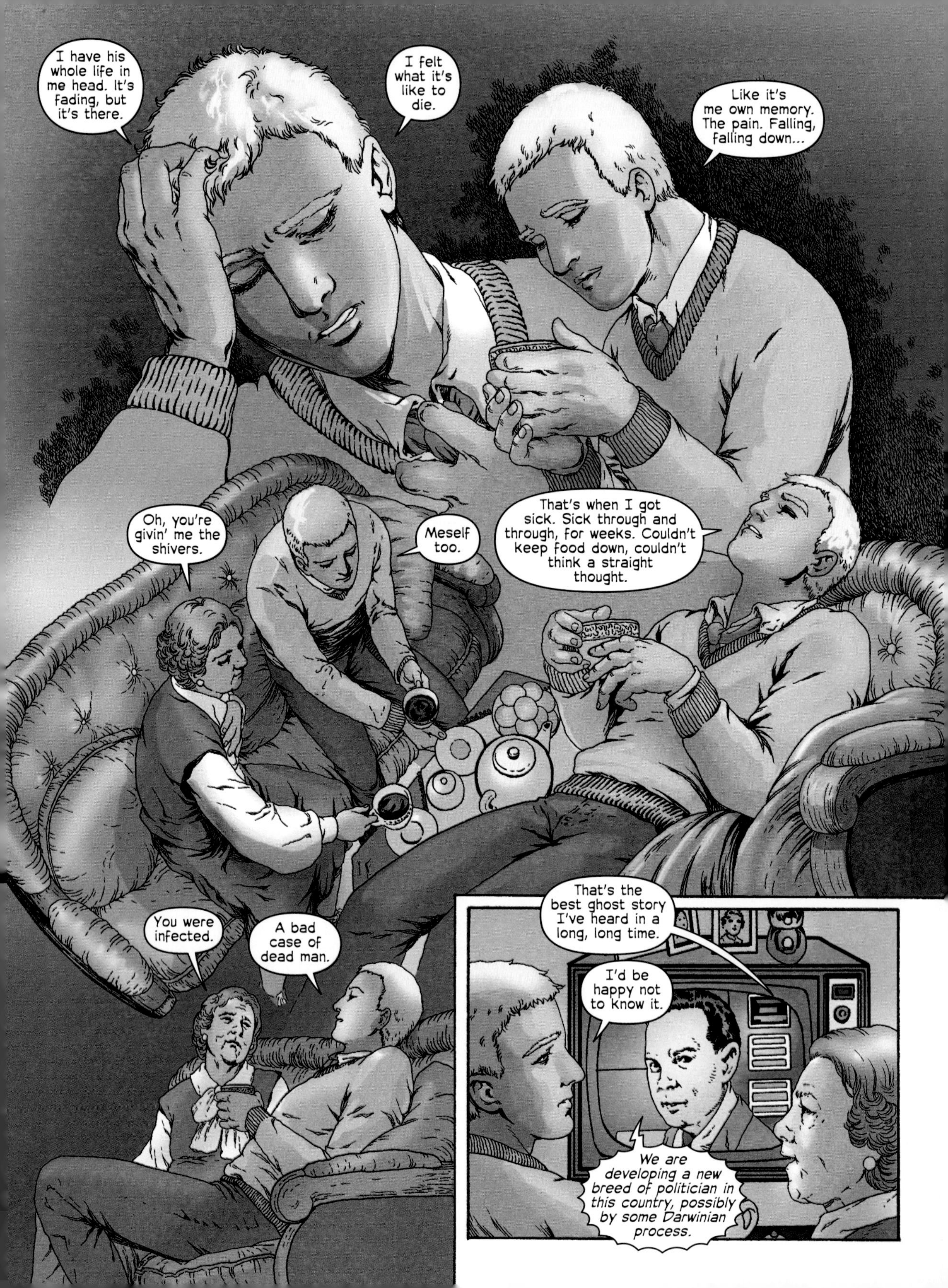
I have his whole life in me head. It's fading, but it's there.
I felt what it's like to die.
Like it's me own memory. The pain. Falling, falling down...
Oh, you're givin' me the shivers.
Meself too.
That's when I got sick. Sick through and through, for weeks. Couldn't keep food down, couldn't think a straight thought.
You were infected.
A bad case of dead man.
That's the best ghost story I've heard in a long, long time.
I'd be happy not to know it.
We are developing a new breed of politician in this country, possibly by some Darwinian process.

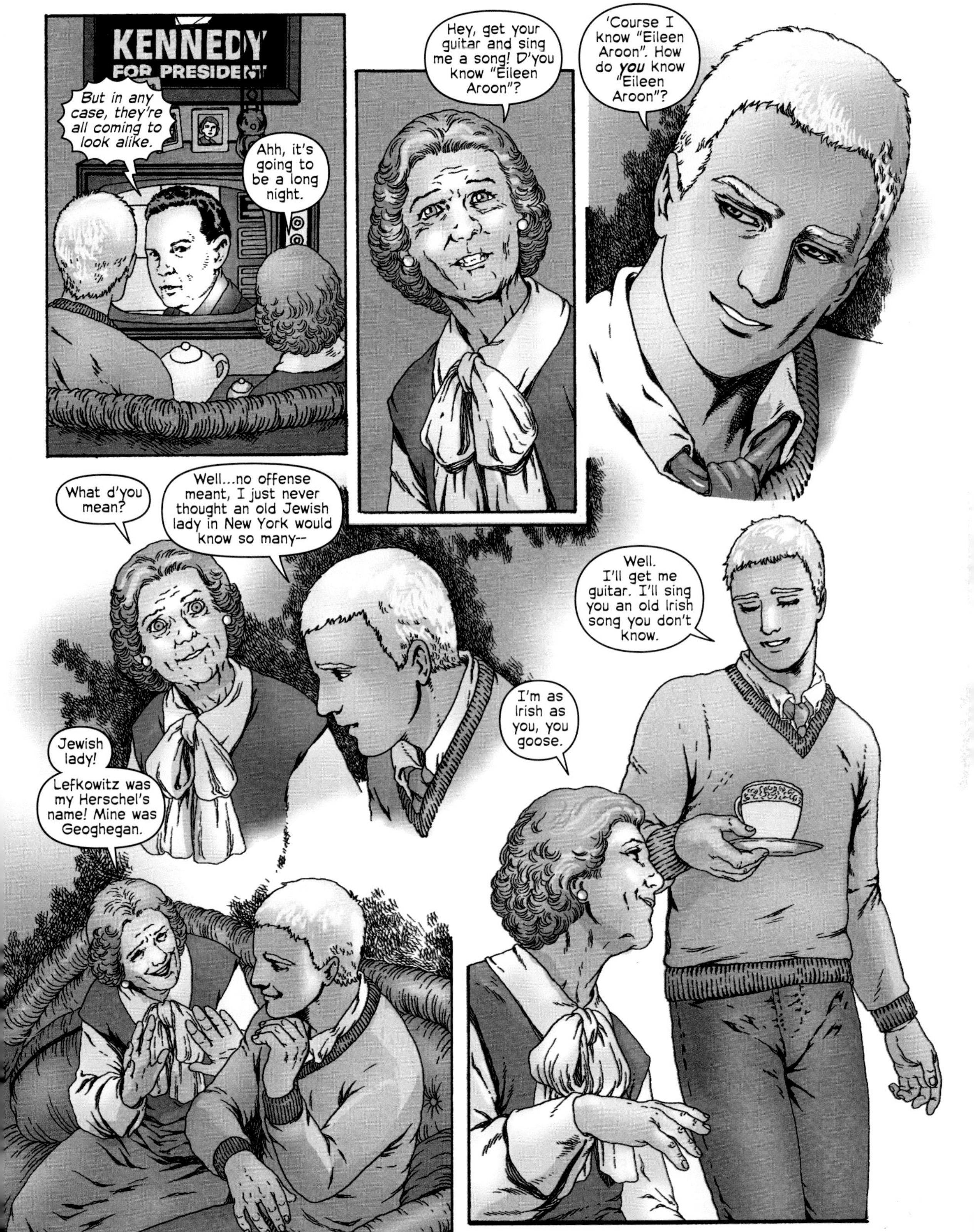
KENNEDY FOR PRESIDENT
But in any case, they're all coming to look alike.
Ahh, it's going to be a long night.
Hey, get your guitar and sing me a song! D'you know "Eileen Aroon"?
'Course I know "Eileen Aroon". How do *you* know "Eileen Aroon"?
What d'you mean?
Well...no offense meant, I just never thought an old Jewish lady in New York would know so many--
Jewish lady!
Lefkowitz was my Herschel's name! Mine was Geoghegan.
I'm as Irish as you, you goose.
Well. I'll get me guitar. I'll sing you an old Irish song you don't know.

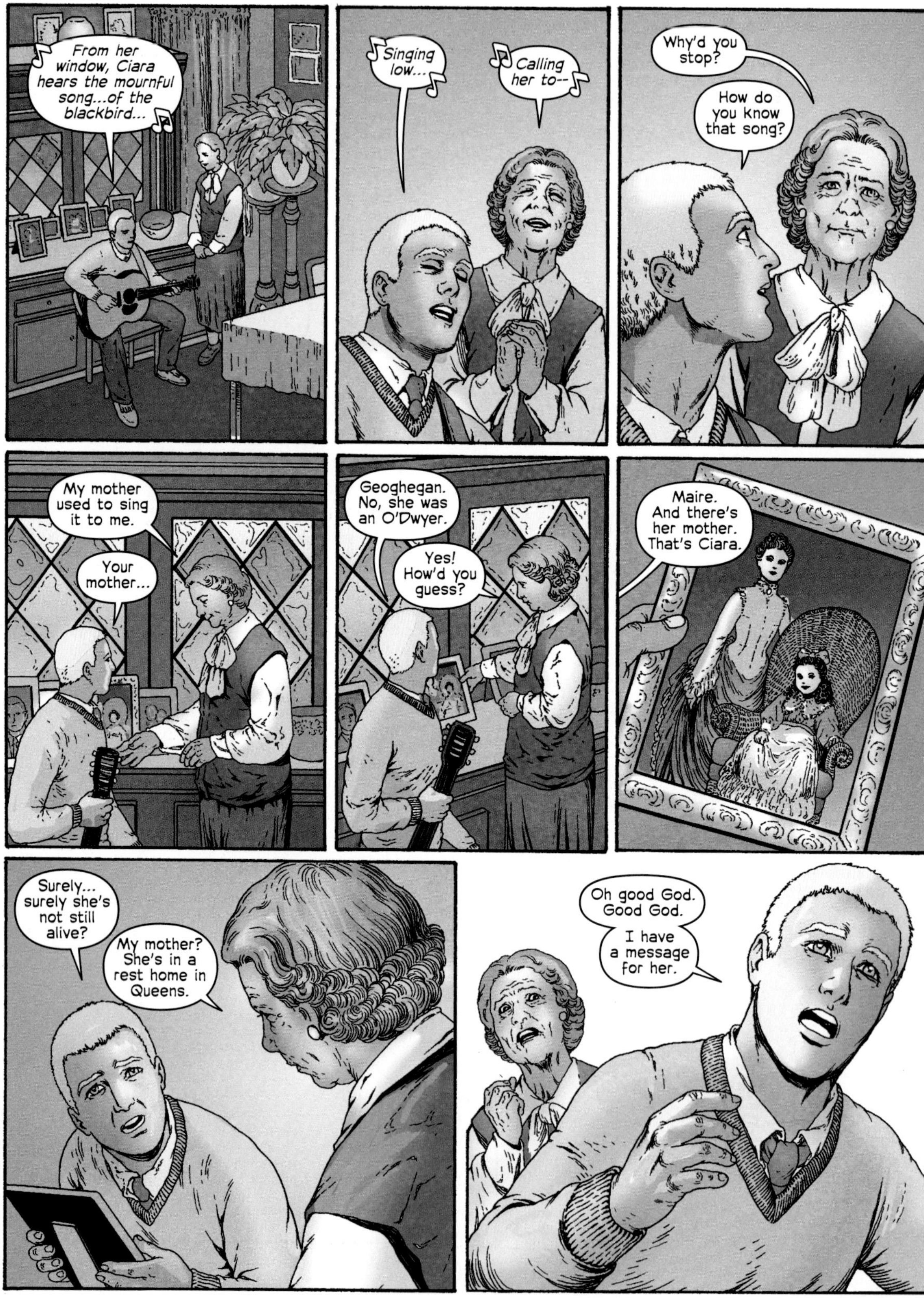
From her window, Ciara hears the mournful song...of the blackbird...
Singing low...
Calling her to--
Why'd you stop?
How do you know that song?
My mother used to sing it to me.
Your mother...
Geoghegan. No, she was an O'Dwyer.
Yes! How'd you guess?
Maire. And there's her mother. That's Ciara.
Surely... surely she's not still alive?
My mother? She's in a rest home in Queens.
Oh good God. Good God.
I have a message for her.

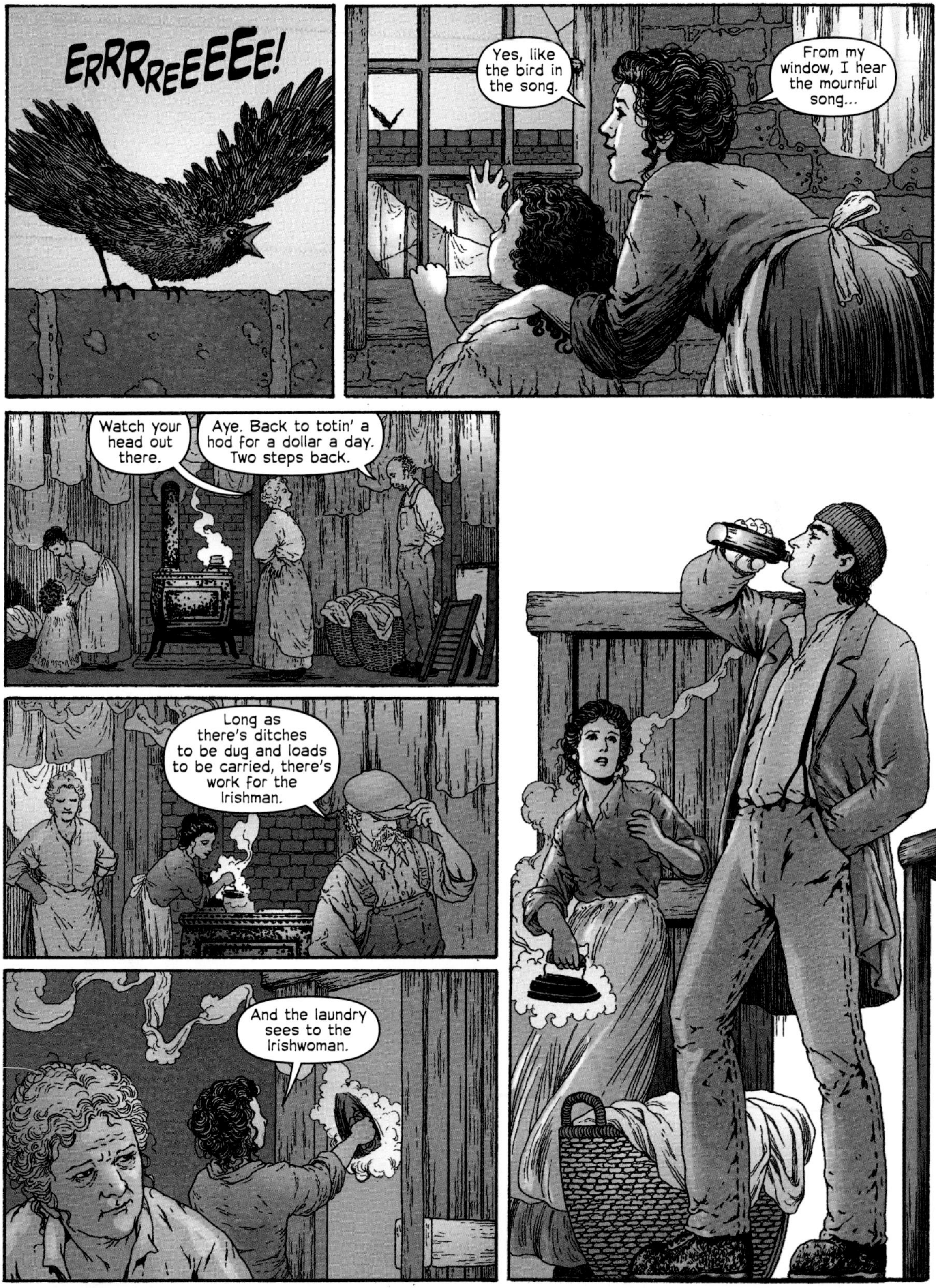
ERRRREEEEEE!
Yes, like the bird in the song.
From my window, I hear the mournful song...
Watch your head out there.
Aye. Back to totin' a hod for a dollar a day. Two steps back.
Long as there's ditches to be dug and loads to be carried, there's work for the Irishman.
And the laundry sees to the Irishwoman.

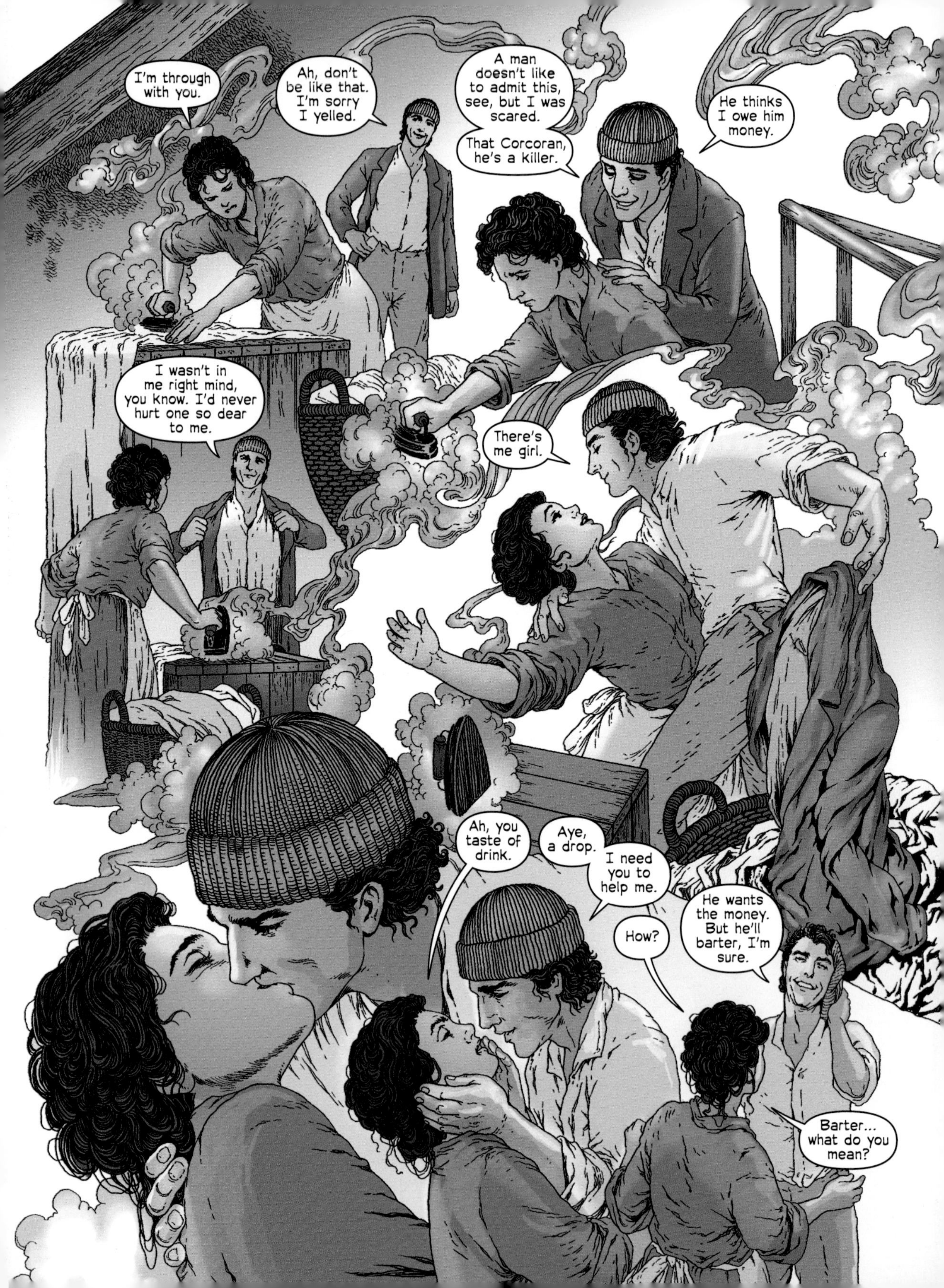
I'm through with you.
Ah, don't be like that. I'm sorry I yelled.
A man doesn't like to admit this, see, but I was scared.
That Corcoran, he's a killer.
He thinks I owe him money.
I wasn't in me right mind, you know. I'd never hurt one so dear to me.
There's me girl.
Ah, you taste of drink.
Aye, a drop.
I need you to help me.
How?
He wants the money. But he'll barter, I'm sure.
Barter... what do you mean?

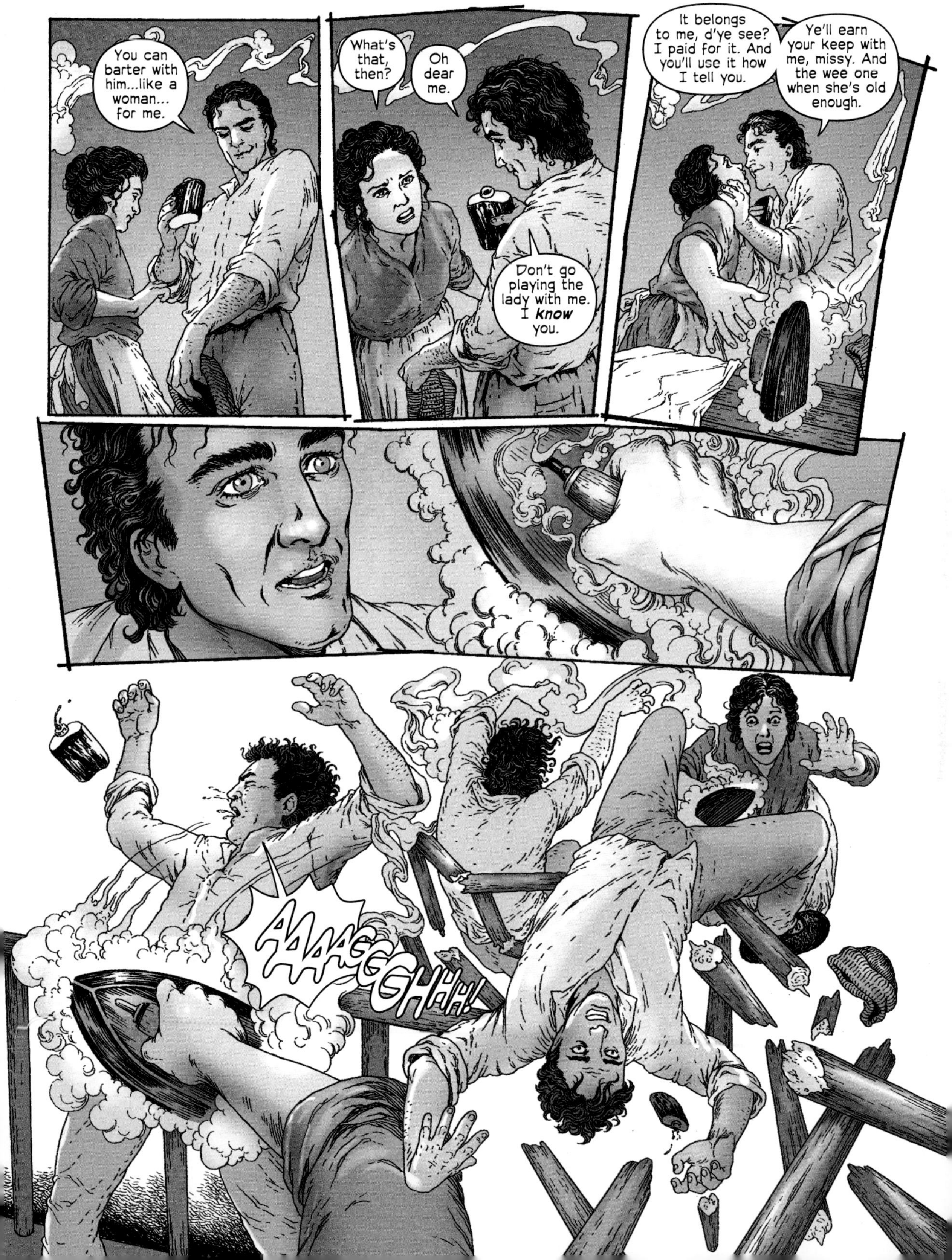

You can barter with him...like a woman... for me.
What's that, then?
Oh dear me.
Don't go playing the lady with me. I **know** you.
It belongs to me, d'ye see? I paid for it. And you'll use it how I tell you.
Ye'll earn your keep with me, missy. And the wee one when she's old enough.
AAAAGGGHHHH!

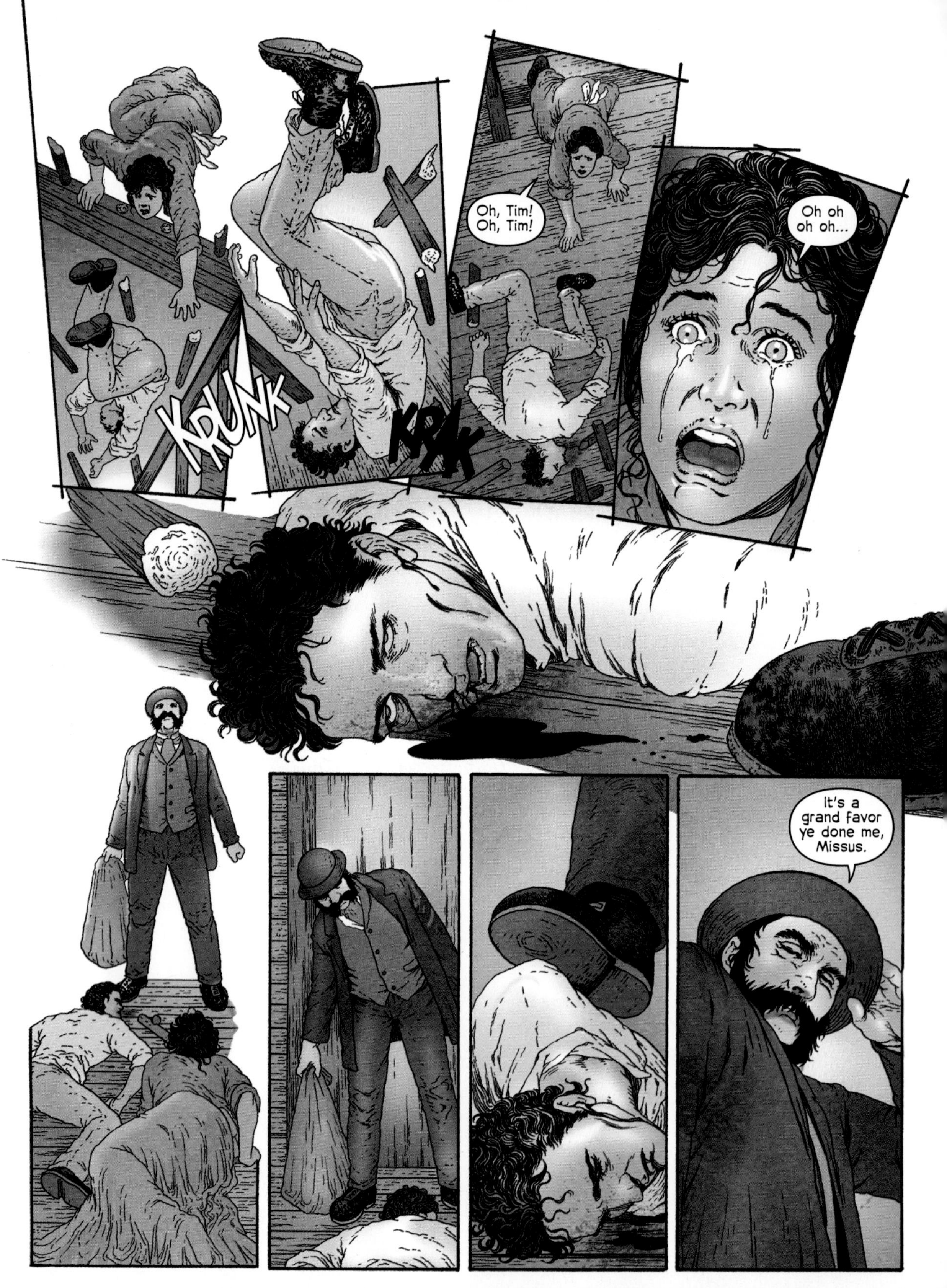
KRUNK
KRAK
Oh, Tim! Oh, Tim!
Oh oh oh oh...
It's a grand favor ye done me, Missus.

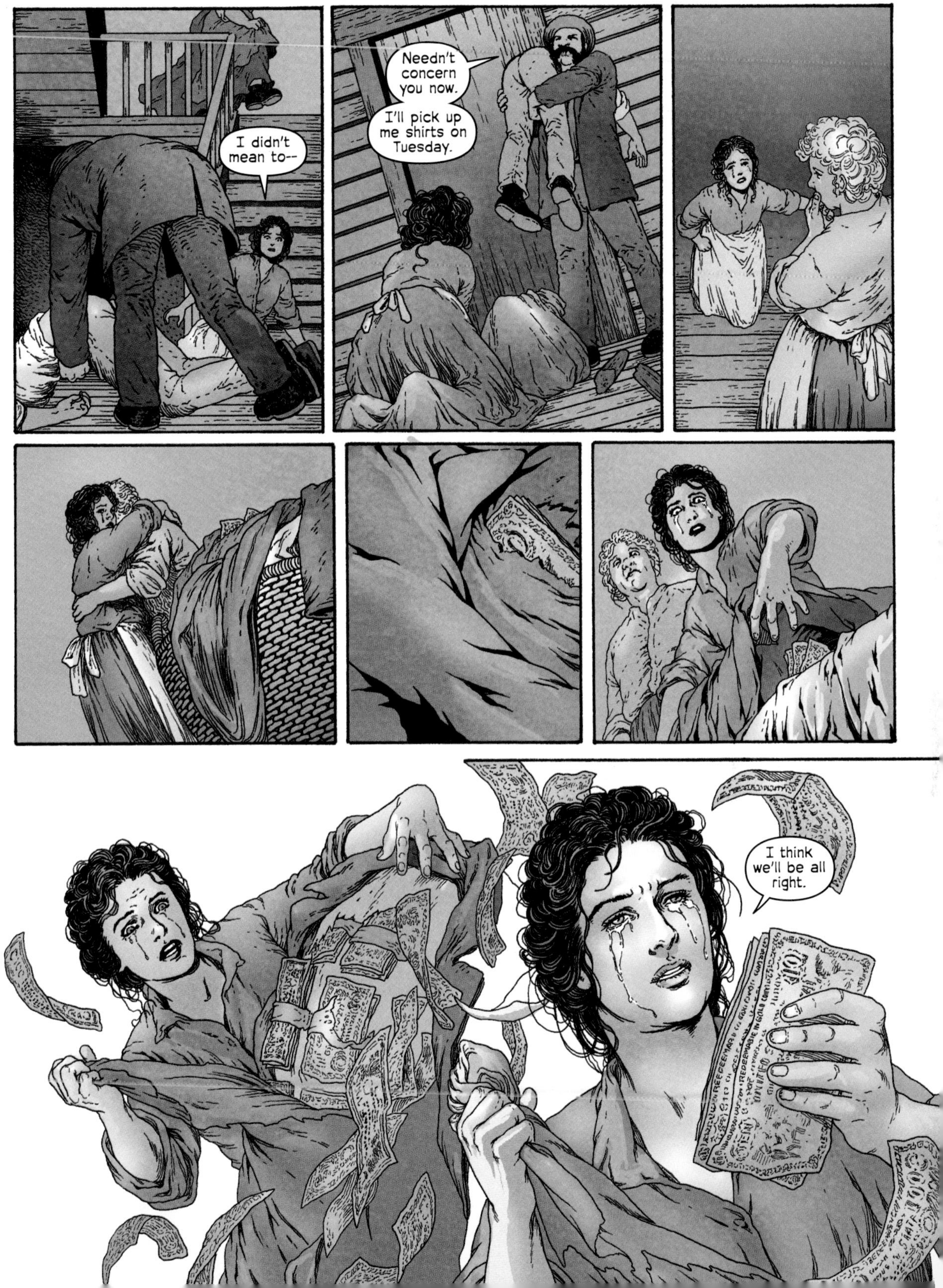
I didn't mean to--
Needn't concern you now.
I'll pick up me shirts on Tuesday.
I think we'll be all right.

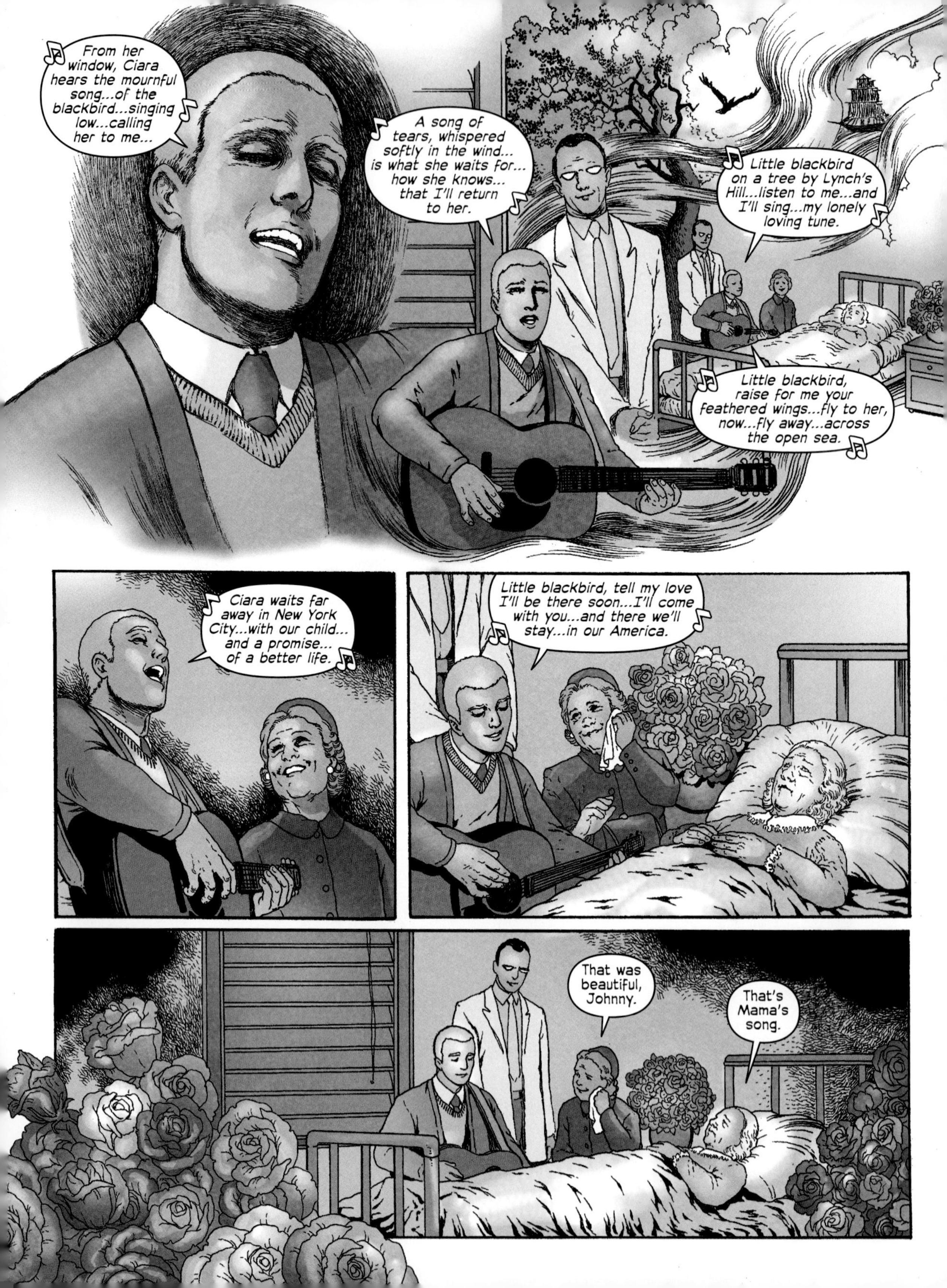

From her window, Ciara hears the mournful song...of the blackbird...singing low...calling her to me...
A song of tears, whispered softly in the wind... is what she waits for... how she knows... that I'll return to her.
Little blackbird on a tree by Lynch's Hill...listen to me...and I'll sing...my lonely loving tune.
Little blackbird, raise for me your feathered wings...fly to her, now...fly away...across the open sea.
Ciara waits far away in New York City...with our child... and a promise... of a better life.
Little blackbird, tell my love I'll be there soon...I'll come with you...and there we'll stay...in our America.
That was beautiful, Johnny.
That's Mama's song.

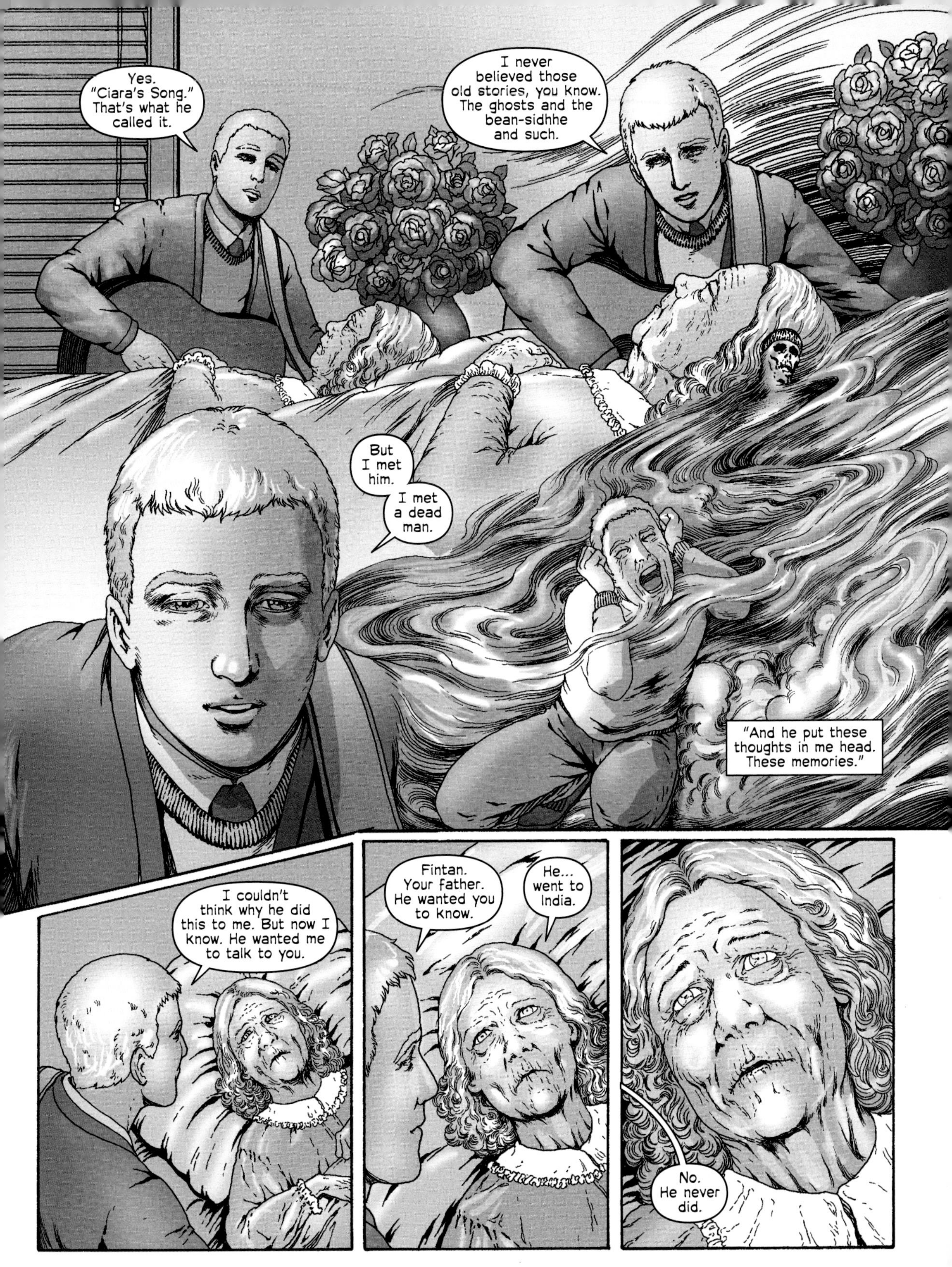
Yes. "Ciara's Song." That's what he called it.
I never believed those old stories, you know. The ghosts and the bean-sidhhe and such.
But I met him.
I met a dead man.
"And he put these thoughts in me head. These memories."
I couldn't think why he did this to me. But now I know. He wanted me to talk to you.
Fintan. Your father. He wanted you to know.
He... went to India.
No. He never did.

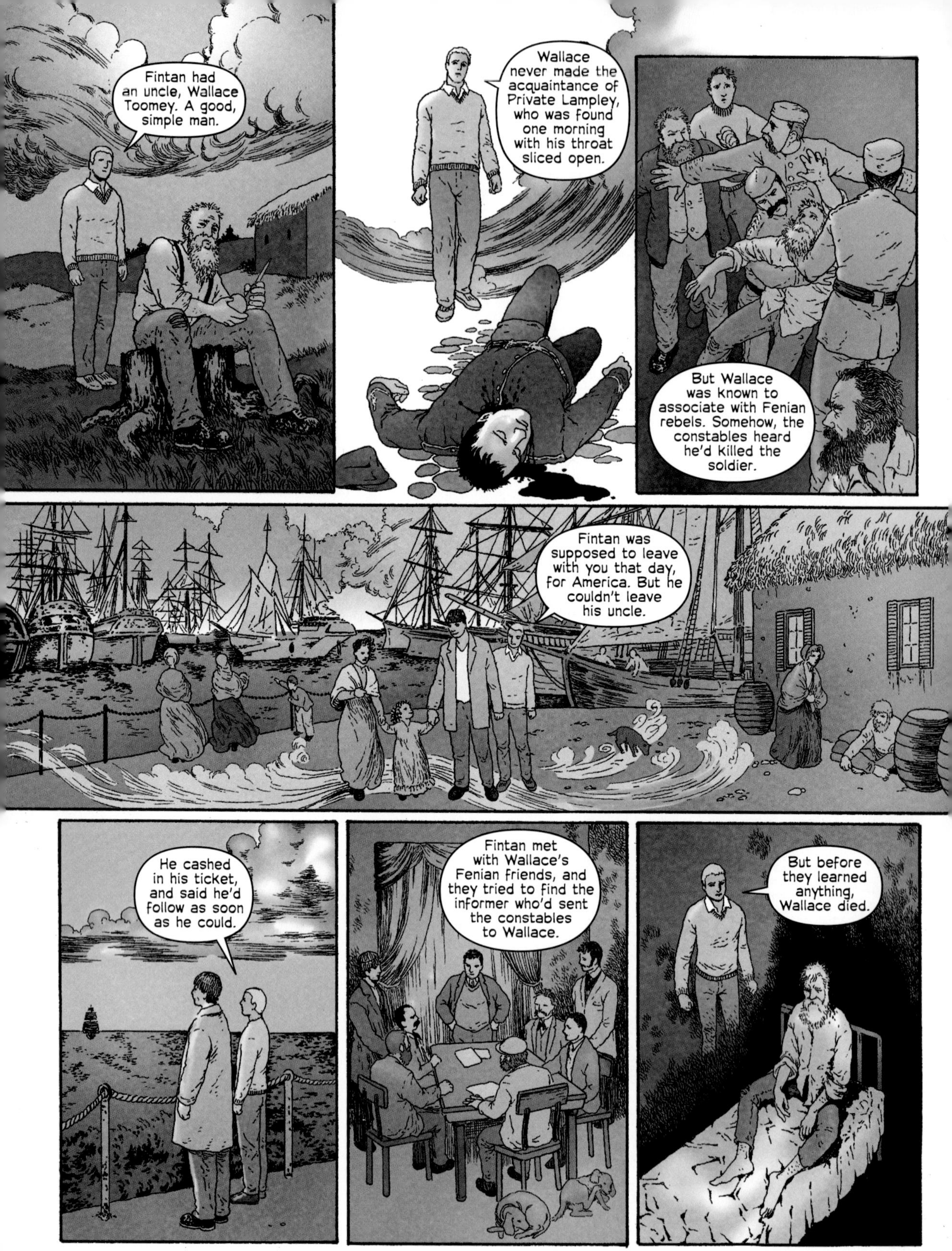
Fintan had an uncle, Wallace Toomey. A good, simple man.
Wallace never made the acquaintance of Private Lampley, who was found one morning with his throat sliced open.
But Wallace was known to associate with Fenian rebels. Somehow, the constables heard he'd killed the soldier.
Fintan was supposed to leave with you that day, for America. But he couldn't leave his uncle.
He cashed in his ticket, and said he'd follow as soon as he could.
Fintan met with Wallace's Fenian friends, and they tried to find the informer who'd sent the constables to Wallace.
But before they learned anything, Wallace died.

With nothing to keep him in Ireland, Fintan sailed for America.

He didn't notice Tim Shea. But Tim Shea noticed him. And worried.

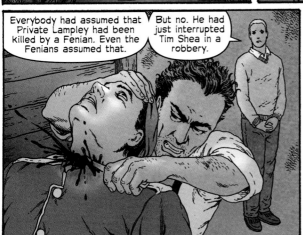

Everybody had assumed that Private Lampley had been killed by a Fenian. Even the Fenians assumed that.

But no. He had just interrupted Tim Shea in a robbery.

And then Tim told the police that he'd seen the Fenian Wallace Toomey with a bloody knife.

Tim made a mistaken assumption, too. He couldn't believe it was a coincidence that they were on the same ship. He thought Fintan was after him for revenge.

Tim watched and waited until the opportunity came.

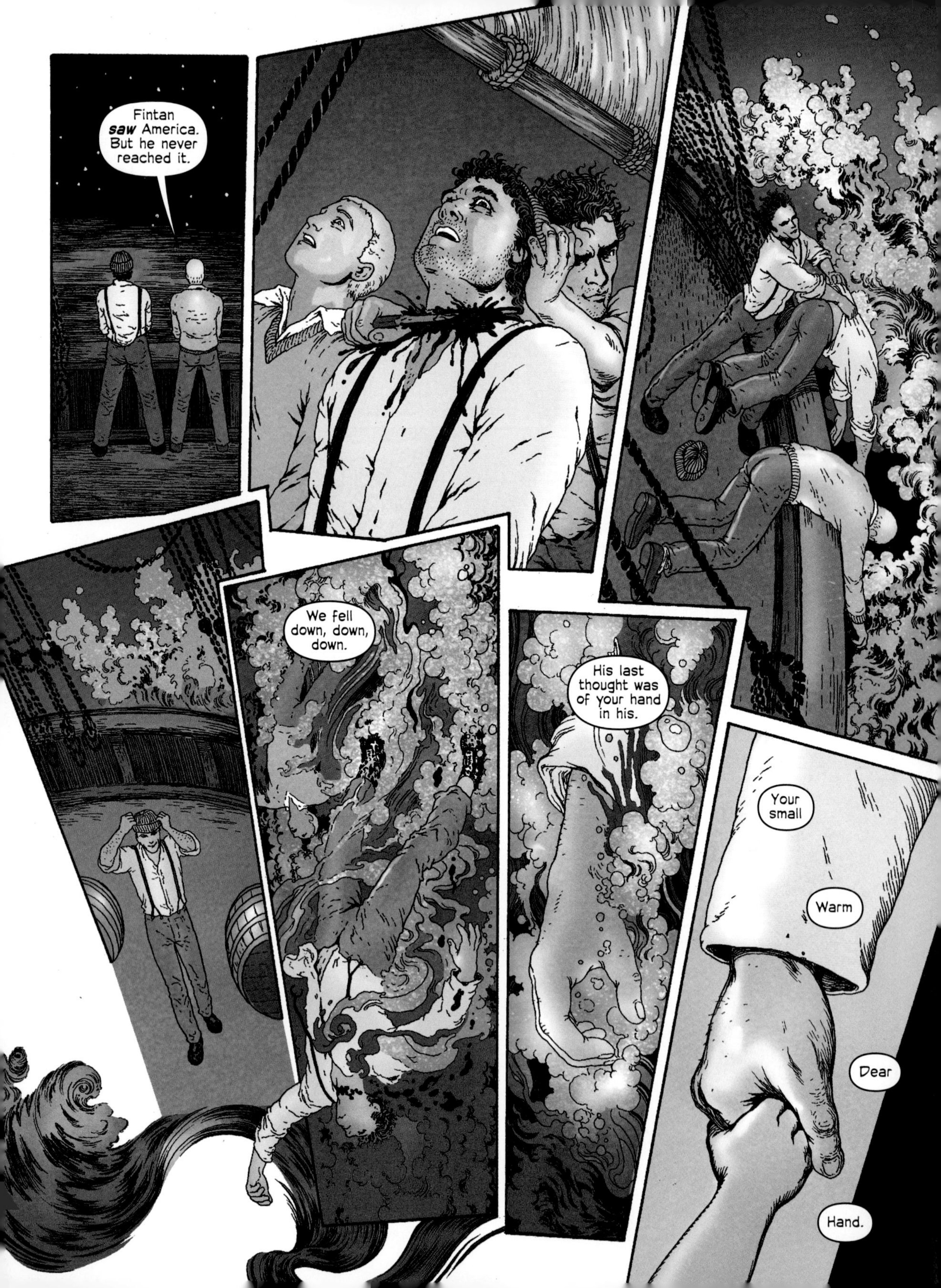
Fintan *saw* America. But he never reached it.
We fell down, down, down.
His last thought was of your hand in his.
Your small
Warm
Dear
Hand.

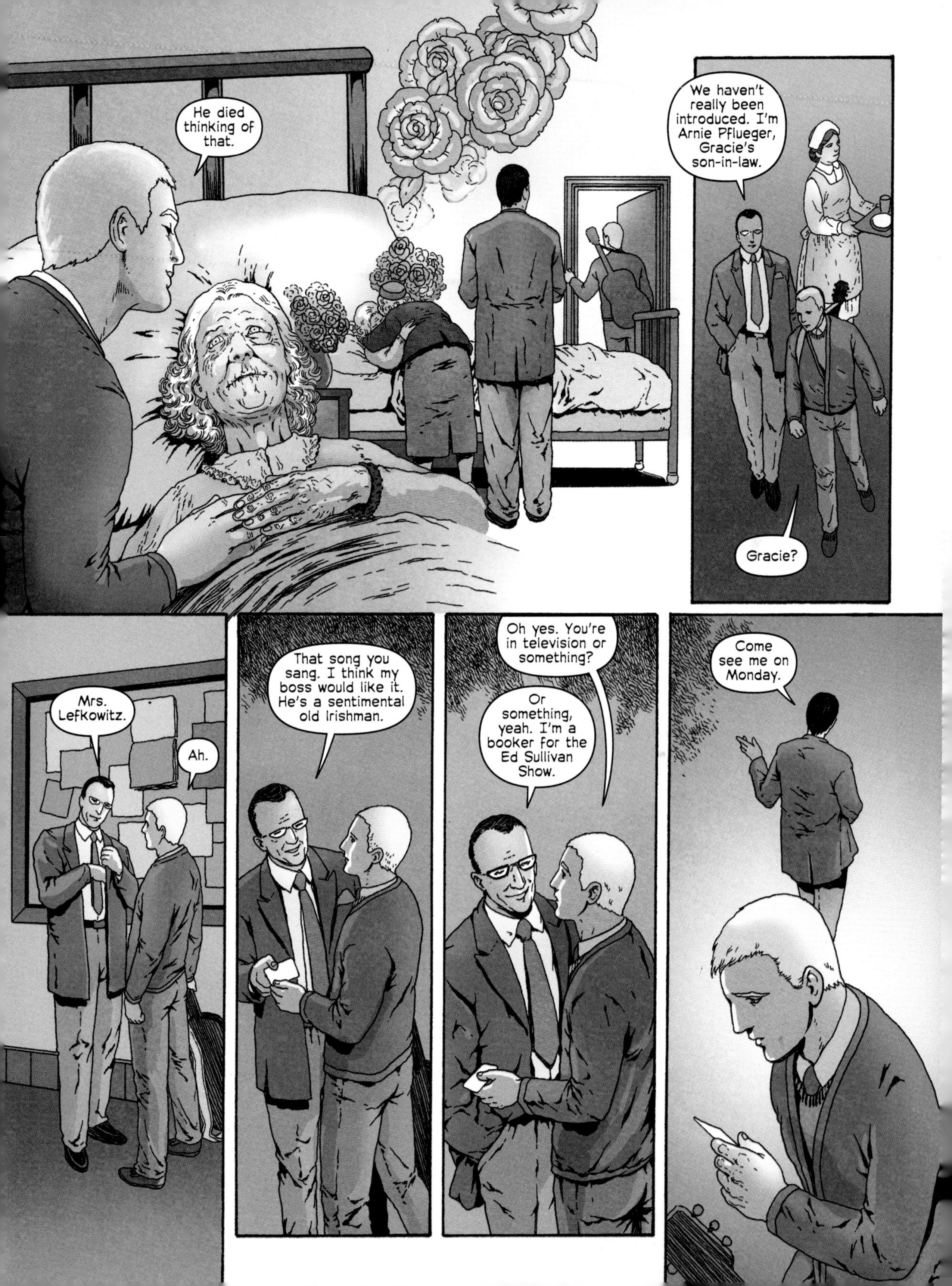
He died thinking of that.
We haven't really been introduced. I'm Arnie Pflueger, Gracie's son-in-law.
Gracie?
Mrs. Lefkowitz.
Ah.
That song you sang. I think my boss would like it. He's a sentimental old Irishman.
Oh yes. You're in television or something?
Or something, yeah. I'm a booker for the Ed Sullivan Show.
Come see me on Monday.

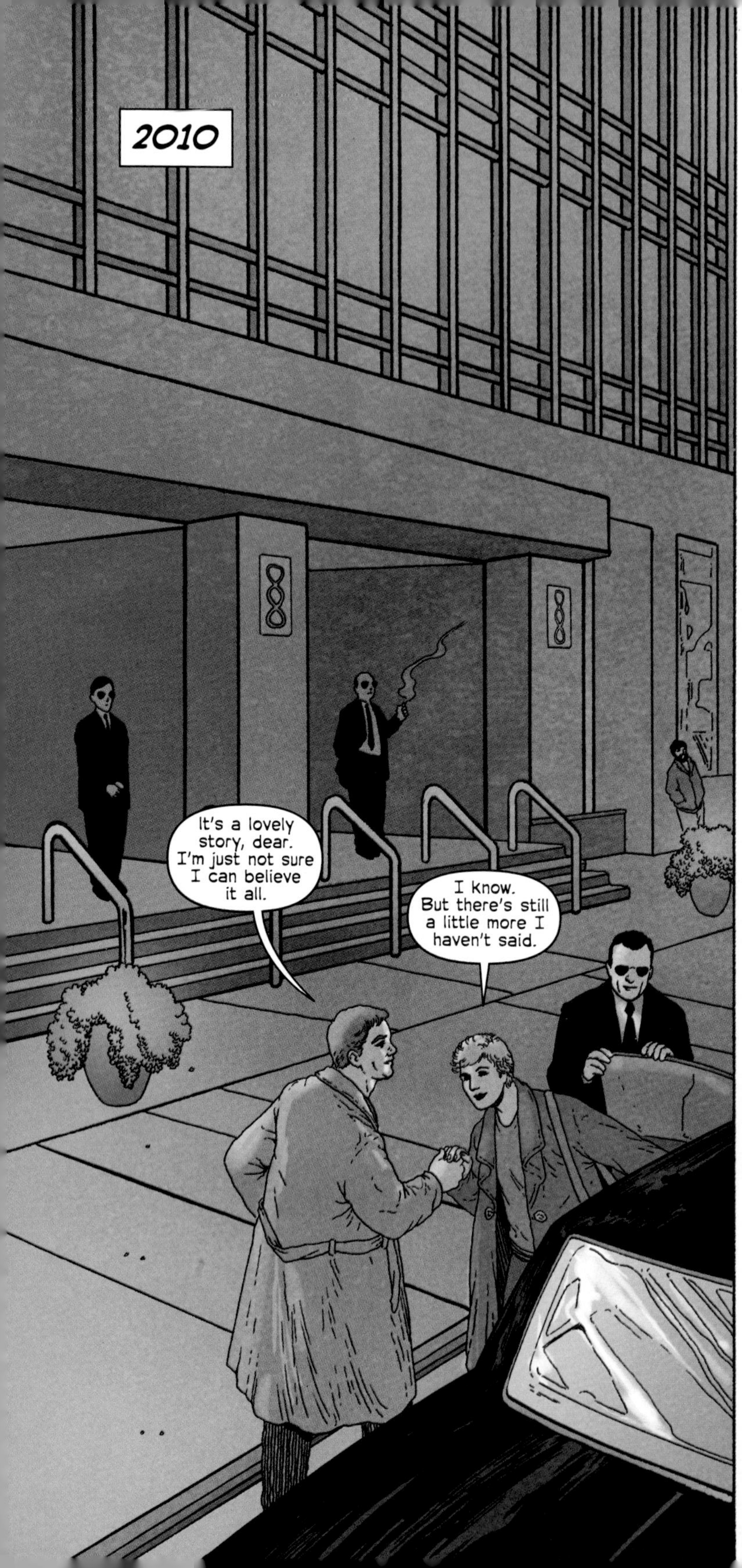
2010
It's a lovely story, dear. I'm just not sure I can believe it all.
I know. But there's still a little more I haven't said.

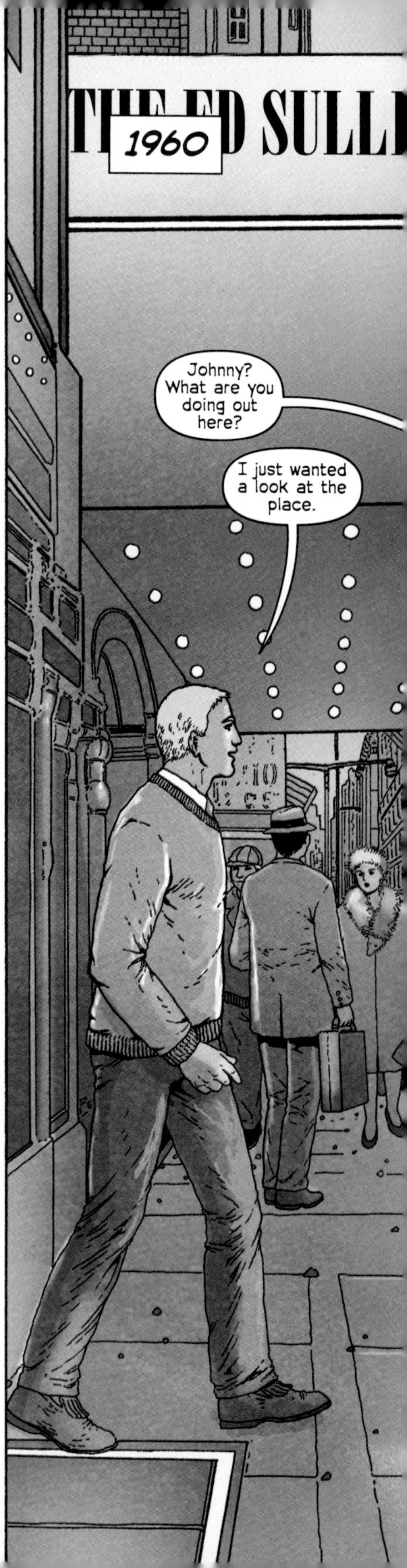
THE ED SULL
1960
Johnny? What are you doing out here?
I just wanted a look at the place.

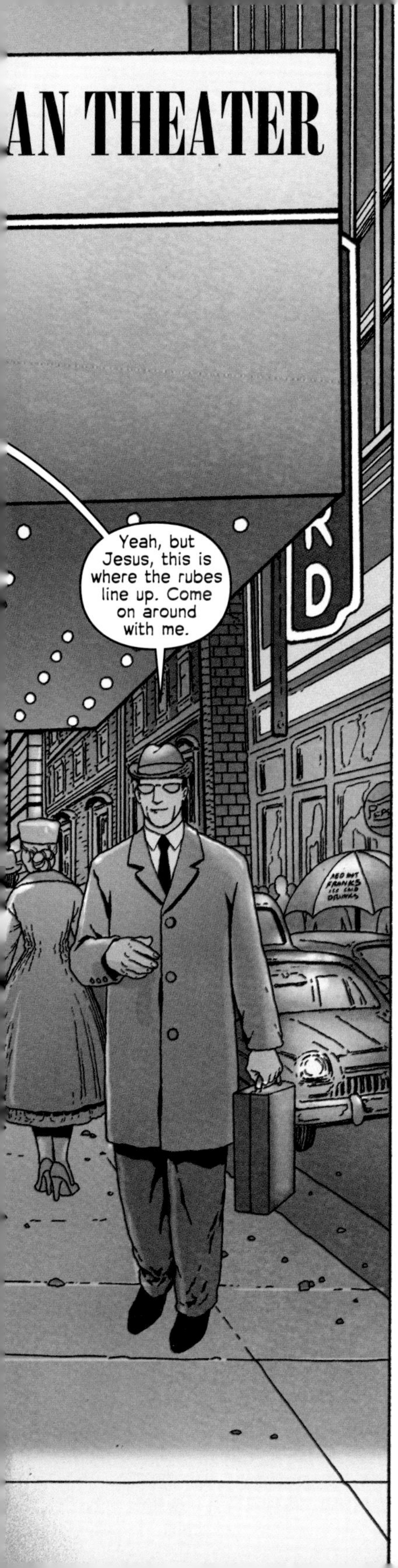
AN THEATER
Yeah, but Jesus, this is where the rubes line up. Come on around with me.

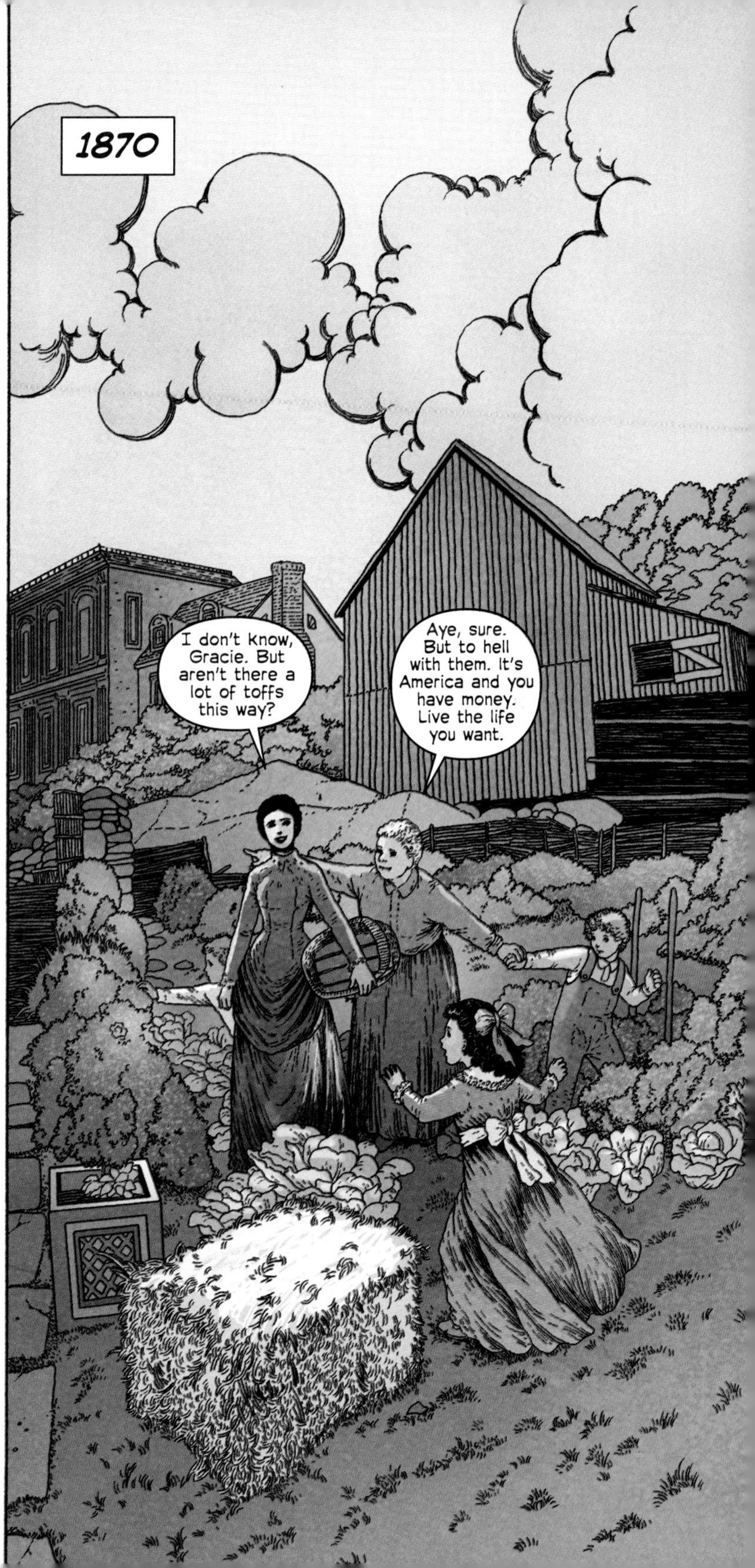
1870
I don't know, Gracie. But aren't there a lot of toffs this way?
Aye, sure. But to hell with them. It's America and you have money. Live the life you want.

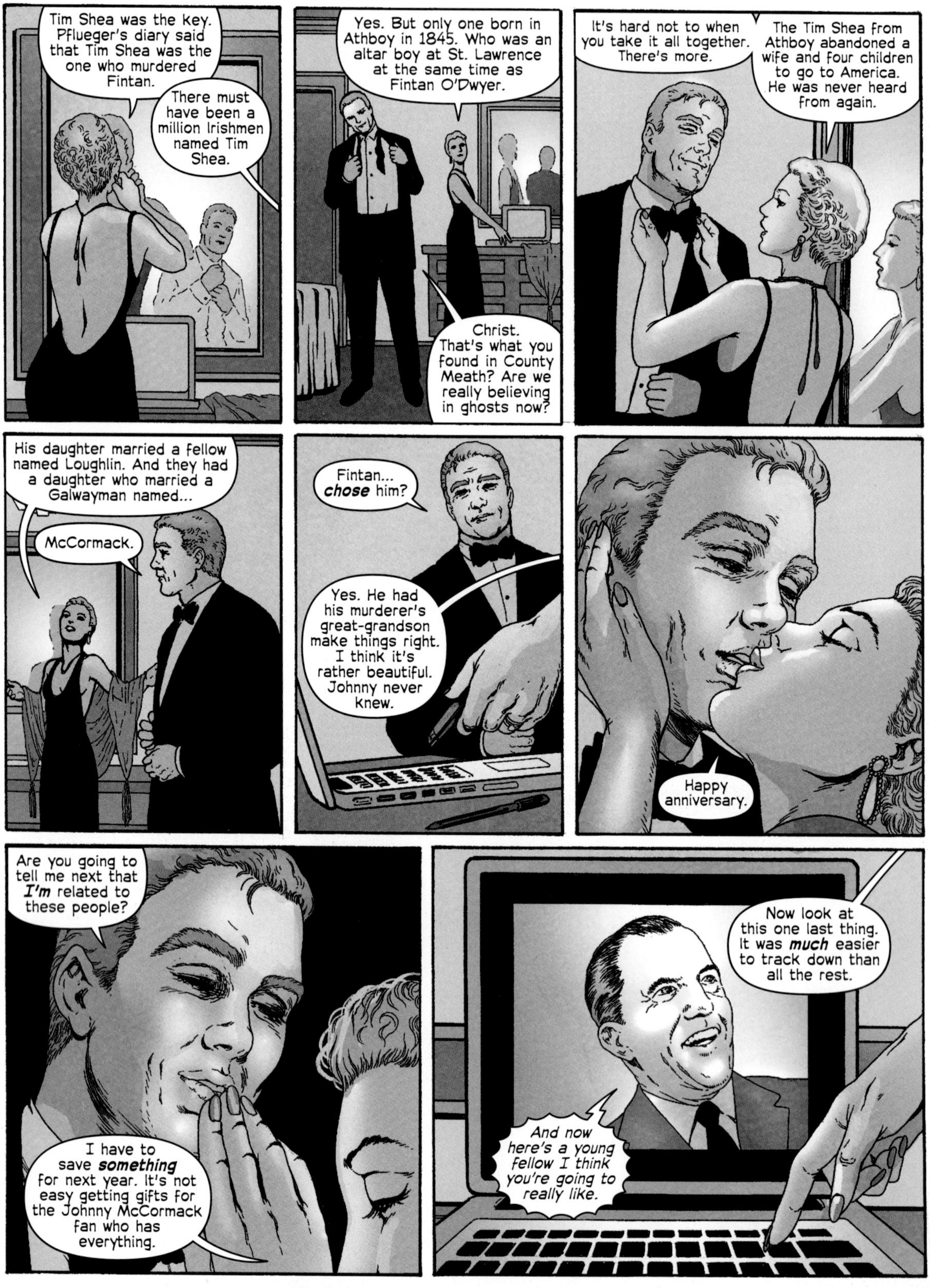
Tim Shea was the key. Pflueger's diary said that Tim Shea was the one who murdered Fintan.
There must have been a million Irishmen named Tim Shea.
Yes. But only one born in Athboy in 1845. Who was an altar boy at St. Lawrence at the same time as Fintan O'Dwyer.
Christ. That's what you found in County Meath? Are we really believing in ghosts now?
It's hard not to when you take it all together. There's more.
The Tim Shea from Athboy abandoned a wife and four children to go to America. He was never heard from again.
His daughter married a fellow named Loughlin. And they had a daughter who married a Galwayman named...
McCormack.
Fintan... *chose* him?
Yes. He had his murderer's great-grandson make things right. I think it's rather beautiful. Johnny never knew.
Happy anniversary.
Are you going to tell me next that *I'm* related to these people?
I have to save *something* for next year. It's not easy getting gifts for the Johnny McCormack fan who has everything.
Now look at this one last thing. It was *much* easier to track down than all the rest.
And now here's a young fellow I think you're going to really like.

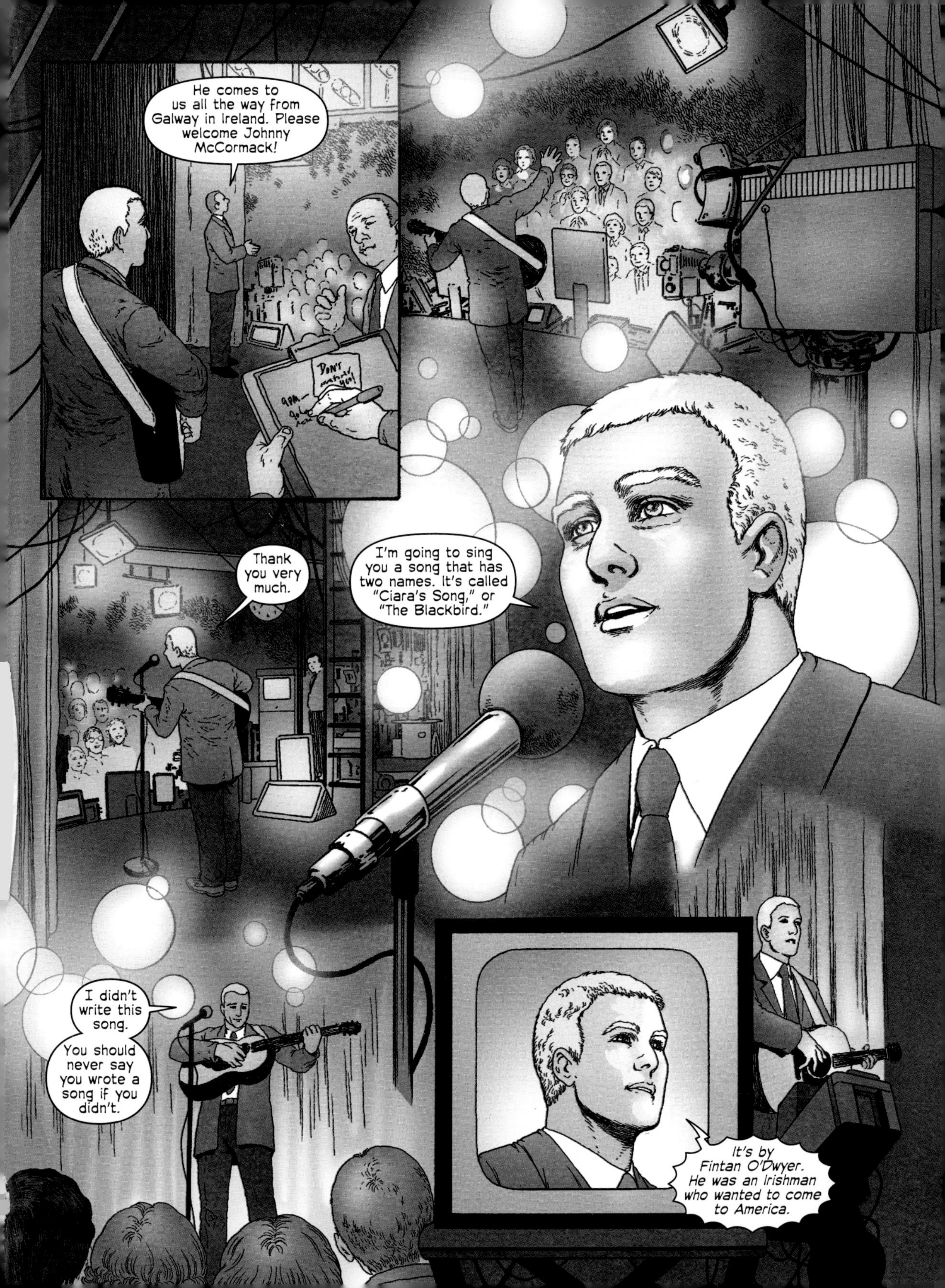
He comes to us all the way from Galway in Ireland. Please welcome Johnny McCormack!
Thank you very much.
I'm going to sing you a song that has two names. It's called "Ciara's Song," or "The Blackbird."
I didn't write this song.
You should never say you wrote a song if you didn't.
It's by Fintan O'Dwyer. He was an Irishman who wanted to come to America.

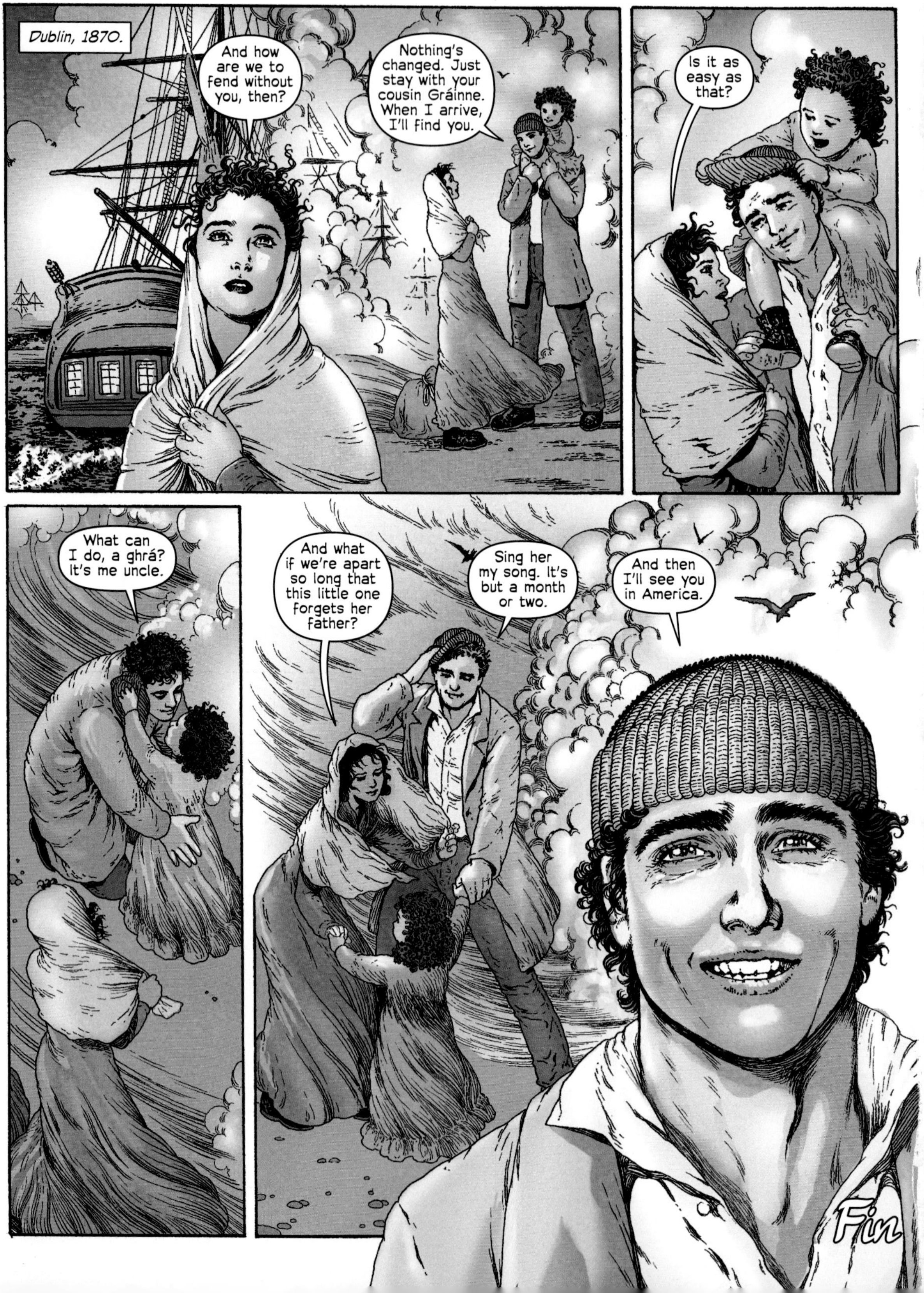

Dublin, 1870.
And how are we to fend without you, then?
Nothing's changed. Just stay with your cousin Gráinne. When I arrive, I'll find you.
Is it as easy as that?
What can I do, a ghrá? It's me uncle.
And what if we're apart so long that this little one forgets her father?
Sing her my song. It's but a month or two.
And then I'll see you in America.
Fin